SPEAKING
OF
WRITING

SPEAKING
OF
WRITING
A BRIEF RHETORIC

Allegra Goodman and Michael Prince

Illustrated by Emmeline Pidgen

broadview press

BROADVIEW PRESS – www.broadviewpress.com
Peterborough, Ontario, Canada

Founded in 1985, Broadview Press remains a wholly independent publishing house. Broadview's focus is on academic publishing; our titles are accessible to university and college students as well as scholars and general readers. With over 600 titles in print, Broadview has become a leading international publisher in the humanities, with world-wide distribution. Broadview is committed to environmentally responsible publishing and fair business practices.

Library and Archives Canada Cataloguing in Publication

Title: Speaking of writing : a brief rhetoric / Allegra Goodman and Michael Prince ; illustrated by Emmeline Pidgen.
Names: Goodman, Allegra, author. | Prince, Michael (Michael B.), author. | Pidgen, Emmeline, illustrator.
Description: Includes bibliographical references and index.
Identifiers: Canadiana 20190076712 | ISBN 9781554814343 (softcover)
Subjects: LCSH: Academic writing—Textbooks. | LCSH: English language—Rhetoric—Textbooks. | LCSH: Report writing—Textbooks. | LCGFT: Textbooks.
Classification: LCC P301.5.A27 G66 2019 | DDC 808/.042—dc23

Broadview Press handles its own distribution in North America:
PO Box 1243, Peterborough, Ontario K9J 7H5, Canada
555 Riverwalk Parkway, Tonawanda, NY 14150, USA
Tel: (705) 743-8990; Fax: (705) 743-8353
email: customerservice@broadviewpress.com

Distribution is handled by Eurospan Group in the UK, Europe, Central Asia, Middle East, Africa, India, Southeast Asia, Central America, South America, and the Caribbean. Distribution is handled by Footprint Books in Australia and New Zealand.

Canadä
Broadview Press acknowledges the financial support of the Government of Canada for our publishing activities.

Edited by Michel Pharand
Book Design by Em Dash Design

PRINTED IN CANADA

Contents

9 Writing and Research
Writing a Research Paper.
Crafting a Multi-Modal Portfolio.

Most of the brief readings included in this book are available in complete form online, and can be accessed through the companion website for *Speaking of Writing*, at https://sites.broadviewpress.com/speakingofwriting/. Passcode: BVSoW6TGWAS

Note to Students

What is college writing? This book explores the question through cartoons depicting students grappling with diverse assignments, limited time, mysterious expectations, and fundamental questions. What is a thesis statement, and how do I come up with one? How can I fill five pages when I only have a paragraph and it's 2:30 in the morning, and the essay is due tomorrow? Can I use Wikipedia as a source for my research paper? How is an economics essay different from a history essay? When is collaboration okay? What is the difference between collaboration and copying?

The four characters in this book face the challenges of college writing in their composition courses and in other classes. They come to college with different interests, backgrounds, and abilities. Zach is from Redmond, Washington. He likes analytic writing but can't stand what seem to him fuzzy open-ended writing assignments. Anna came to Los Angeles from Mexico in high school. She enjoys composition but feels nervous at times about writing in idiomatic English. Kate grew up in South Bend, Indiana. She is pre-med and loves to write. She has returned to school after several years away. Jordan is from Boston and might major in government. He loves writing and public speaking—both debate and improv poetry.

The chapters follow Zach, Anna, Kate, and Jordan as they tackle assignments in composition and courses across the humanities, social sciences, and natural sciences. Some of these assignments offer explicit directions; others are vague. Some focus on analysis of texts and images. Others focus on everyday forms of writing such as reports and interviews. Student work culminates in written pages, but also in oral or multi-media presentations.

We provide brief texts we call **micro-readings** throughout this book because writers learn by example. Think of the way athletes and dancers watch, and the way musicians listen to learn. Observing and practicing are key. Our readings come from many fields and genres. Some are pure text. Some are graphic. Some incorporate word and image together. We draw from advertisements, charts, speeches, interviews, news articles, transcripts, abstracts, papers, posters, poems, and famous essays. Of course, the readings you encounter in your courses will be longer, sometimes much longer.

Using this book as a portal, you can access the complete version of most micro-readings online at https://sites.broadviewpress.com/speakingofwriting/, passcode: BVSoW6TGWAS. We shrink these texts for the same reason a coach reviewing film asks athletes to focus on one bit of tape—so that you can study them closely.

The micro-readings are representative texts. When we say **representative**, we mean that whether the reading is about climate change or a Renaissance prince, the challenges of understanding and evaluation are characteristic of those you will face in your courses.

The same goes for writing assignments. No textbook could teach you all the genres you will be called upon to write in college and at work. However, our cartoons, our text, and our exercises teach you methods you can use in many disciplines on many occasions. In Chapter One, students write a literacy narrative, reflecting on their history as readers and writers. A student can successfully draw upon personal experience for a literacy narrative. However, other assignments require students to investigate different material. In one class you could find yourself writing about the rhetorical appeals of an advertisement. In another, you might review a movie. Learning to interpret your assignment and gauge your **purpose**, your **audience**, and the **genre**, or form, your writing will take is a vital skill we discuss in Chapter Two: Rhetoric and the Rhetorical Situation.

You will often need to decipher and respond to course material in writing. That material could include written or visual texts that require careful study. In Chapter Three: From Reading to Writing about Texts, we demonstrate annotation, note taking, paraphrase, summary, and analysis of written texts. In Chapter Four: From Reading to Writing about Images, we dramatize critical reading and analysis of images and graphs.

College instructors expect you to understand the readings in your courses, but they usually require your own take on that material, as well. They expect you to develop various forms of argument, or writing with a strong sense of purpose. Chapter Five: Building an Argument: Claims and Support demonstrates how to make claims and how to support those claims with evidence. We show students developing arguments in diverse real-world situations.

Assignments in college courses often require a formal **thesis**, the assertion or claim that motivates and controls your argument. In

Chapter Six: Academic Argument, we discuss what is and what is not a thesis statement. We talk about how to come up with a thesis, and how to use your thesis to organize your argument.

In each of these chapters we discuss writing with integrity, identifying and documenting sources, describing, reporting, explicating, and entertaining objections.

Sitting down and hammering out a draft is in many ways the most mysterious part of the writing process. In Chapter Seven: Draft and Revision, we offer several illustrations of that process. We also dramatize different ways to start revising: on your own, with peer review, and after a meeting with your instructor.

Chapter Eight: Responding to Other Voices/Other Sources extends and applies our discussion of writing with integrity. In college courses your instructors will expect you to draw upon diverse media to support and augment your written work. These sources could be text or film, images or events or objects. You may find yourself conducting, transcribing, and quoting an interview. You may cut and paste images and sound clips into your written work. You might write about a graph or about a painting or about a song. In all cases, your instructors expect you to introduce your sources, document them accurately, explain them clearly, and assess them critically. We call this process IDEA: Introduce, Document, Explain, Assess. Emphasizing the importance of documentation, we discuss plagiarism in its many guises and suggest ways to avoid compromising your writing and your integrity.

Following directly from writing responsibly, Chapter Nine: Writing and Research shows how to apply skills of note-taking, summary, close and critical reading, along with the practices of argumentation, draft, and revision to tackle longer research assignments. We follow two students as they grapple with research projects. Kate writes and revises a research paper drawing upon contemporary accounts and scholarly discussion of the Great Fire of Chicago in 1871. Anna compiles and curates a multi-media online portfolio on the gender pay gap. These precise assignments will no doubt differ from yours. However, as they define a topic, identify sources, and organize evidence, Kate and Anna follow a process applicable to many projects.

Finally, Chapter Ten: Voice and Style, illustrates the ways writers set a tone, signal a genre, and reach specific audiences. We discuss the difference between voice and style, and we address a fundamental question: How do I maintain my own voice while adapting to other people's conventions and expectations?

This book teaches and models college writing, but it focuses on what you bring to the task: your knowledge, your experience, your voice, your point of view. The students in this book wonder what their instructors really want. What they learn is that instructors want to know what students think. Well-supported arguments and well-expressed insights never get old. Good thinking and clear writing intrigue most readers, including college instructors. Engaging with your material, writing with purpose and conviction, you invite your reader to engage with you.

1

WHAT YOU BRING/
WHAT YOU CAN EXPECT

Writing a Literacy Narrative.

ANNA What's up?

ZACH Just my personal reflection, which will probably take me all day. We had to go to the museum to look at Greek urns and now we have to reflect on them.

ANNA What's so hard about that?

ZACH Nothing—except I don't know what to say.

ANNA Just think. How did it feel to stand there and look at something so old?

ZACH Annoyed. That's how going all the way down there and looking at an urn made me feel.

Attitudes

Some love to write. Some hate the very thought. Many students enjoy certain kinds of writing, but not others. Your success in college and beyond will depend in part on the attitude you bring to your work. How can you develop a positive attitude toward writing, even if you've struggled at times? Or, if you have always loved to write, how can you apply your love of writing to diverse assignments? Perhaps you feel ambivalent. You have done well with writing assignments previously, but you worry about how you will measure up in your new classes. How might you build on past experience to make the transition to writing in college?

What You Bring

What do you say to yourself when you sit down to write? One student might say—*This will be interesting. Now I have a chance to express myself.* Another might say—*Okay, a three-page paper. I may as well get started.* Clearly Zach tells himself a different story. *Writing is confusing. You're supposed to feel free, but you never really know what your instructor is looking for.*

These are just some of the assumptions that students bring to composition. Over time, such statements can become self-fulfilling prophecies. If you enjoy writing, chances are you will approach your assignments optimistically if not with complete confidence. You may have discovered that writing about a topic helps you to understand it better. On the other hand, if you approach writing with anxiety, you may end up delaying and then rushing the task.

Zach is heading for an all-nighter. Waiting until practically the last moment, he loads up on caffeine, and scrambles to finish his assignment as the sun rises. Anxiety leads to avoidance, which leads to a miserably pressured writing process.

You can't change long-held attitudes and preferences overnight, but you can learn to understand them and work with them—or around them. To this end, it's useful to reflect on your personal history as a writer—both positive and negative experiences.

Jordan

I've won poetry slams, and I get into the performance aspect of writing.

I like responding creatively to a prompt, like Animal. Go. Death of loved one. Go.

A negative writing experience is any three-to-five-page paper where I have to analyze something. I can crank it out, but there's no joy.

Anna

I enjoy writing of all kinds. I keep a journal, and I also wrote for my high school newspaper.

I had a great experience with an article I wrote about endangered elephants. I felt like I was getting the word out.

Far more negative was when I came to America and did my first writing in school. My teacher marked many errors and asked me to get help from a tutor. I was embarrassed by this.

Kate

I'm a returning student, so it's been a while since I've written an essay. I remember I used to write great papers, but that was years ago, before nursing school—and before kids!

I remember a positive experience in eleventh grade when I wrote a research paper on the Battle of Gettysburg. I really got into my sources—especially the eye-witness accounts: letters and photographs. I wrote 11 pages.

I had a negative experience with an essay test where I had 30 minutes to answer the question and I ran out of time. I start freezing up when I'm writing against the clock.

Zach

In general, I prefer assignments where I'm answering a specific question or presenting information. I had a positive experience putting together a science fair poster about probability.

I had negative experiences in high school with "creative" assignments like write a story from the point of view of a dolphin or write about your hopes and dreams.

When it comes to writing, there is no universal method. Indeed, if you ask professional writers about their writing processes, each will tell you a different story. Some write at night, some at dawn. Some work in coffee shops, others at a desk. There are those who write by hand on yellow legal pads, and those who type on laptops, those who prefer large blocks of time, and those who write a little every day. As you reflect on your own process, consider what is working, and what could be causing frustration or stress. Consider what you would like to learn, but also remember what you have to offer.

Approaching an assignment, you bring your history and experience with language. Jordan's history as a writer includes some public speaking, and improv poetry slams. Anna's history includes learning English as a foreign language in school. Kate returns to college with experience writing and editing a healthcare newsletter. Zach arrives with minimal writing experience. In high school he focused on math

REFLECT: How would you characterize your attitude toward writing? Looking back, describe a positive writing experience. Describe a less-than-positive writing experience.

and music, and his English teachers did not assign many long essays. However, he has thought deeply about many social and political questions.

What You Can Expect

In an ideal world you would be able to apply your intellectual ability and experience directly to your work as a writer. However, it is not always easy to adapt your experience to your instructor's expectations. The fact is that instructors in college expect a great deal. They expect you to understand course material, and to show them in writing that you understand it. They expect you to follow certain conventions for this writing, and, beyond this, to come up with your own ideas and develop cogent arguments. They hope to read your work without stumbling over tangled run-on sentences, or jumbled paragraphs, or multiple spelling mistakes and typos.

Writing in college, you know that your instructor will read your work. Your instructor will also expect a certain awareness of audience beyond the classroom. That audience could be general. Kate writes a paper on genetically modified food that could be provocative for anyone interested in the issue. On the other hand, your audience could be extremely specific. Zach plans to write a letter to a particular person. As we shall see in Chapter Two, successful student writers don't just think about what they will write and how. They consider their audience, real and imagined.

As they read your work, instructors look for well supported claims and reasonable arguments. They want to move step by step through your written work, guided by the transitions you provide. And, of course, they want you to do all this on time. With rare exceptions, they insist on receiving written work by an announced due date.

Cogent arguments, lucid sentences, good transitions, correct documentation, clean copy—how will you get all of this done? You will need to develop a process that works for you as you meet the multiple expectations of courses that require writing.

Developing a Writing Process

When Anna describes her process, she talks about doodling before she begins writing. Jordan describes talking to himself. In contrast, Zach focuses on producing the draft itself. It's true that generating a draft is a huge part of the writing process, but how do you get to a point where you can generate that draft? Where do you begin?

Before drafting, many successful writers allow themselves time to reflect on their assignment, ask questions, explore ideas. Instead of starting with complete sentences and finished paragraphs, many begin by doodling and scribbling notes. Another strategy—often overlooked—is to talk through ideas with others. Jordan is on to something when he mentions trying out ideas—even arguing with friends. This is an excellent way to test something you want to say—before committing to writing. Maybe your idea sounds great—or maybe it's got some flaws, as your friends will tell you. Speaking, listening, and responding to comments or objections is a highly effective way to start the writing process. Anna decides to try this strategy as she tackles the first assignment in her freshman seminar: a literacy narrative.

Anna

When I am concentrating, I can type many paragraphs. The hard part is beginning, because I get nervous when I am not sure what I am going to say. When I am trying to think what to do, I will start at times by doodling words and even pictures on paper before I begin typing on my computer.

Jordan

It's easier for me to talk than to sit and type, so I start by walking around, talking to myself. Sometimes I talk to other people, too, just to try out ideas. I'll start arguing my point with friends, like I'm rehearsing for a debate. This gets me in the mood to start writing.

Zach

I go to a coffee shop with a lot of background noise, and I try to trick myself into thinking I'm not really working. I write the first few sentences. Then I take a break. Then I think about how many words I have to go. With a big open-ended assignment, it's torture—but if I'm answering a specific question, I can be efficient. I'm a very concise person.

Kate

I have a lot going on with kids and work in addition to school, so when I get a writing assignment I try to plan ahead, breaking down the job so it's not so overwhelming, and then doing a little each day, until the assignment is due.

REFLECT: How would you describe your writing process? What's working for you? What would you like to change? Have you discovered one process that helps you get a lot done? Or does your writing process change according to your assignment?

Writing a Literacy Narrative

A literacy narrative is an account of the speaker or author's history with language—with reading, writing, and verbal expression. The narrative can be simple or elaborate, brief or extensive, but ideally it reflects on something people often don't think about consciously—our relationship with words.

Anna's instructor asks students to take the first part of class to write down their own memories and reflections on reading and writing. Two students volunteer to read their work aloud. The first describes learning to read.

> I am sitting on the floor pretending I can read *Green Eggs and Ham*. I can't actually read it, but I know it by heart because my mom read it to me so many times. I know what to say for each picture, and I know exactly when to turn the pages. When I'm done, I close the book and I say, "I read it myself!" Later on, in kindergarten, I find out that actual reading means you have to pay attention to printed black letters, and pictures won't always help you ...

Another focuses on the physical act of writing.

> There is a reason I type everything. I have dysgraphia, which is a disorder that in my case means I have trouble getting a pencil to do what I want. I can't get my letters and words spaced correctly, either. They end up jumbled together, or too far apart, and all the wrong sizes. I used to get frustrated when I was younger, but a conversation with my seventh-grade teacher helped me a lot.
>
> I said, "I feel so dumb."
>
> He said, "But I know you, and I know that's not true. You are not your handwriting. In the early grades, neatness counts the most. As you get more advanced, neatness counts less and less, and it's your thinking that really matters."

The class discusses using specific details to make a narrative come alive. They also talk about how a writer can use a certain moment or incident or memory to focus a narrative. Each literacy narrative grabs you with that moment or incident, right at the start. "I am

DR. B. Responses? Anna?

ANNA I liked them.

DR. B. Why?

ANNA Because they're relatable.

DR. B. How so?

KATE Because they're talking about real situations—but not in a general way, in a detailed way.

DR. B. Okay, can you give some examples?

KATE The name of the book, *Green Eggs and Ham*, the sight of the kid sitting on the floor ...

JORDAN The conversation with the teacher. The details wake you up.

sitting on the floor ..." takes you right to that kid pretending to know how to read. "There is a reason I type everything" takes you right to the student's challenges with dysgraphia. Each narrative develops from an incident or situation to tell a larger story (how I learned to read from pictures!) or make a significant point (I am not my handwriting).

In discussion, the class identifies several important narrative qualities:

- A specific moment, incident, or memory focuses a narrative and draws in the reader right from the start.
- Concrete details bring the narrative to life.
- Talking about a challenge, or describing a process engages the reader.
- An effective narrative develops and grows, using an incident or situation to tell a larger story or make a significant point.

Anna thinks about these points when she gets her assignment:

Write a literacy narrative about your experience learning to read and write. Search your memory and try to recreate your experience for the rest of us. Use your narrative to talk about how your history with words has shaped you as a writer today.

PREWRITING

Before sitting down to draft her work, Anna adopts Jordan's strategy of trying out ideas on friends. This is one form of prewriting, an activity done to prepare for writing a draft.

ANNA   So I learned to read twice — once in Spanish and once in English. I'm not sure which I should write about.

ZACH   Do both. It's like extra credit!

ANNA   Yeah, but that makes it more complicated. Aren't we supposed to focus on one incident or memory?

ZACH   Can't you tie them together?

Talking about an assignment allows you to try out ideas—and speak about potential challenges. A friend may offer a new perspective or suggest a strategy that had not occurred to you. Why not tie together two memories? Will that work?

Anna tries listing her memories of learning to read. Again, she is not composing a draft. Listing is another form of prewriting.

1. First time I could read a sign at the store.
2. Writing down letters on newsprint paper.
3. Coming to the USA.
4. Going to school and learning to read English.
5. In America—watching television, listening to people talk, reading signs on buses ...

Anna finishes her list and starts doodling. She jots down more memories and draws arrows and lines between them. In class, her instructor called this prewriting technique clustering.

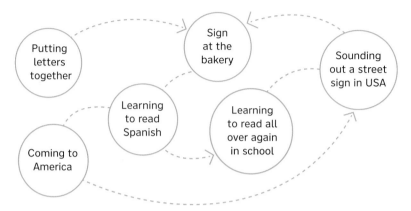

Clustering her ideas, Anna uses pen and paper, literally drawing out her thoughts. She tends to worry about getting her sentences just right, but in a drawing, she feels she can loosen up. After doodling, she begins typing whatever sentences come to her. While typing, she copies and pastes a bakery sign in Spanish, PANADERÍA, and then a NO STOPPING sign in English to illustrate her points.

FREEWRITING

Talking, or typing, or handwriting your sentences without editing or correcting is known as freewriting. This is a great technique for exploring questions and expressing ideas. When you are freewriting, no thought is off limits, no connection impossible. Freewriting may not produce the lucid prose your instructors expect, but it's a great way to get started on an assignment. Glancing at her doodles for inspiration, Anna writes the first thing that comes to mind.

> The first thing I remember reading is the *panadería* and
> this is because I loved going there as a kid. I was like
> when can we go? I loved the treats especially *sopapillas*
> which are like these puffy crispy deep fried very light
> pastries well anyway you remember what's important,
> right? In the US I had to learn to read all over again but
> ironically bakery was not my first word I read on my own

Anna

This paragraph is rambling, but while writing it I figured out my first words in Spanish and English were both on big signs, so that ties them together. Maybe I can use that! Also, it brought back memories of *sopapillas* ...

it was no stopping on a sign on my street where you were not allowed to stop your car and I think I read it because I knew no and stop and I put those together, so not so interesting but kind of part of the theme since that was a sign too.

DRAFTING

Using this point of connection between the bakery sign and the street sign, Anna starts drafting her literacy narrative.

I learned to read twice, and both times, I read my first words on a sign. The first sign was in Spanish. *Panadería* means bakery and I'm sure I learned that word because I loved it there so much. Even the letters looked delicious, painted in black. As soon as I saw this word I thought of *sopapillas*, those crispy, delicate, deep-fried pastries dusted in sugar. The second sign was when I got to the U.S. and started learning in English in school. The first words I could decipher by myself were on a street sign that said no stopping ...

SHARING A DRAFT

In class, students exchange drafts of their literacy narratives for comments. Anna shows hers to Kate.

KATE   I like it.

ANNA   Really? I feel like something is missing.

KATE   What do you mean?

ANNA   It just seems kind of flat and boring—except for the *sopapillas*.

KATE   Yeah, those sound so good.

ANNA   That's where I got inspired. I wish I could bring the rest up to that level!

KATE   Why don't you start with *sopapillas* and take off from there?

REVISING THE NARRATIVE

Anna takes Kate's advice and starts with what she thinks is the best detail in her narrative.

> Light, airy, delicate, deep-fried *sopapillas*. Those were my favorite dessert. No wonder the first word I could read on my own was *Panadería*. Even the black letters on the sign looked good enough to eat. Spanish is my first language and it came easier to me because I learned when I was a baby. English is my second language and I learned it in high school when I was much older, so I associated English with a lot more rules and regulations. No wonder that the first words I read on my own in English were NO STOPPING, which I figured out by putting together the words no and stop. A lot of signs are about what you can't do, and for a while that was what English meant to me. STOP and NO and also CLOSED and DO NOT ENTER. It took a while for me to enjoy the funny side of English—by watching comedy shows on television, and the interesting side—by listening to the news, and even the delicious side—by watching cooking videos. Gradually I filled in English words with my experience, so that now the word ice cream looks good to me, and sorbet, and molten chocolate.

Starting from one detail, Anna develops her narrative and introduces an interesting idea about her relationship with language. She fills in words with her experiences. Anna does not come up with all of this at once. She begins by thinking, and doodling, and talking to other people and considering their comments. She tries out ideas in conversation and in class, and also on paper and onscreen. Then she sits down for freewriting. She drafts her work, shows it to a friend, and then clarifies her ideas by writing again. Of course, not all writers do all of this on every occasion. Certain aspects of Anna's process may be useful to you, while other aspects may be relevant to someone else. The important thing to understand is that effective writing does not happen all in one go. Writing is a process, involving thinking and some form of prewriting, gathering of supporting details or evidence, time for drafting and revision, and ideally, a chance to respond to comments. In this book, you will learn about each step so that you can develop a reliable process of your own.

As you start college, consider your own history and attitudes toward writing: What has worked in the past? What has not? What would you like to change?

A literacy narrative allows you to reflect on your history with language. An effective literacy narrative:

- Focuses on a specific moment, incident, or memory
- Uses concrete details to bring the narrative to life
- Develops an incident or situation to tell a larger story or make a significant point

Writing is a multi-step process. Ideally, these steps include:

- Thinking
- Prewriting, which might include talking, listing, clustering, doodling
- Drafting
- Sharing work
- Responding to comments

ACTIVITIES

1 Below you will find several writers reflecting on their work. Choose one passage and write one to two paragraphs discussing the writer's process. What attitudes does the writer reveal? Are there aspects of the writer's process that you might consider applying to your own work?

From historian David McCullough (b. 1933). His books include 1776, John Adams, *and* Truman.

There's no question that the sheer effort of writing, of getting it down on paper, makes the brain perform as it rarely does otherwise. I don't understand people who sit and think what they're going to write and then just write it out. My head doesn't work that way. I've got to mess around with it on paper. I've got to make sketches, think it out on paper. Sometimes I think I'm not a writer, I'm a *re*writer. When a page isn't working, I crumple it into a ball and throw it in the wastebasket. Always have. Our son Geoffrey, when he was a little boy, would come out where I work and look in my wastebasket to see how many "wrong pages" I had written that day. If the basket was full, it had been a good day. I'd worked things through.

McCullough, David. "The Art of Biography No. 2." *The Paris Review*, no. 152, Fall 1999, www.theparisreview.org/interviews/894/the-art-of-biography-no-2-david-mccullough. Accessed January 17, 2019.

From comic book writer and editor Scott Peterson (b. 1968). His works include Batman: Gothic Adventures *and* Batgirl.

First I write the story out in prose, which takes one and a half to three pages ... This is the document called "Plot."

Then I have a document that simply lists from page one to page twenty-two and I fill in what happens on each page with between one and a dozen words:

> Page Three
> More fight
> Page Thirteen
> Batman checks out alibi, realizes truth

This is the document called "Outline." All along I have another document called "Thoughts" or "Ideas" or "Notes" ... stuff I want to remember to put in the story to add to the subplot or subtext or just a cool visual move for later in the issue when Batman has the fight scene in the bakery or whatever …

And then I start writing the actual script. I've found that if I go through all these steps, the process, from beginning to end (including all those steps, plus the actual writing of the script) is not very long, but if I try to skip one of the steps, I usually actually lose time.

Peterson, Scott. Qtd. in *The DC Comics Guide to Writing Comics*. Watson-Guptill, 2001, p. 80.

From science writer Ed Yong depicting his process writing an article for Discover ***magazine.***

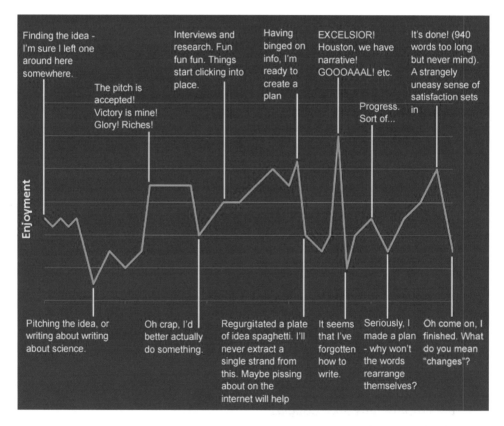

Yong, Ed. "Not Exactly Rocket Science: The Writing Process." *Discover Magazine* blog, 30 Mar. 2011. http://blogs.discovermagazine.com/notrocketscience/2011/03/30/the-writing-process/#. XEDMtGIIDIU. Accessed 17 Jan. 2019.

From an interview with Mary Coleman, Senior Development Executive, on the screenwriting process at Pixar.

One of many reasons that the writer being part of the creative team is so important is that while writing that second draft they're working side by side with the eight or so story artists who are drawing the movie. There's a lot of back and forth. It's really a unique experience for a screenwriter because they're not only collaborating with the director, but also with this very talented group of visual storytellers. The drawings feed the written word just as much as the written word feeds the story boards. The writers who have lasted here love that process. And then there are the ones who ran out of here screaming "too many chefs!!"

So the second draft of the screenplay is also the first reel screening. And it's always bad. It's just bad. That's okay. Andrew [Stanton] likes to say "Be wrong fast." On the one hand, we'll take a whole year to get to a first draft. But once we have that, we put it up on reels an average of eight times and that's eight visual rough drafts of the movie. That translates to many more than eight drafts of the script. At a certain point the back and forth is so fluid you lose count.

Coleman, Mary. "GITS Q&A, Part 4: Mary Coleman (Pixar)." Interview by Scott Myers. *Go into the Story* blog, 28 Feb. 2012, www.gointothestory.blcklst.com/gits-q-a-part-4-mary-coleman-pixar-cfea02a390e5. Accessed 20 Sept. 2018.

---

2   How would you describe your own writing process? Discuss the way you tackled a recent assignment. Alternatively, create a graph, timeline, cartoon, or infographic, like Ed Yong's above, to present your process visually. Are you satisfied with your writing process? Is there anything you would like to change? If so, why?

---

3   Read the following literacy narratives and answer these questions. What situation, incident, or challenge focuses the narrative? What details does the author use? How does the author use these details to make a larger point about reading, writing, speaking, and thinking?

Born a slave, Frederick Douglass (1818–85) became an abolitionist, writer, and social reformer.

Very soon after I went to live with Mr. and Mrs. Auld, she very kindly commenced to teach me the A, B, C. After I had learned this, she assisted me in learning to spell words of three or four letters. Just at this point of my progress, Mr. Auld found out what was going on, and at once forbade Mrs. Auld to instruct me further, telling her, among other things, that it was unlawful, as well as unsafe, to teach a slave to read. To use his own words, further, he said, "… there would be no keeping him. It would forever unfit him to be a slave. He would at once become unmanageable, and of no value to his master. As to himself, it could do him no good, but a great deal of harm. It would make him discontented and unhappy." These words sank deep into my heart, stirred up sentiments within that lay slumbering, and called into existence an entirely new train of thought. It was a new and special revelation, explaining dark and mysterious things, with which my youthful understanding had struggled, but struggled in vain. I now understood what had been to me a most perplexing difficulty—to wit, the white man's power to enslave the black man. It was a grand achievement, and I prized it highly. From that moment, I understood the pathway from slavery to freedom. It was just what I wanted, and I got it at a time when I the least expected it. Whilst I was saddened by the thought of losing the aid of my kind mistress, I was gladdened by the invaluable instruction which, by the merest accident, I had gained from my master. Though conscious of the difficulty of learning without a teacher, I set out with high hope, and a fixed purpose, at whatever cost of trouble, to learn how to read. The very decided manner with which he spoke, and strove to impress his wife with the evil consequences of giving me instruction, served to convince me that he was deeply sensible of the truths he was uttering. It gave me the best assurance that I might rely with the utmost confidence on the results which, he said, would flow from teaching me to read. What he most dreaded, that I most desired. What he most loved, that I most hated. That which to him was a great evil, to be carefully shunned, was to me a great good, to be diligently sought; and the argument which he so warmly urged, against my learning to read, only served to inspire me with a desire and determination to learn. In learning to read, I owe almost as much to the bitter opposition of my master, as to the kindly aid of my mistress. I acknowledge the benefit of both.

Douglass, Frederick. *Narrative of the Life of Frederick Douglass, an American Slave*. Broadview Press, 2018, pp. 112–13. [Note: We have omitted racial slurs used by Mr. Auld. You can find the complete text in the Broadview edition or online.]

Temple Grandin (b. 1947) is a professor of animal science, a consultant to the livestock industry on animal control and humane slaughter, and a writer and speaker on what it is like to live with autism.

Growing up, I learned to convert abstract ideas into pictures as a way to understand them. I visualized concepts such as peace or honesty with symbolic images. I thought of peace as a dove, an Indian peace pipe, or TV or newsreel footage of the signing of a peace agreement. Honesty was represented by an image of placing one's hand on the Bible in court. A news report describing a person returning a wallet with all the money in it provided a picture of honest behavior.

The Lord's Prayer was incomprehensible until I broke it down into specific visual images. The power and the glory were represented by a semicircular rainbow and an electrical tower. These childhood visual images are still triggered every time I hear the Lord's Prayer. The words "thy will be done" had no meaning when I was a child, and today the meaning is still vague. Will is a hard concept to visualize. When I think about it, I imagine God throwing a lightning bolt. Another adult with autism wrote that he visualized "Thou art in heaven" as God with an easel above the clouds. "Trespassing" was pictured as black and orange NO TRESPASSING signs. The word "Amen" at the end of the prayer was a mystery: a man at the end made no sense.

Grandin, Temple. *Thinking in Pictures: And Other Reports from My Life with Autism*. Vintage Books, 2006, p. 17.

Author and artist Grace Lin (b. 1974) is known for picture books such as Red Is a Dragon ***and young adult novels such as*** When the Mountain Meets the Moon.

I grew up in upstate New York where there were very, very few minority families. Except for my sisters, I was definitely the only Asian in my elementary school. That gave me kind of a weird sense of identity, though when I was younger all I did was try really hard to forget that I was Asian. I wanted to forget that I was different from everybody else as much as possible, and I did a really good job of that. I remember walking down the street when I was young and seeing my reflection in a window and saying, "Oh, there's a Chinese girl there." I completely forgot that I was Asian because I had done such a good job forgetting all about that. My Asian heritage was something that I purposely tried not to know anything about until much, much later. Then I realized what a shame it was and how sad it was.

I remember the first time I really, really felt that tragedy. I was in Rome, Italy. I went to Rome as part of the Rhode Island School of Design's European honors program. I studied in Rome for a year, and the Italians immediately thought that I was Chinese or Japanese. The idea of me being an Asian American was not their first thought. They would talk to me and ask me all these things about China or Taiwan in Italian, and I knew nothing—but I could speak to them in Italian. I realized how strange it was that I knew Italian, but I didn't know any Chinese—my parents' native tongue. I knew no Chinese at all, yet I knew all these things about Italy. I knew about Michelangelo's girlfriends and where he bought his tomatoes, but I didn't know anything about my own family. I didn't even know why my parents moved from Taiwan to the United States, and all of a sudden I felt really ashamed. That was probably the first time I realized how much I didn't know and what I was missing out on. That was the start of trying to embrace my roots more.

Lin, Grace. "In-depth Written Interview." *Teachingbooks.net*, 23 May 2011, www.teachingbooks.net/interview.
cgi?id=95&a=1. Accessed 20 Sept. 2018.

From My Beloved World, *by Sonia Sotomayor (b. 1954), an Associate Justice of the United States Supreme Court.*

One day the doorbell rang, and my mother opened the door to a man carrying two big briefcases. It wasn't the man who made the rounds of the projects selling insurance. It wasn't the old man who came to collect two dollars every Saturday for the drapes he'd sold us months before. My mother sat down with the salesman at the kitchen table, and they talked for a very long time, looking at books, adding up numbers. I was in the other room, overhearing bits and pieces: "priceless gift of knowledge ... like a library of a thousand books ... easy monthly payments ..."

When the two big boxes labeled *Encyclopedia Britannica XXX* arrived, it was Christmas come early. Junior and I sat on the floor surrounded by piles of books like explorers at the base of Everest. Each of the twenty-four volumes was a doorstop, the kind of book you'd expect to see in a library, never in someone's home and certainly not twenty-four of them, including a whole separate book just for the index! As I turned the densely set onionskin pages at random, I found myself wandering the world's geography, pondering molecules like daisy-chains, marveling at the physiology of the eye. I was introduced to flora and fauna, to the microscopic structures of cells, to mitosis, meiosis, and Mendel's garden of peas. The world branched out before me in a thousand new directions, pretty much as the salesman had promised, and when it became overwhelming, all I had to do was close the book. It would wait for me to return.

Sotomayor, Sonia. *My Beloved World*. Vintage Books, 2014, p. 89.

4   Write a brief literacy narrative about your experience learning to read and write. Can you remember yourself before knowing how to read and write? How do you remember learning? If you know more than one language, how would you describe your relationship with each? Reflect on how your history with spoken and/or written words has shaped you as a writer today.

2

RHETORIC AND THE RHETORICAL SITUATION

Writing a Persuasive Letter.

ZACH Okay, got my coffee. Got my table. Got my laptop. *Assignment. Write a one-page letter about a real-world issue that affects your life.* Great. I have to write a letter, even though nobody writes letters anymore.

BEEP BEEP

Low battery! Excuse me. Sorry. I'm looking for an outlet. Could I just ... Doesn't reach!

BEEP BEEP BEEP

Keep your audience in mind ...

BEEP BEEP BEEP

Why are there only two outlets in this coffee shop?
Consider the rhetorical situation ...

BEEP BEEP BEEP BEEP

Zach pleading with his computer. You're dying on me now? Wait, wait. What's a rhetorical situation??

What Is Rhetoric and Why Does It Matter?

There are many ways to convey a message. Effective writers weigh their options carefully. *What will I say? And how will I say it?* These are such important questions that an entire field has developed to study them. Rhetoric is the study of effective communication in speech and writing, and also in images, symbols, gestures—in every form of human interaction. Greet a friend, ask a question, provide directions, apply for a job: each of these interactions carries a purpose—whether that message is long and involved or just a quick ☺ to a friend. In every case, you have a **purpose**, you communicate to a real or imagined **audience**, and choose a **genre**, or form, to convey a message. Each of these elements interacts within a certain **context**—the circumstances, conditions and framework—for communication. Context can be personal—we talk at lunch—or geopolitical—world leaders meet to sign a treaty on climate change. We communicate in private and public ways, in intimate and socio-economic frameworks, and sometimes all of these frameworks at once. But no matter how we communicate, when taken together, purpose, audience, and genre comprise what rhetoricians call the **rhetorical situation**.

If people communicate all the time without thinking twice, why is it important to understand the rhetorical situation and its elements? First, rhetorical knowledge enables us to **read critically**, providing tools and vocabulary for evaluating texts and images. Second, rhetorical knowledge helps us to **write effectively**, as we consider the best way to convey a message to a particular audience. Let's look more closely at the key elements of the rhetorical situation.

PURPOSE

Purpose is your motivation, the desire, the need that drives you to communicate. Sometimes rhetorical purpose is straightforward. You ask the waiter for a spoon, because yours fell on the floor and you need a clean one. Sometimes purpose is complex. When Martin Luther King Jr. wrote his "Letter from a Birmingham Jail," he had at least two motives in mind—to argue directly with a group of ministers who advised against immediate protests against racial injustice and to make a larger statement defining human freedom and dignity. In each case, purpose drives communication.

In college, your purpose depends on the assignment. Some assignments require you to inform. Reporting the results of a chemistry experiment, you inform your reader. Some assignments require you to persuade. You write a speech arguing for campaign finance reform. Still other assignments require a mix of information and persuasion. You set up an argument by informing your reader about previous research on campaign finance and the electoral system, and then you try to persuade your reader of your own viewpoint. There are those assignments which ask for a written analysis of a document or an image or an event or a data set. Alternatively, an instructor may ask you to entertain with storytelling, or to move your reader with poetry, or to spark debate with your reporting, or to provide a record of an event. The possibilities are endless, but in each case your purpose provides a reason or **motivation** for writing.

Sometimes students lose that motivation, or sense of purpose. Writing can seem artificial, compared to the quick flow of everyday communication. After all, you are writing in college to fulfill an assignment. It's possible to take that as your sole purpose. However, if you write *only* to fulfill an assignment, your work could become a mechanical exercise, tedious to write and to read. When you bring your own interests, concerns, and experience to the assignment, your writing comes alive. Instructors know this, and so you will find that many assignments provide an opening for you to think beyond the classroom. Zach's instructor asks for a letter about a real world issue that affects Zach personally. This language urges Zach to write about an issue or problem he cares about—to write with a real-life sense of purpose.

Anna

I wrote a one-page statement about my experience as a camp counselor. My purpose was to persuade the camp to accept me for a summer leadership program.

Kate

I wrote down a list of names and phone numbers for my babysitter. My purpose is to help her contact adults in an emergency.

Jordan

I sent flowers to my grandmother. My purpose was to wish her a happy birthday, but also to apologize for not calling her all semester.

Zach

I told a bad joke to my roommate. My purpose was to cheer him up after he got his midterm back.

REFLECT on your day so far and consider two or three communications. Identify your purpose or purposes for each.

AUDIENCE

An audience receives your messages. Your audience can be big or small, familiar or anonymous, knowledgeable or uninformed,

Zach

I am supposed to write a letter to an actual human, but I am actually writing *for* my instructor.

Anna

I am posting on my class discussion forum. The other students are my audience— but I know the prof will be lurking there as well!

Jordan

I am writing a movie review for my film class. My audience is my instructor, but in order to write a useful review, I have to think about what moviegoers want to know— like should they actually pay money to see this movie?

Kate

I am writing a lab report. My audience is the teaching assistant who already knows how the experiment is supposed to turn out—but I need to imagine a reader who does not know all the details and the outcome, so I can explain my experiment step by step.

REFLECT on a writing assignment. Do you need to imagine an audience in addition to your instructor? Who might that audience be? What choices will you make to communicate effectively with your imagined audience?

friendly, hostile, or undecided. You tailor messages to different audiences all the time. You ask a friend for directions. *Hey, where's the party?* But you ask a stranger for directions quite differently. *Excuse me. Do you know where I can find Hemmingway Gym?* Generally, you would not approach a stranger the way you would a close friend. By the same token, you would not speak in class the way you would to a small child. You give an oral presentation on famine. *Drought, economic decline, political chaos, and isolation are known contributors to famine in the developing world.* But you make different rhetorical choices when your audience is your eight-year-old nephew. *Sometimes when countries have terrible weather and don't get enough help, people don't have enough to eat.* Notice how quickly tone and content shift when you address a new audience. The very details you highlight in a public presentation are those you would avoid when speaking to a child.

As a speaker you usually communicate directly. You speak up in class and see your classmates and your instructor sitting together in the room. When you whisper to a friend, you communicate immediately and directly as well. You are confiding in a particular person. However, when you write, your audience is usually not present physically. Nor can you see your audience respond in real time as you communicate your message. Often, as a writer, you need to visualize the audience you cannot see. Sometimes imagining that audience is easy. Send a text and you can imagine the expression on your friend's face. You may even anticipate your friend's response. At other times, imagining an audience is more complex. Who is your audience when you write an essay for class? You know your instructor will read and evaluate your work—so on one level your instructor is your audience. However, your instructor may ask you to envision another audience as well—and even if your instructor doesn't ask, it helps to imagine a reader outside the classroom.

GENRE

With a specific purpose in mind, a writer chooses a form in order to communicate to an audience. This specific form of communication is called a genre. The term genre is often used to delineate categories of creative expression. Painting, photograph, sculpture are all genres of visual art. A poem, novel, essay, play are genres of literature. Pop, Country, Rock, R&B, Folk, Funk, Jazz, Blues, Gospel, Classical—these are all genres of music with their own stations on the radio. One way to study art—and creativity—is to investigate the way artists work with and against the conventions of genre.

Genre is also a useful term for understanding everyday communication. A birth announcement, an obituary, a propaganda poster, a dictionary definition, a reality show, a crossword puzzle, a three-page essay, a yearbook picture, a newspaper article, a diary entry—each of these is a distinct genre. Genre is important because it signals the content of a message. The words *knock knock* prepare the listener for a joke. These set words invite the formulaic response *Who's there?* A list of ingredients beginning *one cup flour, one half cup sugar* signals a recipe and prepares the reader for baking instructions. Knowledge of genre helps a reader categorize and decode messages. You see the words *Dear Aunt Paula* and you think personal letter. You see the words *To Whom It May Concern* and you think this is an open letter to anyone who will listen. **LIMITED TIME OFFER!!!** in all caps, boldface print, with three exclamation points signals a sales pitch. *Once upon a time* signals a fairy tale.

Zach

A lot of times mathematical proofs start with Let X = something and Y = … Or, take two numbers such that …

Jordan

Not all the time—but a lot of the time—you can tell it's a poem by the short lines, the white space on the page, and the missing punctuation.

Kate

When you see tiny print with phrases such as *valid only in* … or *Other restrictions may apply* … you know you're getting into legal language.

Anna

When you see *To all who read these letters, greetings* … and there's a university seal at the bottom and a lot of signatures, you're reading a diploma.

REFLECT on the genres you read, see, and hear in your everyday life. How do you identify these genres? What signals tip you off?

ZACH Kate, could you look at this?

KATE Okay, let's see. *The Quest for Power, by Zachary Akino. Power is a necessity in modern times to get any work done. So there should obviously be more than two outlets in a coffee shop ...* Wait, I'm confused. What's this essay about?

ZACH It's not an essay.

KATE Oh! I thought it was, because it had the title and author on top.

ZACH No, the assignment is to write a persuasive letter.

KATE Who's it for?

ZACH Well—my instructor.

KATE So you're going to write *Dear Instructor*?

ZACH No, of course not!

Many of your assignments will require you to write in a certain genre and to understand its conventions. A lab report requires you to present information in specific ordered sections. In contrast, a genre such as a discussion forum might forbid offensive language but does not require a certain structure for written comments.

Some genres set strict limits on length—for example, a one-paragraph summary, or a three-to-five-page paper. Some dictate a specific format. A pie chart is round. A half-hour television show breaks for commercials at the ten-minute mark. A sestina is a poem that repeats certain words in a specific pattern. On the one hand, these conventions restrict expression. On the other hand, they can provide welcome guidance. If you have ever thought of writing as open-ended, or fuzzy, look to genre for rules and structure. But what if you are unsure which genre to use, and what its rules might be? It is crucial to study your assignments to learn what form your writing should take.

An essay is one genre, and a letter quite another. Each carries its own conventions. Zach's formal title *The Quest for Power* sounds like the title of a formal essay or book, not a personal appeal. If he is going to write a letter, he needs to begin differently. Most letters begin with some kind of greeting, or more formal heading.

Okay, a letter. I need to write to a human—preferably somebody who can do something about the lack of power outlets. *Dear Manager of the Atomic Bean.* Wait, that would be Lorraine. *Dear Lorraine …*

New Genres, Unfamiliar Situations

In conversation, you can see a speaker's face and gestures. You can hear even the subtlest changes in tone and voice. In writing you cannot rely on these signals. You must communicate onscreen or on the page, adopting specific conventions to convey your ideas. Often the appropriate strategy seems obvious. You are inviting friends to dinner. You know your audience, you know what you want to say, you know how to say it, and you know the form your message will take—a quick text. *Dinner @ 8. Bring food!*

Sometimes, however, you will find yourself in a situation where you do not know quite what to say. For the first time, you need to send a message of condolence. How do you write with respect and sympathy? You need to draft a report for your boss. How long should it be? How much detail should you include? And how should you present your work? Email attachment? PDF? Hard copy? Slide show? What should it look like on the page or screen?

As you reflect on these questions, remember to consider the elements of the rhetorical situation. Ask yourself, what is my purpose here? Who is my audience? What's the best approach? These are not trivial questions. The stakes are high when we communicate. A carelessly worded condolence letter might hurt the recipient. A message sent to the wrong recipient could cost you your job. Information sent through unapproved channels could compromise company security. The opposite is also true. A heartfelt letter can comfort a reader. A well-directed message could earn you a fair hearing. Information sent through appropriate channels could enhance your company's productivity.

At times college classes present students with new rhetorical situations. Your instructor may ask you to write in a genre you have not tried, such as an annotated bibliography, an abstract, a specific kind of lab report, a research paper, or a multi-modal presentation. Even when a genre seems familiar, you may find that instructors' expectations differ. An essay in this class may not look the same as an essay in the class you took last year. Often your assignment will provide guidance, explaining expectations. Even with these guidelines, it helps to break down an unfamiliar assignment by answering the rhetorician's key questions:

- What is my purpose?
- Who is my audience?
- What is the genre?

If you have not worked in a particular genre before, try asking for examples to study. Writing an annotated bibliography is much easier when you can look at an example in the format your instructor requires. Reading scientific abstracts will give you a better sense of the length and level of detail your instructor expects. Of course, looking at examples will only get you so far. Working in a new genre can be daunting. When in doubt, it makes sense to pause and consider how to address your audience. This is the fundamental question. How do you present a message your audience will understand, or believe, or enjoy, or answer?

ZACH

So I am writing to Lorraine, the manager of the Atomic Bean, and I envision my letter as frustrated but rational, polite but also urgent, laser-focused without sounding too crazy ... How do I get all that in writing?

Rhetorical Appeals

How can I convey my message effectively? Rhetoricians have studied this question for thousands of years. The philosopher Aristotle (384–322 BCE) suggests that when we communicate we use three different rhetorical strategies, or **appeals**: ethos, pathos, logos. He adds a fourth term, kairos, to convey the dimension of time and timeliness.

ETHOS

Ethos is the Greek word for character. An appeal to ethos is an appeal to the character and credibility of the speaker or writer. A candidate for school board might say, *I have lived and worked in this community for 30 years. I have served as both a teacher and a school* *principal. Both my children attend our public schools.* These are appeals to ethos. The speaker is saying Don't just vote for what I've done. Vote for who I am—your neighbor, your teacher, your fellow parent.

Advertisements often appeal to ethos. Consider the images of men and women dressed like scientists in white lab coats to sell cosmetics, and the phrases you've heard. *Dentist-recommended.* Or *Nine out of ten doctors ...*

Credibility can mean expertise, honesty, integrity, and authenticity. It can also mean audacity and edge. There is a reason companies pay so much for movie stars or sports heroes to wear certain shoes or carry a certain phone. We look up to these people when it comes to style. A celebrity spokesperson for a brand makes a huge impression—especially to a young audience. Indeed, advertisers consider audience carefully when they make appeals. They consider such factors as age, gender, ethnicity, income, and education. After all, what counts as expertise and authority for a middle-aged woman may look quite different to a 12-year-old girl.

Appeals to ethos can manipulate an audience. I want to run like her. I want to look like him. I admire them, and so I'll buy their products. However, appeals to ethos extend beyond advertising. In everyday conversation a friend appeals to ethos when he says, *Trust me. I've been commuting here for four years. I've tried both routes and this one is faster.* In academic debate, a scholar might declare, *I have not only read every source available on this topic, but I have edited the definitive edition of these texts.* In each case, the appeal to ethos tries to establish trust. A careful writer appeals to ethos with an argument well supported by reliable sources and sound reasoning. A student who proofreads and corrects errors appeals to ethos by submitting a clean draft. The reader's first impression is that this writer takes pride in her work.

PATHOS

Appeals to ethos often focus on the speaker, but appeals to **pathos** focus on the audience. Appealing to pathos, the speaker or writer attempts to influence emotions. You see a picture of a wide-eyed shelter kitten along with the words *Will you be my forever family?* You're looking at an appeal to pathos. Your friend asks, *Aren't you* *angry about the litter on campus? Don't you want to do something about it?* That's an appeal to pathos. Activists declare, *Don't stand by and watch. Join us and we can change the world for the better.* Often, even when the speaker or writer highlights her own feelings,—she does so to reach out to the audience. *I am outraged, and you should be too!*

Advertisers appeal to pathos. Pictures of farms and country porches, golden light, and fields of wheat evoke feelings of nostalgia that help to sell—granola. Images of a starry sky, a swooping eagle, and a spaceship make us think of speed, flight, and cutting-edge technology, all of which advertise—a luxury car.

Politicians appeal to pathos when they campaign for election. Candidates speak to our love for our children and our hope for the future. *Don't you want a better tomorrow for your sons and daughters?* Internet trolls appeal to pathos when they try to inflame debate with angry rhetoric and racist or misogynistic language. Charities appeal to pathos when they ask potential donors to identify with those less fortunate—and to feel guilty if they don't. *Have you ever been hungry?* Military recruiters spark feelings of patriotism—*Sworn to defend American soil*—and appeal to ambition and pride—*Be all you can be.*

Appealing to pathos can be highly effective, not only in advertising but in the genres of poetry, sermons, stump speeches, flash mobs, personal letters, and viral videos. Such appeals might be less welcome in genres such as academic essays or factual reports. Think carefully about your assignment and your instructor's expectations before you make emotional appeals. An appeal to pathos could work well in a story for your creative writing class, but derail a lab report in organic chemistry.

LOGOS

Well suited to academic writing are appeals to **logos,** or reason. A scientist explains how experiments demonstrate that even the youngest infants recognize human speech. A debater points out holes in his opponent's argument: *You say now that you would support military action in certain cases, but in your opening statement you said no boots on the ground. Which do you believe?* A mathematician asks you to accept three axioms as the basis of a proof. These are all appeals to logos. Appeals to logos are not all based on formal logic. An appeal to "common sense" and an argument from evidence in a court of law both serve as appeals to logos. As with ethos and pathos, an appeal to logos takes different forms, depending on the rhetorical situation.

Not all appeals to logos are created equal. You hear politicians quoting studies and statistics. You see commercials displaying graphs and charts touting the superiority of one product over another. Where did these numbers come from? What kind of study produced these results? Are these results as compelling as they seem? Advertisers compare their detergent to "a leading brand." What exactly is this leading brand—an arch-rival, or some random cut-rate soap? Like other rhetorical appeals, the appeal to logos can serve many purposes. A scientist appeals to logos, but a car salesman does too. *Let me run the numbers for you. With your trade-in and the cash back, and this low interest rate, your new car will cost less than the one you're driving now ...*

Some appeals to logos are designed to manipulate an audience, and they invite skepticism or even disdain. However, a fair-minded appeal to logos inspires trust and substantive debate. In college your instructors may ask you to develop a well-supported argument. Such assignments require appeals to logos as you make a claim and provide strong evidence for your assertions. By the same token, in class discussion, instructors hope that you will make a point and then explain your reasoning. Such appeals to logos are highly prized in the workplace, in the research community, and in conversation. This is why instructors want you to practice them.

KAIROS

Aristotle uses a fourth term, **kairos,** to refer to time. We include it here because timing is an important variable in the rhetorical situation. Effective communication conveys a sense of timeliness, even urgency, to the audience. Debates on taxation, capital punishment, gun control, and gender equality don't renew themselves year after year simply because these topics are controversial. Some specific event or cause provokes new discussion. *A Department of Labor study released today, shows that women earn only 77 cents for every dollar earned by men. We need to take action now.*

Let's say you are protesting development on your street. You need to rally your neighbors *now*, before the developers receive approval for their plans. Or let's say you are tweeting news you've just received about storm warnings. You don't want to talk about storms in general, or limit yourself to phrases like "stay safe." You need to emphasize that storms are expected tonight. Without using the term, you invoke kairos, the urgency of the moment.

Salespeople use kairos to expert effect as they try to close a deal: *Don't delay. These prices won't last.* Politicians declare: *Now is the time. This is the moment to act.* Kairos figures strongly in songs and poetry. Robert Herrick (1591–1674) uses kairos in his poem "To the Virgins, to Make Much of Time."

> Gather ye rosebuds while ye may,
> Old Time is still a-flying:
> And this same flower that smiles to-day
> To-morrow will be dying.

Herrick, Robert. "To the Virgins, to Make Much of Time." *Hesperides*. London: John Williams, 1648.

In a love song, kairos sounds intimate and intense. In academic writing, investigators appeal to kairos to demonstrate the timeliness of certain findings, the urgency of a problem, and the need for new solutions. A medical report states: *The mortality rate has not changed in 20 years, and more funding for clinical studies is urgently needed.* Charitable organizations assert: *Every three minutes a child goes missing. Join with us to prevent abduction today.* Environmentalists declare: *Without immediate action the golden-cheeked warbler will soon die out.* The dateline on a news story, the time and date of an instant message, the appeal to act now: kairos frames the rhetorical situation in time.

Jordan

When my mom said, "Picture your grandma sitting alone in her tiny room waiting to hear from you," that was an appeal to pathos, for sure.

Zach

I saw a sign: HUGE DISCOUNTS, ONE DAY ONLY! That was an appeal to kairos.

Anna

The president of the university came to talk to us at orientation, and he started by saying, "I was a first-generation college student, just like you." I felt like wow. He gets it. That was an amazing appeal to ethos.

Kate

I appealed to logos when I reasoned with my son. "Wait for the cookies to cool. They'll be just as yummy, and they won't burn your tongue."

REFLECT on an exchange you've had recently in conversation or text. How would you describe the appeals used?

Using Rhetorical Appeals

Students of rhetoric learn to identify and use the three rhetorical appeals, along with kairos, in their own work. Zach begins his letter to the manager of the Atomic Bean with a strong appeal to pathos.

> Dear Lorraine,
> Has your computer ever shut down while you are struggling to make a deadline? Can you picture the total frustration and panic as your computer starts beeping and then ominously goes dark? Not to mention losing your train of thought—possibly forever?

Zach's instructor reads the draft and suggests that he might make some initial adjustments.

DR. B.   Zach, this is a good start, but your letter sounds a little ... hysterical.

ZACH   That's my appeal to pathos.

DR. B.   You're coming on strong. Remember keeping your audience in mind?

ZACH   Yeah, I've got that covered. *Dear Lorraine*.

DR. B.   Hmmm.

ZACH   You think using her first name is too personal?

DR. B.   It's personal and it's also aggressive. Keeping Lorraine in mind means considering her point of view. How is she going to react to this attack?

Zach rewrites his letter. Keeping his audience in mind, he expands his repertoire of rhetorical appeals as he tries to address Lorraine's possible objections. Read his work below and see if you can identify appeals to ethos, pathos, logos, along with a reference to kairos.

Dear Ms. Malloy,

I have been a loyal Atomic Bean customer since classes began two weeks ago. In fact I show up almost every day for your amazing coffee. However, when it comes to power outlets, the Atomic Bean is seriously lacking.

Do you really expect a coffee shop with ten tables and a counter (total seating 26) to get by with just two power outlets? Students come to drink coffee and see each other, but also to work. Imagine finding the perfect seat, the most inspiring muffin (banana chip), and the perfect noise level. You are just reaching the crucial point where your whole paper is coming together and then your battery runs out. Both outlets are being used. Only two choices are left to you. Trudge a mile to the library, or give up and retreat to your room, where you see your bed and instantly fall asleep.

Adding new outlets would improve my life and that of countless other students. New outlets would also boost your business, attracting repeat customers at all hours of the day and night. It's true that some of us work at tables for hours at a time, but we fill the Bean during off hours, providing a constant source of revenue with our continuous coffee refills.

I know I speak for a lot of students when I say that I can't keep working at the Atomic Bean without more outlets available. Last weekend I tried Branwell's and counted at least ten convenient power outlets. You've got better music and much better coffee. Please don't make me leave. Bring in an electrician and add some outlets right away.

Sincerely Yours,
Zachary Akino

Zach begins his letter with an appeal to ethos. I am a loyal customer. Therefore, you should listen to me. He also reaches out to create common ground with his audience. He uses a bit of humor, suggesting that he not only likes but needs the café's banana chip muffins—the most inspiring kind—to work effectively. This kind of detail is disarming, as is Zach's admission that the Atomic Bean might have a problem with customers camping out all day with their laptops. This concession appeals to ethos, building respect between writer and reader, and sets up an appeal to logos, establishing a willingness to think through the problem with Lorraine—whom he now addresses respectfully as Ms. Malloy.

Zach also develops his appeal through logos—look, do the math. Two power outlets cannot serve 26 customers. If you add some outlets, you will not only provide better customer service but serve your own interests, boosting your business and making more money. However, he does not limit himself to rational appeals. He does not forget his appeal to pathos. Imagine what it's like to reach that moment of inspiration and then suddenly run out of power. Using vivid language, Zach asks his reader to picture the poor student who must "trudge" to the library. Finally, Zach concludes with an appeal to kairos, underlining the urgency of his request. His appeal, "Please don't make me leave," is actually a veiled threat. Act now, before I give up on the Atomic Bean and take my business elsewhere. Each appeal serves a central purpose—to argue for more outlets in the coffee shop.

You may have heard the expression "empty rhetoric." Sometimes people associate rhetoric with ineffective hand-waving and clichés. In fact, rhetoric is hugely powerful. Rhetoric can serve as a weapon, to cheat, to bully, to slander, to incite violence. Rhetoric can also serve as a tool. A brilliant sales pitch can launch a successful product. A well-crafted defense can convince a jury to acquit a murder suspect. On a global level, the language in a treaty and its accompanying maps can shape the world for generations to come. On a personal level, a serious, well-worded apology could save a friendship, or your job. In every case, rhetoric can change minds and lives.

Consider: What is the most effective way to address my audience? How might my audience respond?

Every communication involves:

- **Audience**
- **Purpose**
- **Genre**

Together, these comprise the rhetorical situation.

Rhetorical Appeals

- **Ethos** appeals to the credibility of speaker or writer
- **Pathos** appeals to emotions
- **Logos** appeals to reason
- **Kairos** frames a message in time

Use Rhetorical Knowledge While Writing

Break down assignments with these questions:

- What is my purpose?
- Who is my audience?
- What is the expected genre?
- What appeals would be effective in this situation?

Use Rhetorical Knowledge While Reading

These questions can help you think critically as you read:

- What is the author's purpose?
- What genre or genres does the author use?
- What appeals does the text make?
- Are these appeals effective?
- Why or why not?

ACTIVITIES

1 Try your hand at writing for different audiences. Write a few sentences for each prompt.

Tell your best friend what you did over the weekend.
Tell your parents.

Ask your instructor for help with an assignment.
Ask your roommate.

Describe your car's problems to your mechanic.
Describe mechanical problems to the person interested in buying your car.

Contemplate the future with your academic advisor.
Contemplate the future in your journal.

Choose one pair above and write a paragraph reflecting on the rhetorical adjustments you made to address a different audience.

2 Have you ever mistakenly hit "reply all"? It's embarrassing to send a private message to a large group. Scrambling a rhetorical situation can lead to laughter. It can also lead to serious misunderstanding. Sometimes the trouble is what you say. Sometimes it's where—and to whom—you say it. Sometimes it's when you say it. Sometimes it's *how* you say it. Describe a rhetorical blunder—either one you have made or one you have witnessed. What went wrong?

3 Read the following passages. See if you can identify the genre of each. What rhetorical cues tipped you off? If in doubt, consult the sources at the end for more clues. Once you identify the genre, what can you infer about the author's purpose and audience?

A. Preheat oven to 300° F.
   In medium bowl combine flour, soda, and salt. Mix well with a whisk. Set aside.

B. I do not remember when I first realized that I was different from other people; but I knew it before my teacher came to me. I had noticed that my mother and my friends did not use signs as I did when they wanted anything done, but talked with their mouths. Sometimes I stood between two persons who were conversing and touched their lips. I could not understand, and was vexed. I moved my lips and gesticulated frantically without result. This made me so angry at times that I kicked and screamed until I was exhausted.

C. Dearly beloved, we are gathered here …

D. Don't let the name fool you: a black hole is anything but empty space. Rather, it is a great amount of matter packed into a very small area—think of a star ten times more massive than the Sun squeezed into a sphere approximately the diameter of New York City. The result is a gravitational field so strong that nothing, not even light, can escape. In recent years, NASA instruments have painted a new picture of these strange objects that are, to many, the most fascinating objects in space.

E. **QUANTIFIERS**
When all the variables in a propositional function are assigned values, the resulting statement has a truth value. However, there is another important way, called **quantification**, to create a proposition from a propositional function. Two types of quantification will be discussed here, namely, universal quantification and existential quantification.

F. Saturday, 21st. Winds Southerly, a Gentle breeze, and Clear weather, with which we coasted along shore to the Northward. In the P.M. we saw the smoke of fire in several places; a Certain sign that the Country is inhabited. At 6, being about 2 or 3 Leagues from the land, we shortned Sail, and Sounded and found 44 fathoms, a sandy bottom. Stood on under an easey sail until 12 o'Clock, at which time we brought too until 4 A.M., when we made sail, having then 90 fathoms, 5 Leagues from the land. At 6, we were abreast of a pretty high Mountain laying near the Shore, which, on account of its figure, I named Mount Dromedary (Latitude 36 degrees 18 minutes South, Longitude 209 degrees 55 minutes West).

G. Friends and Fellow-citizens: I stand before you to-night, under indictment for the alleged crime of having voted at the last Presidential election, without having a lawful right to vote. It shall be my work this evening to prove to you that in thus voting, I not only committed no crime, but, instead, simply exercised my citizen's right, guaranteed to me and all United States citizens by the National Constitution, beyond the power of any State to deny.

H. PICKERING [gently]. What is it you want, my girl?
THE FLOWER GIRL. I want to be a lady in a flower shop stead of selling at the corner of Tottenham Court Road. But they won't take me unless I can talk more

genteel. He said he could teach me. Well, here I am ready to pay him—not asking any favor—and he treats me as if I was dirt.

I. The upper surface of the table, known as the playing surface, shall be rectangular, 2.74m long and 1.525m wide, and shall lie in a horizontal plane 76cm above the floor.

The playing surface shall not include the vertical sides of the tabletop.

The playing surface may be of any material and shall yield a uniform bounce of about 23cm when a standard ball is dropped onto it from a height of 30cm.

A. Fields, Debbie. "Blue-Ribbon Chocolate Chip Cookies." *Mrs. Fields Cookie Book: 100 Recipes from the Kitchen of Mrs. Fields*. Time-Life Books, 1992.

B. Keller, Helen. *The Story of My Life*. Doubleday, 1903, p. 10.

C. Episcopal Church. *The Book of Common Prayer and Administration of the Sacraments and Other Rites and Ceremonies of the Church: Together with the Psalter or Psalms of David According to the Use of the Episcopal Church*. Seabury Press, 1979, p. 423.

D. "Black Holes." *NASA Science*, www.science.nasa.gov/astrophysics/focus-areas/black-holes. Accessed 20 Sept. 2018.

E. Rosen, Kenneth H. *Discrete Mathematics and Its Applications*. 4th ed., McGraw-Hill, 2011, p. 23.

F. Cook, Captain James. *"21 April 1770." Captain Cook's Journal,* www.southseas.nla.gov.au/journals/cook/17700421.html. Accessed 26 Nov. 2018.

G. Anthony, Susan B. "Is It a Crime for a Citizen of the United States to Vote?" National Woman Suffrage Association Meeting, Washington, DC, 16 Jan. 1873.

H. Shaw, George Bernard. *Pygmalion: A Romance in Five Acts*. London: Constable, 1920, p. 217.

I. The International Table Tennis Federation. "The Laws of Table Tennis." *Handbook 2018*, ITTF, 2018, p. 34, www.ittf.com/handbook/. Accessed 20 Sept. 2018.

4   Each of the following authors has a strong sense of purpose. Choose one text and discuss the rhetorical situation. Identify the purpose of each message, the audience you think the author is trying to reach, and the genre he or she uses. What rhetorical appeals does each author make? How does the author use these appeals to communicate to his or her audience?

> *Raymond Anthony Lewis Jr. (b. 1975) was a defensive lineman for the Baltimore Ravens. He won numerous awards during his career, including Most Valuable Player for his performance in the 2001 Super Bowl. Here he speaks to the football team at his alma mater, the University of Miami.*

There is not a person on my team who has consistently beat me to the ball. That ain't got nothing to do with talent. It's just got everything to do with effort. Nothing else. Fifteen straight years, twelve pro-bowls later, if you want the numbers. It's all effort. And the only thing that's kept me around is effort.

Effort, which is between you and you. Nobody can give you effort.

Ask yourself the question personally. How much time do you really waste? I sat in the same chairs you sat in, man. If you want to do something, work at it. If you want a better relationship with God, work at it. This is where it all came from. The same path you all walk ... I had one pair of jeans at college.

What drives you? Like for real?

Gotta stop leaving each other. Gotta stop hanging out without each other. There's many temptations out there. Stay focused, man. As a team, though. As a TEAM. That's all I knew when I was here. It kept me focused.

It's up to you to carry that. Every Sunday. Every Saturday.

Know what you carry when you carry this U on your chest. Know what you carry. A legacy of greatness. And greatness is a lot of small things done well. Day after day. Workout after workout. Obedience after obedience. Day after day.

Lewis, Raymond Anthony, Jr. "Speech to Miami University." 2 Sept. 2011., *YouTube*, www.youtube.com/watch?v=uu4aVQ-qR8U. Accessed 26 Nov. 2018.

Sheryl Sandberg is a tech executive and founder of Leanin.org.

Today in the United States and the developed world, women are better off than ever. We stand on the shoulders of the women who came before us, women who had to fight for the rights that we now take for granted. In 1947, Anita Summers, the mother of my longtime mentor Larry Summers, was hired as an economist by the Standard Oil Company. When she accepted the job, her new boss said to her, "I'm so glad to have you. I figure I am getting the same brains for less money." Her reaction to this was to feel flattered. It was a huge compliment to be told that she had the same brains as a man. It would have been unthinkable for her to ask for equal compensation.

We feel even more grateful when we compare our lives to those of other women around the world. There are still countries that deny women basic civil rights. Worldwide, about 4.4 million women and girls are trapped in the sex trade. In places like Afghanistan and Sudan, girls receive little or no education, wives are treated as the property of their husbands, and women who are raped are routinely cast out of their homes for disgracing their families. Some rape victims are even sent to jail for committing a "moral crime." We are centuries ahead of the unacceptable treatment of women in these countries.

But knowing that things could be worse should not stop us from trying to make them better. When the suffragettes marched in the streets, they envisioned a world where men and women could be truly equal. A century later, we are still squinting, trying to bring that vision into focus.

The blunt truth is that men still run the world.

Sandberg, Sheryl. *Lean In: Women, Work, and the Will to Lead*. Knopf, 2013, p. 5.

From the website of Community Blood Center.

Why Give Blood?

Blood donation is a community responsibility. While you're reading this, a local area patient needs blood.

- Blood is needed every two seconds.
- About one in seven people entering a hospital needs blood.
- Blood is always needed for treatment of accident victims, cancer patients, hemophiliacs and surgery patients.
- Blood cannot be manufactured or harvested.
- Only 37 percent of our country's population is eligible to give blood, and less than 10 percent donate annually.

What if everyone eligible to donate became complacent and decided they didn't need to donate because someone else would?

What if there wasn't enough donated blood available when you, a loved one — anyone — needed it?

Our blood supply comes from caring donors like you. It takes about one hour of your time.

When you give blood, it gives someone another smile, another hug, another chance. It is the gift of life.

Be a Hero. Give Blood.

"Why Give Blood." *Community Blood Center*, www.givingblood.org/donate-blood/why-give-blood.aspx. Accessed 20 Sept. 2018.

5 Sometimes a writer will send a private letter to one person or organization with the knowledge that the letter could be read by others as well, now or in the future. Read the following letter in which one writer protests the banning of his books. How would you describe the audience here? What is Vonnegut's purpose? Does he have more than one? What rhetorical appeals can you identify? Are they effective?

Kurt Vonnegut (1922–2007) was an American writer best known for his novels **Slaughterhouse Five** *(1969) and* **Cat's Cradle** *(1963).*

November 16, 1973

Dear Mr. McCarthy:

I am writing to you in your capacity as chairman of the Drake School Board. I am among those American writers whose books have been destroyed in the now famous furnace of your school.

Certain members of your community have suggested that my work is evil. This is extraordinarily insulting to me. The news from Drake indicates to me that books and writers are very unreal to you people. I am writing this letter to let you know how real I am.

I want you to know, too, that my publisher and I have done absolutely nothing to exploit the disgusting news from Drake. We are not clapping each other on the back, crowing about all the books we will sell because of the news. We have declined to go on television, have written no fiery letters to editorial pages, have granted no lengthy interviews. We are angered and sickened and saddened. And no copies of this letter have been sent to anybody else. You now hold the only copy in your hands. It is a strictly private letter from me to the people of Drake, who have done so much to damage my reputation in the eyes of their children and then in the eyes of the world. Do you have the courage and ordinary decency to show this letter to the people, or will it, too, be consigned to the fires of your furnace?

I gather from what I read in the papers and hear on television that you imagine me, and some other writers, too, as being sort of ratlike people who enjoy making money from poisoning the minds of young people. I am in fact a large, strong person, fifty-one years old, who did a lot of farm work as a boy, who is good with tools. I have raised six children, three my own and three adopted. They have all turned out well. Two of them are farmers. I am a combat infantry veteran from World War II, and hold a Purple Heart. I have earned whatever I own by hard work. I have never been arrested or sued for anything. I am so much trusted with young people and by young people that I have served on the faculties of the University of Iowa, Harvard, and the City College of New York. Every year I receive at least a dozen invitations to be commencement speaker at colleges and high schools. My books are probably more widely used in schools than those of any other living American fiction writer.

If you were to bother to read my books, to behave as educated persons would, you would learn that they are not sexy, and do not argue in favor of wildness of any kind. They beg that people be kinder and more responsible than they often are. It is true that some of the characters speak coarsely. That is because people speak coarsely in real life. Especially soldiers and hardworking men speak coarsely, and even our most sheltered children know that. And we all know, too, that those words really don't damage children much. They didn't damage us when we were young. It was evil deeds and lying that hurt us.

After I have said all this, I am sure you are still ready to respond, in effect, "Yes, yes—but it still remains our right and our responsibility to decide what books our children are going to be made to read in our community." This is surely so. But it is also true that if you exercise that right and fulfill that responsibility in an ignorant, harsh, un-American manner, then people are entitled to call you bad citizens and fools. Even your own children are entitled to call you that.

I read in the newspaper that your community is mystified by the outcry from all over the country about what you have done. Well, you have discovered that Drake is a part of American civilization, and your fellow Americans can't stand it that you have behaved in such an uncivilized way. Perhaps you will learn from this that books are sacred to free men for very good reasons, and that wars have been fought against nations which hate books and burn them. If you are an American, you must allow all ideas to circulate freely in your community, not merely your own.

If you and your board are now determined to show that you in fact have wisdom and maturity when you exercise your powers over the education of your young, then you should acknowledge that it was a rotten lesson you taught young people in a free society when you denounced and then burned books—books you hadn't even read. You should also resolve to expose your children to all sorts of opinions and information, in order that they will be better equipped to make decisions and to survive.

Again: you have insulted me, and I am a good citizen, and I am very real.

Kurt Vonnegut

Vonnegut, Kurt. "Letter to Charles McCarthy, November 16, 1973." *Letters of Note: Correspondence Deserving of a Wider Audience*, compiled by Shaun Usher. Canongate, 2014.

---

6 Letters come in many shapes and sizes. Chats, blogs, letters to the editor, product reviews—to name just a few. In a form appropriate for your purpose and audience, write a letter about a problem that affects your life. Examples might include a complaint to the manufacturer of a defective product, an open letter lobbying for change, a response to a news story. The letter might address a small annoyance—bad service at a restaurant—or something more profound—hate speech on campus. After writing the letter, write a paragraph reflecting on any aspect of the rhetorical situation you found especially important.

3

FROM READING TO WRITING ABOUT TEXTS

Writing a Paraphrase and Summary.
Writing an Analysis of a Text.

ANNA   How's it going?

ZACH   I don't know where to start.

ANNA   Let me see that assignment again. *In his* Paris Review *interview, Nigerian writer Chinua Achebe talks about his vocation. Why did Achebe become a writer? How would you characterize his sense of purpose? What is the purpose of writing in your life?* Okay, that's not so bad.

ZACH   The purpose of writing in my life? What does that even *mean*?

ANNA   What does Achebe say?

ZACH   Um ...

ANNA   Have you read the interview?

What Makes Reading Difficult?

In college, most of your writing begins with an assignment, and many of those assignments will require a response to other people's ideas. Those ideas may take the form of a movie in a film course, or an article in a psychology class, or a diagram in biology class. Zach doesn't know where to begin with his writing, but his instructor provides a starting place with the assigned reading. When you do your reading and study your course material, you lay the foundation for a strong written response.

It's easy to say *do the reading*, but sometimes that reading is difficult. The sheer volume may seem daunting, especially when you are juggling assignments from other courses. Even when your reading is brief, it can present challenges. Perhaps you encounter **unfamiliar vocabulary,** the author's choice of words. You may stumble on specialized language or technical terms.

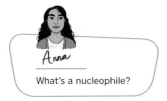

Anna

What's a nucleophile?

Perhaps the **syntax,** or sentence structure, is complicated, and the vocabulary is technical as well. You may run into a long, convoluted sentence like this one: *Observation of nature finds the notion realized in inorganic nature, laws, whose moments are things which at the same time are in the position of abstractions* (Hegel 170).

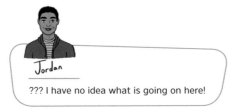

Jordan

??? I have no idea what is going on here!

Perhaps you need some **background knowledge** to decipher your reading because the text comes from a distant time or place. You may find yourself staring at a passage with all kinds of references you don't understand. *Europe is too thickly planted with Kingdoms to be* *long at peace, and whenever a war breaks out between England and any foreign power, the trade of America goes to ruin ...* (Paine 66).

Wait. Which kingdoms? Which wars?
How did trade go to ruin?

REFLECT on the reading you are doing in your own courses. Is there a text that you find difficult? How would you describe the challenges? Technical language? Complex syntax? A need for background knowledge? Figurative language? If a passage is difficult, what is your preferred strategy for deciphering it?

Perhaps the text uses **figurative language**—words and phrases used in expressive and sometimes unexpected ways, departing from literal meaning. *It is Spring, moonless night in the small town, starless and bible-black, the cobblestreets silent and the hunched, courters'-and-rabbits' wood limping invisible down to the sloeblack, slow, black, crowblack, fishingboat-bobbing sea* (Thomas 1).

HELP!

When you find a text difficult, it may be helpful to use what you hear in lecture or class discussion to support your reading. You may also need to consult dictionaries on- and offline. But what about texts with everyday vocabulary and straightforward syntax? These can present difficulties of their own. Zach's instructor asks him to read an interview with Nigerian writer Chinua Achebe (1930–2013). The interview appears online in the archives of a literary magazine, *The Paris Review*, which publishes a series of interviews with writers about their lives and their work. When Zach starts reading, he is not sure where to find the answer to his instructor's question: *Why did Achebe become a writer?*

The interview doesn't have technical terms I have to look up, but it's frustrating because it rambles on about Achebe's family, his books, and education. It's hard to find the important points in one long conversation.

Previewing as a First Step

Zach's instructor advises the class to preview, or quickly look over, the reading first. When previewing your reading, imagine yourself flying over the text in a small plane. You get a sense of how big the area is, and begin to orient yourself, preparing for the landmarks and obstacles, the mountains, forests, and bogs you will encounter when you go in on foot. Previewing a text, you don't stop to look up every difficult word. You don't worry about what every paragraph means. You are getting the lay of the land. How long is this text? How is it formatted? In other words, how does it look on the page or screen? Is it divided into sections? Does the passage include words in bold face? These are often important terms. Does the text include illustrations? Graphs? Charts? Is it, like the Achebe interview, presented as a series of questions and answers?

Previewing his reading, Zach looks at the interviewer's questions, while keeping his instructor's question in mind. How did Achebe become a writer? Zach stops at this place in the interview: "Would you tell us something about the Achebe family, and growing up in an Igbo village, and whether in your early education there was anything that pointed you that early in the direction of writing?"

This question seems to point toward a discussion of why Achebe became a writer. While he reads the whole interview, Zach pays particular attention to Achebe's answer to this question. This is going to be an important passage. Zach will study it carefully.

Note-taking as a Second Step

How do you study a passage? You have probably heard that taking notes is an excellent place to start—but what kind of notes? That depends on you, the nature of your course, the assigned material, and your goals as a reader. With note-taking, as with any kind of writing, it is important to ask yourself, *What is my purpose? Am I taking notes to prepare for a test? Am I taking notes to gather information for a paper?* It also makes sense to ask *Who is the audience for these notes? Am I preparing notes to post online for a class review session? Or am I writing notes for myself alone?* Effective students may have a personal note-taking style, but they are able to adapt that style to the demands of a specific assignment.

Note-taking as Active Learning

You are driving along, and you stop to ask for directions. After listening, you repeat back. *Okay, turn right at the light, drive half a mile past the gas station and then a sharp left....* Instinctively, you know that repeating the directions will help you to remember them better. By the same token, when you write or type information, you rehearse it to yourself, retracing material step by step, allowing your mind to linger and remember better. If you have ever studied for a test with flashcards you may have noticed that the most useful part of the exercise is writing up the flashcards in the first place. You review material when you write out equations, or dates, or words and definitions.

Beyond helping you to remember material, notes help you to organize your ideas about that material. Choosing what to jot down, you make a decision about what is significant. The film you watch for your contemporary culture class is two hours long, but you take just one page of notes, choosing the moments you want to remember. The math midterm is open notes, but not open book. You write down the equations you think you will need. At its best, note-taking is a process of selection. Instead of trying to copy down every bit of information from a lecture or book, you select and record the key ideas, the essential formulas, the turning point in an argument.

Many instructors post their own lecture notes online. These notes are packed with information and provide excellent study guides. However, your instructor's notes cannot substitute for yours. Why?

Jordan

Usually I don't take a lot of notes. I might jot down a few questions for myself. However, for psychology, I have to post a response to the reading in the class discussion forum. I usually post several questions, and reply to other people's notes as well.

Anna

I try to look up words I don't know. I create a vocabulary list which I can look back at later. It's great for studying because a lot of times those words or technical terms are on the exam.

Zach

I use an online annotation tool to comment on the reading as I go. As I read on screen, I'm filling the margins with comments.

Kate

I'm old school. For chemistry I write major formulas and equations on notecards. I scan the cards so I can access the info on my computer. However, for political science, I write in pencil in my book. We are reading Machiavelli. At first, I wrote in the book just to stay awake. Now I'm writing in the book because Machiavelli's ideas make me angry!

REFLECT: How would you describe your approach to note-taking? Do you adapt your note-taking to the demands of an assignment? How so?

Because when you read course notes you follow your instructor's thought process. When you write your own notes *you lead*, selecting, organizing, and explicating material. Taking notes, you prioritize ideas. Whether you are typing, or writing by hand, jotting down key words or drawing diagrams, you engage with the material as an active reader. You may find yourself connecting concepts, events, and examples. Ultimately, note-taking may lead you to make connections between the text and class discussion, between course material and lecture and your own experience. Forging these connections, you **synthesize** material, bringing together and combining ideas and information for the purpose of greater understanding.

Strategies for Note-taking

You have many options for note-taking. You might use an app to take notes online, as Zach does. You might prepare old-fashioned notecards like Kate, or simply write in the margins of your book. Whatever style you use, keep one thing in mind: notes on a text should respond directly to that text. Key your comments and questions to specific language in the passage you are reading, and you will understand and discover more. You will also set yourself up for writing about your reading later. Returning to your notes, you will know exactly where you found that amazing example, or graph, or language, and you can cite it easily.

USING A T CHART

Zach's instructor asks the class to take notes in a **T Chart**. This is a simple and useful note-taking style. You paste text for study on one side of the page and write your comments and questions on the other. Zach creates two columns onscreen. He pastes Achebe's text into the left side. Then he comments freely on the right. The text he chooses is the passage he singled out while previewing. It is Achebe's answer to why he became a writer. Achebe talks about the stories he heard as a child, and then the books he began to read. Take a look at the notes Zach takes. Many of them are simply questions.

Then I grew older and began to read about adventures in which I didn't know that I was supposed to be on the side of these savages who were encountered by the good white men. I instinctively took sides with the white people. They were fine! They were excellent. They were intelligent. The others were not ... they were stupid and ugly. That was the way I was introduced to the danger of not having your own stories. There is that great proverb—that until the lions have their own historians, the history of the hunt will always glorify the hunter. That did not come to me until much later. Once I realized that, I had to be a writer. I had to be that historian. It's not one man's job. It's not one person's job. But it is something we have to do, so that the story of the lion will also reflect the agony, the travail—the bravery, even, of the lions.	Who are the savages? Did black Africans appear like savages in the books Achebe read as a kid? How did Achebe realize his mistake— identifying with the white men in the books? Hunters = white? Lions = black victims? Okay, here suddenly he decides to be a writer!!! Why does he have to be a historian? Couldn't he have been something else?
Achebe, Chinua. "The Art of Fiction 139." Interview by Jerome Brooks. *The Paris Review*, no. 139, www.theparisreview.org/interviews/1720/chinua-achebe-the-art-of-fiction-no-139-chinua-achebe. Accessed 13 Mar. 2018.	

There is a lot Zach doesn't understand about this passage, and his questions reflect that. His questions are open, searching, and raw. He doesn't pretend he knows exactly what's going on. He is not trying to develop a conclusion or build an argument about this reading—not yet. He is just trying to figure it out. And that's fine! That's the beauty of note-taking. You don't have to write polished prose. You don't have to provide answers. Your questions are good here. You are exploring, trying to find out what the writer, or in this case, the speaker, is saying. Entering his questions and comments into the T Chart, Zach enters into a dialogue with Achebe. *You say hunters. Does that mean white people? You say you have to be a historian. But why? Could you have chosen some other profession?*

ANNOTATION

Zach is practicing **annotation,** a form of note-taking that allows you to engage a text where it lives, on the page or on the screen. Annotating a text, you can mark confusing words, or startling ideas, or questionable assumptions right there as you see them. Also, with annotation, you can respond to an author directly. If you find yourself dozing off as you read, the act of annotation may keep you awake. If you tend to lose focus while studying dense material, annotation will help. It is particularly useful for approaching difficult texts, because the process of annotation allows you to mark words you don't know, and points that confuse, inspire, or provoke you. As you annotate a passage, you can follow—or challenge—the turns an author takes.

Many students use annotation tools to mark electronic texts. Annotating online, you can type your comments. Your work will be legible—and easily shared. In some classes, the annotated text becomes a public space, and note-taking becomes a group activity. Students mark a text and then others respond with annotations of their own.

In addition to annotating electronically, you may find it useful to use pen or pencil to annotate your own books and papers. Your marginalia, or notes in the margins, will provide you—and later readers—with a record of your thoughts as they occur.

Annotation allows you to respond in the same space as the text, often on the same line. *What does this mean? Is this true? What if this is NOT the case?* Annotation, by its very nature, hews closely to the text.

The advantage of annotation is that it forces you to read closely and look at text in detail. But can annotation help you figure out the big picture? What if you need to find the main idea in your reading? The answer is that annotation will help you there as well. Reading a passage closely, you will uncover clues and collect the information you need to figure out the writer's message.

Identifying Verbal Signals

Zach reads with his instructor's question in mind. *Why did Achebe become a writer?* As he annotates, he looks for clues. Like a trail-marker painting blazes on trees, the writer provides **verbal signals** for the reader to follow. These signals are particularly useful.

- **Word choice:** Writers have enormous choice in the words they use. A friend could use the word *disappointed* but chooses *devastated* instead. A writer could state that *legal reforms are advisable* but chooses to say *legal reforms are necessary*. These choices reveal a great deal about the message.
- **Repetition:** Repeating a word, or phrase, or verbal pattern often signals an important idea. *It's not one man's job. It's not one person's job.* Repetition serves as emphasis.
- **Transitional words and phrases:** Writers use certain words and phrases such as *in addition*, *also*, and *by the same token* to guide the reader from one point to another. They use words and phrases such as *however*, *nevertheless*, *although*, and *in contrast* to signal some change or turn in the message.
- **Words and phrases making rhetorical appeals:** Certain words and phrases signal an appeal to ethos, pathos, logos, and kairos. (For more on these appeals, see Chapter Two). In academic writing, phrases such as *Without a doubt ...* or *We must conclude ...* or *There are, of course ...* make strong claims to ethos with their confident wording. *Without a doubt* suggests that it's impossible to imagine any other situation or outcome. *Of course* signals common knowledge and shared consensus. *Obviously, you know this, because you are one of us.*
- **Words and phrases introducing a new point of view.** In class discussion, students use certain phrases to acknowledge others and then introduce their own ideas. *Building on what you said, I would add ... I agree with the first part of that, but ... In addition to that, I would say ...* Writers use similar phrases to acknowledge the ideas of others and then assert their own point of view. *This study builds upon work done over the past five years ... I agree with the premise of this article, but ... In addition to these three points, we would add ...*

As Zach annotates Achebe, he begins to uncover verbal signals. For example, Achebe does not say "I had to be that writer." He says "I had to be that historian." This word choice suggests that for Achebe becoming a writer means telling an accurate story of his people, not simply making up fiction or entertaining his audience.

Zach finds repetition, as well. Achebe says of writing, "It's not one man's job." Then he repeats this idea, using the same sentence structure, but making the point in slightly broader terms. "It's not one person's job." Repetition suggests that this idea is especially important.

Zach notes phrases signaling the passage of time.

Then I grew older ...
That did not come to me until much later ...
Once I realized ...

Underlining each of these phrases, Zach marks three stages in Achebe's evolution as a writer.

These phrases signaling a journey, or a natural progression, may remind you of Aristotle's kairos, as they introduce the element of time into the narrative. Many authors use the element of time to structure their writing. Even formal academic writers signal the process of an investigation with words such as *Then ... Next ... After ...* and phrases such as *In time ... Over the course of ... We later discovered ...*

Zach finds other rhetorical appeals as well. The sentences: "I had to be a writer. I had to be that historian," make a strong appeal to ethos. He is saying this is who I am, and this is what it means to be a writer.

Signals like *As we have shown ...* or *This demonstrates ...* appeal to logos, as they indicate the steps of a formal argument. When Achebe says "That did not come to me until much later," he makes a quiet appeal to logos. He suggests that his understanding of his role as a writer developed over time as a process of step-by-step thinking.

In personal or persuasive messages, signals in arguments may appeal to pathos. Often these signals invoke the feelings of the audience, personalizing an argument, and leaning heavily on the relationship between audience and speaker. *To be honest ... Let's agree that ...* When Achebe uses the word *we*, he reaches out to his listeners and readers in a subtle appeal to pathos. Telling one's own story isn't just something I have to do. It's something *we* have to do. Zach underlines the sentence "It's not one person's job."

Annotation Inspires Larger Questions

Taking notes inspires questions Zach might not have asked if he were just skimming. However, he is still not sure that he understands why Achebe suddenly became a writer. Nor is Zach confident that he can come up with a personal response to this passage. He goes to see his instructor.

ZACH   I can't really relate. Since I never wanted to become a writer, it's hard for me to compare my experience to Achebe's. I'm not really sure what he means when he says he *had* to become a writer.

DR. B.   Okay, why don't we look at this one passage and break it down? Just tell me what you think Achebe is saying.

ZACH   What do you mean?

DR. B.   Just tell me what Achebe is saying in your own words.

Paraphrase

A **paraphrase** is literally a retelling of a text. It is an excellent method for learning difficult material. A paraphrase is not the mechanical substitution of one word for another; paraphrase is an actual retelling, as if you were describing the text in different words to someone who has not read it. A paraphrase is often as long as the original text—sometimes longer—because it retells each point in turn. Please note that this retelling should always be in your own words. If any language from your source material ends up in your paraphrase, you could end up **plagiarizing** your source, dishonestly passing off the work of others as your own. Always use your own words and cite your source. (For more on plagiarism and citation, see Chapter Eight.) Note as well that some instructors frown on paraphrase because they do not want you to regurgitate the assigned reading. Paraphrase is no substitute for your own thinking. However, it is a useful tool for breaking down a difficult passage and teaching yourself how it works.

ZACH   Okay here goes. Achebe is talking about how he became a writer. He heard stories when he was younger that glorified white people and made his own people look bad, so he realized the only way to counteract that would be to write his own stories.

DR. B.   That's a start, but you're rushing. Don't skip over the stages in Achebe's gradual realization that he wanted to be a writer. Try sitting down with the text and writing out your paraphrase, step by step.

Zach takes this advice and rewrites his paraphrase. In order to paraphrase fully, Zach follows Achebe's narrative closely. In addition, he finds that he needs to read between the lines, connecting the dots between Achebe's ideas. Achebe jumps from his childhood experience enjoying stories of heroic white men to his realization much later that those stories were biased. Zach spells out Achebe's thought process.

Paraphrase of a passage from "Chinua Achebe, The Art of Fiction"

In this passage from his *Paris Review* interview, Achebe describes how he came to an important realization about writing. As he grew older, Achebe realized that the books he'd been reading led him to sympathize with whites and not his own people who were black. Once he realizes the indoctrinating power of reading, he decides *he* must become a writer, so that he can tell the history of his own people. In the interview, he recalls a proverb about men hunting lions. The hunters get to tell the story, and the lions do not. The implication is that as long as the hunters (whites) tell the history of the hunted (Africans), they will narrate the story in a way that makes them look glorious and Africans subordinate. Thus, Achebe concludes that he had to become a writer in order to restore dignity and heroism to his people.

Achebe, Chinua. "The Art of Fiction 139." Interview by Jerome Brooks. *The Paris Review*, no. 139, www.theparisreview.org/interviews/1720/chinua-achebe-the-art-of-fiction-no-139-chinua-achebe. Accessed 13 Mar. 2018.

Zach includes a full citation of his source in the MLA style his instructor requires. (For more on where, when, and how to cite sources, see Chapter Eight.)

This paraphrase is more successful than Zach's first attempt, because he highlights connections beneath the surface of Achebe's account and explains points that are difficult or confusing. He also explains points that Achebe relates symbolically or suggestively with figurative language, comparing whites to hunters and blacks to lions.

Summary

DISTILLING THE MAIN IDEA

If a paraphrase provides a detailed map, a summary provides a pocket guide. Paraphrase explains. Summary distills. A **summary** is a concise statement of essential points. If you want to write a good paraphrase, assume your reader wants to trace every step the writer takes. If you want to write a good summary, assume your reader wants to know the essence of the text. Writing a summary requires discernment. As you consider which points to include, you decide which are the most important. How do you make these decisions? Begin by annotating the passage. Then imagine you need to explain the gist to a friend who has not read it and does not have time to hear every detail.

By the time he finishes his paraphrase, Zach has a thorough understanding of Achebe's message. When his instructor asks him to summarize what Achebe says, Zach is well prepared. Here is Zach's summary of the Achebe passage. Notice how short it is!

> In this passage from his *Paris Review* interview, Achebe describes gradually realizing the power of stories. Over time, Achebe began to see that the victor writes history. Ultimately, he decided to become a writer to rewrite the white man's version of history and to show his people their own history and heroism.

BREVITY AND ACCURACY

As with paraphrase, good note-taking will help you write your summary. Rereading your notes, you can review the key points you have identified. When you summarize, you retell those key moments in your own words. You do not need to account for every detail, only the key points. Nor must you follow every twist and turn in order. A good summary reorders points to convey the central message.

You want to be accurate in your summary, but you need to be concise as well. When a friend asks *How was dinner?* she probably does not want to hear about every single thing you ate. By the same token, your reader doesn't want you to retell every detail in your summary. Challenge yourself to summarize a page in one paragraph. Now try summarizing that paragraph in one sentence.

> Zach's one-sentence summary: Chinua Achebe becomes a writer to reclaim his people's history.

Can you be even more concise? Think of a newspaper headline. Can you capture your summary in just a few words?

> Zach's headline: African Writer Takes Back History

After writing a paraphrase and a summary, Zach feels more confident about his reading of Achebe. In fact, he uses his summary as the foundation for his response to his instructor's question *What is the role of writing in your life?*

> It is very humbling to see that Achebe became a writer because he saw that writing shapes history. I have not experienced writing in my own life in such a deep way. Usually for me writing is about getting information out there and fulfilling assignments (sometimes painfully). Also, I admit that when I thought about writing in the past I considered it "creative expression" more than anything else. I had not thought as much about writing as a tool for standing up for people, telling another side of the story, or making sure certain perspectives are not forgotten.

Using Paraphrase and Summary as Ends in Themselves

Zach's instructor asks him to paraphrase and summarize the reading to help him break it down and understand it better. Paraphrase and summary are great study aids, but they serve other uses as well. In some genres, paraphrase and summary become ends in themselves. An abstract introducing a journal article summarizes results and methods. *In a longitudinal study of over 200 adults, we show that sleep deprivation is not only a symptom, but a cause of depression....*

An obituary summarizes a life. In concise language, the obituary sums up major events and accomplishments. *Born in Nigeria in 1930, Chinua Achebe was a revered writer and thinker. His works include* Things Fall Apart *(1958)....*

Outside school you may not need to write a scientific abstract or an obituary. However, you could find yourself preparing a summary for an oral or written report. *The study demonstrates that simply reducing access to sugary soft drinks has a significant impact on childhood obesity.* After a meeting, you could be the one writing up and distributing notes "to make sure everyone is on the same page." In this role you need to provide an accurate paraphrase of the discussion. *After the presentation John rose to object to the housing proposal. He stated three reasons for his opposition.*

First, the development plan would add 300 new apartments to a quiet neighborhood. Second, it would increase traffic and parking problems. Third, it could impact wildlife.

Using Summary to Build an Argument

In genres such as research reports, memos, books, and magazine articles, authors use summary to build arguments. An author might summarize an important concept, viewpoint, or historical framework in order to set up her own assertion. *Some historical background is necessary here ... Many scholars in this area have argued ... However, these findings lead us to a different conclusion.* An author might use summary to recapitulate and emphasize a major point. *Simply put, this alliance between competing interests was doomed from the start.*

The words *Simply put* introduce a summary of the argument up to this point. For emphasis and clarity, the author is summarizing her own text as she goes. Watch for these moments as you do your reading. They are the verbal equivalent of bold face or boxed text—mini-summaries within the larger narrative. Common signals for such moments in more formal academic writing include *In other words ... In sum ... In short ... According to ... Simply stated ...* In more conversational texts the author may signal summary with phrases like *As you can see ... The bottom line is ... Here's the thing ...* When you are talking to a friend and you say *To make a long story short ...* you actually define what you are doing as summary!

Public speakers also reiterate and underline key ideas with brief summaries. *Let's be clear here ... Make no mistake ... If there's one thing I've learned ...* In this rhetorical situation, you can't watch for verbal signals; you must listen for them. Next time you hear a speech or lecture, listen for the way the speaker signals a summing up: *This much I know ... So what we're really saying here is ...*

From Reading to Writing: Analysis

A plumber takes apart a broken water heater to diagnose and repair the problem. A chemist analyzes a new material by breaking it down into essential elements. A pathologist analyzes tissue samples to diagnose disease. A historian analyzes a violent public uprising by examining the smaller events leading up to it. **Analysis** is a thorough examination for the purpose of discussion or interpretation. Often analysis involves studying the structure of a substance, or an object, or an event, or whatever requires attention, and then figuring out how its elements fit together. Analysis of a text means identifying what the writer says, and then pushing further to consider how the writer says it.

Much of your writing in college will involve analysis. Any assignment that asks you to *discuss* or *assess* a text invites analysis. When you compare two passages, you use the tools of analysis, juxtaposing the components of each. When your instructor asks you to *respond* to what you read, analysis allows you to move past quick personal judgments such as *I liked it* or *This was really interesting* to more rigorous discussion. *What was really interesting about this piece was the way the author began with an anecdote about a family getting evicted from their home and then zoomed out to discuss a pattern of evictions in poor urban neighborhoods.*

While analysis often means studying the inner workings of a text, it can also involve stepping back to take a broader view. How does this author's message look when compared to other competing claims? How might this reading connect to other materials you have discussed in class? Does this message stand up to fact checking? Are the author's appeals effective? Why or why not? Answering these questions involves analysis as well.

Jordan builds his analysis of a reading in psychology by looking closely at what the writer is saying and then connecting the writer's claims to what he learned in class discussion.

Jordan

My assignment is to write a brief response to an article about happiness. I start by reading and marking up the article. This is the part that interests me the most.

Much of the positive psychology research is focused on what makes people happy. Recent studies, for instance, have found that happiness comes in everyday simple rewards. In research she's conducted, Alice Isen, Ph.D., a professor in the psychology department of Cornell's Arts College, found that people experience a thrill when they get a free sample, find a quarter on the street or receive an unexpected gift — and this emotion makes them feel more generous, friendlier and healthier. They became more flexible, creative and better at solving problems.

How do people get from happier to smarter and more creative? What's the connection here?

In fact, she also found that small inductions of positive emotion make people smarter, more productive and more accurate. In a study of radiologists, for example, she found that when they were given a small present, they made more accurate diagnoses.

?

Are people more accurate in their work when they are feeling good? Maybe the connection is that people work better when they feel appreciated. That motivates them.

"We can induce affective states in small ways," she said. "The fact that we can impact behavior and cognitive processes so strongly with such little manipulation suggests you need to pay attention to people's capabilities and abilities to change as much as we pay attention to underlying strengths."

Kogan, Marcela. "Where Happiness Lies: Social Scientists Reveal Their Research Findings in the Realm of Positive Psychology." www.apa.org/monitor/jan01/positivepsych.aspx. Accessed 11 Nov. 2018.

Although Jordan is drawn to this passage with its new perspective on happiness, he finds it hard to decipher. Therefore, Jordan backs up to look at the text more carefully.

Jordan begins taking notes on this passage by copying the full title and author of the article along with the web-link. It's an extra step, but Jordan's instructor insists on it because if you document material right away, you are less likely to run into trouble later, forgetting where you found a text, or misattributing that text. You are also less likely to mix an author's language with your own. There are many formats for documentation of texts, and we discuss several in Chapter Eight. We use the MLA (Modern Language Association) style throughout this book. This is a style often used in the humanities. However, Jordan's instructor requires the APA (American Psychological Association) style, a format often used in the social sciences, so his citation looks like this:

> Kogan, M. (2001). Where happiness lies. *American Psychological Association, 32*(1). Retrieved from www.apa.org/monitor/jan01/positivepsych.aspx

Always make sure to use the documentation style your instructor requires.

After documenting the text, Jordan types up some brief notes for himself. *What are small inductions of positive emotion?* He looks up induction and finds many definitions online, but when he returns to the reading, he sees that in this context induction means an addition or supplement.

> So, when you supply positive feedback, people get smarter, more productive, etc.

Next, he types up some notes on the text as a whole. These notes don't just report what he finds in the article. They record his response. He does not have time to prepare a T Chart, but he carefully records important points.

> Happiness—it's the little things.
> Surprises—big impact!
> Happiness motivates.

As he writes his notes, Jordan begins to draw connections, and to extrapolate from the text.

> Happiness causes people not just to feel better but to perform better. That's crazy!
>
> So you don't need to provide BIG rewards—you can give small rewards and people will do a better job on their work. They feel appreciated. They feel their work is seen. This motivates them to work at a higher level.
>
> This reminds me of random acts of kindness. Also lecture about types of positive reinforcement.

Jordan uses these private notes to write a very brief summary of the passage.

> This article reports on research that small rewards and everyday surprises have a big impact on people's morale and even their job performance.

Jordan does not post this summary yet. He builds on it to write his own response to the text.

> It's crazy that happiness causes people not just to feel better but to perform better at their jobs. You don't even need much to be so happy, just a small reward. This reminds me of random acts of kindness. As we discussed in class, a satisfying gift is often the one that is "non-transactional." A surprise gift comes with no pressure and no expectations, so it is a lot more fun. As a positive reward, the gift says you are doing great already, not we want more from you. Instead of negative pressure—do more, work faster—workers experience positive reinforcement which motivates them to work harder and better.

Notice how Jordan draws a connection between the reading and class discussion. Synthesizing information in this way, he enriches his reading of the text. In the process, he makes the move from reading to analysis.

The psychology article inspires Jordan. He enjoys responding to this material. Kate finds the reading in her political science class a bit more of a struggle.

Kate's instructor assigns a brief excerpt from *The Prince*, by the Italian writer, politician, and diplomat Niccolò Machiavelli (1469–1527). The book describes the characteristics of a successful prince—but Kate's instructor explains that the book is also about leadership and power. Kate finds the text challenging, because it was written long ago for an audience of courtiers in a society that Kate does not know well.

Kate

I don't know who the princes were or what kind of wars they fought or how they lived. Also, the book was written in Italian, so I'm reading it in translation. It is literally foreign to me.

Because the text is difficult, Kate depends on note-taking, paraphrase, and summary to help her break it down and lay the foundation for her written response. She also uses her notes from class to provide her with some historical background and context.

Kate begins by looking over the entire excerpt. One passage stands out for her because of the focus on what makes a prince successful.

Kate

My assignment is to discuss Machiavelli's definition of a successful prince and say whether I agree or disagree with Machiavelli's characterization. One passage stood out for me—where Machiavelli talks about princes who have achieved great things.

Kate reads this passage slowly, annotating as she goes.

> Everyone realizes how praiseworthy it is for a prince to honor
> his word and to be straightforward rather than crafty in his
> dealings; nonetheless, contemporary experience shows that
> princes who have achieved great things have been those who
> have given their word lightly, who have known how to trick
> men with their cunning, and who, in the end, have overcome
> those abiding by honest principles.
>
> Machiavelli, Niccoló. *The Prince*. Translated by George Bull, Penguin, 2003,
>   p. 56.

The first thing Kate notices is Machiavelli's bold **claim,** or
assertion: Everyone realizes it's praiseworthy for a prince to honor
his word and be straightforward.

> Everybody realizes this? Really?

Reading further, Kate sees that Machiavelli signals a change in
direction with the word *nonetheless*. Everybody likes an honorable
prince. Nonetheless, contemporary experience teaches …

> Okay, the author isn't just focusing on what everybody knows.
> He's focusing on what successful rulers learn from experience.

Kate marks words and phrases she finds striking, confusing, or
provocative. She takes special note of the verbal signals Machiavelli
uses to guide his readers to follow and accept his point of view.
The word *nonetheless* guides us from what we might think to what
Machiavelli wants us to believe.

Who's everyone?

> Everyone realizes how praiseworthy it is for a prince to honor
> his word and to be straightforward rather than crafty in his
> dealings; nonetheless, contemporary experience shows that
> princes who have achieved great things have been those
> who have given their word lightly, who have known how

*is he talking
about lying?*

> to trick men with their cunning, and who, in the end, have
> overcome those abiding by honest principles.

"In the end" signals Machiavelli's own conclusion—that at the end of the day, the cunning triumph.

After annotating the text, Kate paraphrases Machiavelli's argument. She writes out this paraphrase simply because she wants to understand what Machiavelli is doing. She wants to follow his reasoning where it leads.

> Although we all honor leaders who we believe are honest and direct, we know that the leaders who have been most successful in the past are the ones who have been effective liars, willing and able to cheat their way to success.

Notice that Kate's paraphrase, like the excerpt from Machiavelli, has two parts. We praise one thing about princes, but experience tells us that something quite different makes them successful. Drawing this distinction, Machiavelli contrasts the ideal prince with the real prince, and he concludes that the real prince will lie and cheat in order to triumph over the ideal prince.

So what is Machiavelli really saying? Kate distills Machiavelli's argument in a brief summary.

> We all admire princes who behave honorably, but dishonorable princes are quite effective. In fact, the prince who cheats often conquers the noble prince.

As she annotates and summarizes the text, Kate begins to feel more confident. Now it's time to respond. Why does Machiavelli claim that the most successful princes lie and cheat?

With this question in mind, Kate uses her summary of the text to set the stage for her own analysis.

> Machiavelli claims that we all admire princes who behave honorably, but the truth is that dishonorable princes are quite effective. He comes across as a realist who doesn't have a lot of time for "praiseworthy" princes. He suggests that winning praise isn't nearly as important as achieving great things. Is this true?

This is an important question. Kate stops to think. *Is it better to be virtuous or successful? But wait. Why does it have to be either/ or? Can't some people be virtuous and successful?* As she asks this question, Kate identifies a possible flaw in Machiavelli's argument.

Kate

I just don't think it's true that you have to cheat to win. Where is his evidence for that? How is he so confident? Is he telling it like it is? Or is he just trying to provoke people?

Kate continues questioning. *Why would Machiavelli force such a choice on the reader? Maybe he does it for effect. Everything you thought you knew is wrong! You're just naïve if you care about honor and nobility.* In her first response to the text, Kate resists this line of thought.

> Machiavelli writes as though he and only he knows the truth about what makes a prince successful and he dismisses all other points of view. In his opinion you can't be virtuous and successful, but he never says why. He simply presents his own point of view with total confidence. In this way, I believe he manipulates the reader.

When Kate turns in this response, her instructor suggests that she revise her work to focus on exactly *how* Machiavelli manipulates the reader. Kate's instructor asks: *What exactly does he do to manipulate you?*

Kate revises her response to focus on the component parts of Machiavelli's text, his technique, and his rhetorical appeals. She looks at how these elements contribute to a strong but disturbing statement about how to succeed as a prince.

> Machiavelli assumes that you can be virtuous or successful, but not both. But why can't you be both? One thing that bothers me about his work is that he pretends to be very cold-blooded and rational. However,

he is not necessarily so logical. In this passage, I think he could have been much more thoughtful, looking at both sides of the question. However, he does not want to consider alternatives to his point of view. He writes that "everyone realizes" a prince should be virtuous and then says nonetheless this is not true. Who is everyone? Why does he assume the whole world is idealistic? And why are everyone's beliefs unfounded? He does not prove "everyone" wrong. He just says we are because contemporary events prove he's right. Well what are those events? And how long are cunning princes successful? Is Machiavelli talking about long term success? Or short term? He does not say! He just wants to say that honesty is not a realistic expectation. We might assume ethical behavior is best, but he's going to explode our preconceived ideas and tell it like it is. In his argument I think Machiavelli appeals more to pathos than to logos. He seems at times more interested in shocking the reader than in reasoning with the reader.

Kate continues to resist Machiavelli's claims, and she expresses her strong disapproval of his methods, but her response is more effective now because she uses analytic tools to examine the reading. Her written response identifies Machiavelli's main idea and then delves deeper to identify his assumptions and rhetorical claims. Reading carefully and critically, she questions Machiavelli's assertions, pointing out that he does not define "everyone" or support his claims with specific examples.

What do Zach's paraphrase and Kate's response have to do with you? Building on the work they do, you can look for signal phrases. Extrapolating from their process, you can develop your own, as you tackle difficult texts. Reading closely, paraphrasing and summarizing a passage—all these acts spark questions. Those questions might seem small or simple at first. Why does Machiavelli write: "Everyone realizes"? But the smallest questions often turn out to be the most revealing. Think of a reporter establishing basic facts. *What is your full name?* Or a lawyer examining a witness. *Where were you on October eleventh?* Or an archeologist sifting rubble. *Is this a rock or a tooth?* Small questions. Critical questions. Like a lawyer, a reporter, or a scientist, an active reader studies a text, marking, describing, retelling, and then responding to it. The beauty of this process is that it provides a starting place and a foundation for your own work. Taking notes, recording what you find, annotating what you read, you will never face a blank page.

Build analysis from notes, paraphrase, summary, and the questions they inspire.

Take notes to

- remember material
- ask questions
- identify key points
- locate signal phrases

Paraphrase to

- retell a text in your own words
- study each move an author makes

Summarize to

- distill the essence of a text
- lay a foundation for your own response

ACTIVITIES

1 Choose one of the following passages to read and annotate. Note difficult vocabulary, unusual word choice, and signal phrases. Watch for repetition. Write a paraphrase of your chosen passage. Take your time and follow each turn in the text. Now write a brief summary. Finally, write a one-line banner headline. Try to capture the gist of the text.

From a nationally broadcast 27 November 1963 speech to Congress by President Lyndon Johnson, five days after President John F. Kennedy's assassination.

First, no memorial oration or eulogy could more eloquently honor President Kennedy's memory than the earliest possible passage of the civil rights bill for which he fought so long. We have talked long enough in this country about equal rights. We have talked for one hundred years or more. It is time now to write the next chapter, and to write it in the books of law.

I urge you again, as I did in 1957 and again in 1960, to enact a civil rights law so that we can move forward to eliminate from this Nation every trace of discrimination and oppression that is based upon race or color. There could be no greater source of strength to this Nation both at home and abroad.

Johnson, Lyndon B. "Address before a Joint Session of the Congress, November 27, 1963." *The American Presidency Project*, compiled by Gerhard Peters and John T. Woolley, www.presidency.ucsb.edu/ws/?pid=25988. Accessed 20 Sept. 2018.

From "What Jazz Is—and Isn't" by Wynton Marsalis (b. 1961), trumpeter, educator, composer, and artistic director of jazz at Lincoln Center.

My generation finds itself wedged between two opposing traditions. One is the tradition we know in such wonderful detail from the enormous recorded legacy that tells anyone who will listen that jazz broke the rules of European conventions and created rules of its own that were so specific, so thorough and so demanding that a great art resulted. This art has had such universal appeal and application to the expression of modern life that it has changed the conventions of American music as well as those of the world at large.

The other tradition, which was born early and stubbornly refuses to die, despite all the evidence to the contrary, regards jazz merely as a product of noble savages— music produced by untutored, unbuttoned semiliterates for whom jazz history does not exist. This myth was invented by early jazz writers who, in attempting to escape their American prejudices, turned out a whole world of new clichés based on the myth of the innate ability of early jazz musicians. Because of these writers' lack of understanding of the mechanics of music, they thought there weren't any mechanics. It was the "they all can sing, they all have rhythm" syndrome. If that was the case, why was there only one Louis Armstrong?

That myth is being perpetuated to this day by those who profess an openness to everything—an openness that in effect just shows contempt for the basic values of the music and of our society. If everything is good, why should anyone subject himself to the pain of study? Their disdain for the specific knowledge that goes into jazz creation is their justification for saying that everything has its place. But their job should be to define that place—is it the toilet or the table?

Marsalis, Wynton. "What Jazz Is—and Isn't." *The New York Times*, 31 July 1988, pp. 20–21.

From the Nobel Prize Lecture of Malala Yousafzai (b. 1997). Malala is an activist for girls' education. Taliban gunmen shot her in the face, but she recovered and continued her work. She was awarded the Nobel Peace Prize in 2014.

Some people call me a "Nobel Laureate" now.

However, my brothers still call me that annoying bossy sister. As far as I know, I am just a committed and even stubborn person who wants to see every child getting quality education, who wants to see women having equal rights and who wants peace in every corner of the world.

Education is one of the blessings of life—and one of its necessities. That has been my experience during the 17 years of my life. In my paradise home, Swat, I always loved learning and discovering new things. I remember when my friends and I would decorate our hands with henna on special occasions. And instead of drawing flowers and patterns we would paint our hands with mathematical formulas and equations.

We had a thirst for education, we had a thirst for education because our future was right there in that classroom. We would sit and learn and read together. We loved to wear neat and tidy school uniforms and we would sit there with big dreams in our eyes. We wanted to make our parents proud and prove that we could also excel in our studies and achieve those goals, which some people think only boys can.

But things did not remain the same. When I was in Swat, which was a place of tourism and beauty, it suddenly changed into a place of terrorism. I was just ten [when] more than 400 schools were destroyed. Women were flogged. People were killed. And our beautiful dreams turned into nightmares.

Education went from being a right to being a crime.

Girls were stopped from going to school.

When my world suddenly changed, my priorities changed too.

I had two options. One was to remain silent and wait to be killed. And the second was to speak up and then be killed.

I chose the second one. I decided to speak up.

Yousafzai, Malala. "Nobel Lecture." 10 Dec. 2014, Oslo, Norway, www.nobelprize.org/prizes/peace/2014/
    yousafzai/26074-malala-yousafzai-nobel-lecture-2014/. Accessed 20 Sept. 2018.

From a 31 March 1776 letter by Abigail Adams (1744–1818) to her husband John Adams (1735–1826), then a delegate from Massachusetts to the Continental Congress, a convention of delegates from the 13 American colonies. Members of the Continental Congress drafted, adopted, and signed The Declaration of Independence.

I long to hear that you have declared an independency—and by the way in the new Code of Laws which I suppose it will be necessary for you to make I desire you would Remember the Ladies, and be more generous and favourable to them than your ancestors. Do not put such unlimited power into the hands of the Husbands. Remember all Men would be tyrants if they could. If perticuliar care and attention is not paid to the Laidies we are determined to foment a Rebelion, and will not hold ourselves bound by any Laws in which we have no voice, or Representation. That your Sex are Naturally Tyrannical is a Truth so thoroughly established as to admit of no dispute, but such of you as wish to be happy willingly give up the harsh title of Master for the more tender and endearing one of Friend.

Adams, Abigail. "To John Adams." 31 Mar. 1776. *Familiar Letters of John Adams and His Wife Abigail Adams,
    during the Revolution*. Hurd and Houghton, 1876, p. 150.

From The Psychology of Everyday Life *by Sigmund Freud (1856–1939), Chapter 4.*

I believe we accept too indifferently the fact of infantile amnesia—that is, the failure of memory for the first years of our lives—and fail to find in it a strange riddle. We forget of what great intellectual accomplishments and of what complicated emotions a child of four years is capable. We really ought to wonder why the memory of later years has, as a rule, retained so little of these psychic processes, especially as we have every reason for assuming that these same forgotten childhood activities have not glided off without leaving a trace in the development of the person, but that they have left a definite influence for all future time. Yet in spite of this unparalleled effectiveness they were forgotten! This would suggest that there are particularly formed conditions of memory (in the sense of conscious reproduction) which have thus far eluded our knowledge. It is quite possible that the forgetting of childhood may give us the key to the understanding of those amnesias which, according to our newer studies, lie at the basis of the formation of all neurotic symptoms.

Freud, Sigmund. "Childhood and Concealing Memories." *The Psychopathology of Everyday Life*, edited and
     translated by A.A. Brill. T. Fisher Unwin, 1914, p. 62.

2 The following passages come from an interview with feminist Betty Friedan. Read
   and take notes in whatever style you choose. Write a brief summary in three or
   four sentences. After you write the summary, answer the following questions. What
   motivated Friedan to "start the women's movement"? And how does that motivation
   develop? Consider the words Friedan chooses and the details she decides to include.
   How do these shape her message?

   Betty Friedan (1921–2006) was an American feminist and author of **The Feminine
   Mystique,** *published in 1963.*

   My father had a fancy jewelry store, like sort of Tiffany's for that part of the Middle
   West. And my mother was technically a housewife. I mean, she had been the
   women's page editor of the Peoria paper and she had loved that. And she could
   hardly wait for me to get into junior high school to get me to try out for the school
   paper. And she was obviously a bright woman with a lot of my energy. [W]e were
   comfortably middle class. And so, except for the Depression, there was sometimes
   a maid and a cook and so on. [My mother] did everything that women were
   supposed to do, and she did it very well: golf, tennis, bridge, Mah Jongg, shopping.

And, you know, when people, reporters, historians, [ask] why me, why did I start the women's movement, I can't point to any major episodes of sexual discrimination in my early life. But I was so aware of the crime, the shame that there was no use of my mother's ability and energy. And I think [of] her frustration ... she was a beautiful woman and she was a very able woman. But she spent a lot of time in bed with colitis, and she dominated her husband and made her children's life slightly miserable.

And when my father was much older, began to have serious heart trouble, and he taught my mother how to run the business. And she had to start seriously working at running the [business]. Her colitis disappeared, you know....

Well, at Smith [College] we certainly were not geared [toward] having careers. You were going to get married, you were going to have kids and you'd be a leader, a community leader, a leader of the volunteer effort. If you were very bright and you became head of a department, as I did, of the psychology department, you were encouraged to go on to graduate work. But as a woman you didn't even think about discrimination. Nobody asked you, "What do you want to be when you grow up, little girl?" but, "Oh, you're a pretty little girl; you'll be a mommy like mommy," blah, blah, blah. Well, I knew one thing. I did not want to be a mommy like mommy. And I understood somehow my mother's frustration. And that it was no good not only for her, but for her children or her husband, that she didn't have a real use of her ability.

Friedan, Betty. "Betty Friedan Interview." Interview by Ben Wattenberg. www.pbs.org/fmc/interviews/friedan. htm. Accessed 17 Jan. 2019.

---

3 Read the following excerpt from George Orwell's essay "Politics and the English Language" and take notes in whatever style you choose. Now write a brief summary in three or four sentences. After you write the summary, write a paragraph answering the following questions. What is Orwell's main idea here? How does he make his case? Consider Orwell's word choice, and his use of rhetorical appeals. Do you find his appeals effective? Why or why not? Do you think his assertions are still relevant today? What "familiar phrases" might Orwell hear from today's politicians — and their followers?

George Orwell (1903–50) was an English novelist and essayist. His novels include Animal Farm *and* 1984. *"Politics and the English Language" was first published in 1946.*

In our time it is broadly true that political writing is bad writing. Where it is not true, it will generally be found that the writer is some kind of rebel, expressing his private opinions and not a 'party line'. Orthodoxy, of whatever colour, seems to demand a lifeless, imitative style. The political dialects to be found in pamphlets, leading articles, manifestos, White papers and the speeches of undersecretaries do, of course, vary from party to party, but they are all alike in that one almost never finds in them a fresh, vivid, homemade turn of speech. When one watches some tired hack on the platform mechanically repeating the familiar phrases—*bestial, atrocities, iron heel, bloodstained tyranny, free peoples of the world, stand shoulder to shoulder*—one often has a curious feeling that one is not watching a live human being but some kind of dummy: a feeling which suddenly becomes stronger at moments when the light catches the speaker's spectacles and turns them into blank discs which seem to have no eyes behind them. And this is not altogether fanciful. A speaker who uses that kind of phraseology has gone some distance toward turning himself into a machine. The appropriate noises are coming out of his larynx, but his brain is not involved, as it would be if he were choosing his words for himself. If the speech he is making is one that he is accustomed to make over and over again, he may be almost unconscious of what he is saying, as one is when one utters the responses in church. And this reduced state of consciousness, if not indispensable, is at any rate favourable to political conformity.

Orwell, George. "Politics and the English Language." *Horizon*, vol. 13, no. 76, pp. 252–65.

4   Select a passage from one of your course readings and prepare a summary for someone who has not read the text. After summarizing the passage, assess its significance. Be sure to identify and document your source.

4

FROM READING TO WRITING ABOUT IMAGES

Writing an Analysis of an Image.

JORDAN   Which of these pictures do you like better?

ANNA   What's the difference? They're both pictures of you in a white shirt and black shorts playing Ultimate ...

JORDAN   But in this one I'm just starting to jump, and in this one I'm almost horizontal to the ground.

ANNA   Let me see that.

JORDAN   See, in one I'm taking off, but in the other, I'm practically flying! Yeah, that one's better.

ANNA   I thought you wanted to know which one *I* like better!

JORDAN   Not if you can't tell them apart!

Beyond a Quick Glance—Starting to Read Images

At first glance, it is hard to differentiate similar images. Anna only sees two photos of Jordan playing Ultimate. However, if Anna is to choose the image she likes better, she needs to look more closely. Like verbal texts, images reward careful scrutiny—especially because we tend to take in an entire image at a glance. When you write about images, it's important to be aware of this tendency to rush, and to remember that, in fact, seeing is a kind of reading.

We read images and signs and graphics every day, and we read them fast. Signs on the road present a quick visual language. Yield. Danger! Falling rocks. Curves ahead.

Certain articles of clothing present a visual language as well. You see a woman in a white gown and a veil and you think *bride*. You see a student in a long gown and a cap with a tassel and you think *graduate*. These costumes stand out as different from ordinary clothes, and we associate them with specific rituals and occasions. Of course, we aren't born knowing what these symbols represent. We learn to recognize visual conventions gradually. However, once we assimilate the meaning of representative symbols, or **icons**, we decode them in a flash. *Yellow triangle. I'd better yield. Oh, that's a lock. That means this website is secure.*

Consider the international symbol for accessibility.

Now consider another image—also a stylized figure of a person in a wheelchair—a 2012 alternative proposed by designer Sara Hendren and philosopher Brian Glenney, co-founders of the Accessible Icon Project.

The old symbol seems sedentary compared to this dynamic figure. Subtle changes make a huge difference. The first stick figure sits up straight, arms out, feet up, body sinking into the circle representing a wheelchair. The image makes you think of a patient at rest. In contrast, the second stick figure leans in, arm up as if pushing the chair forward. This image makes you think of an athlete racing or playing wheelchair basketball. No feet are included here. The new symbol is all about movement with the wheel cut through on the diagonal to emphasize forward motion. A few subtle changes add up to a picture of wheelchair users as active rather than passive, differently abled rather than disabled. The proposed symbol not only reflects a shift in the way society views disability, it *promotes* that shift, literally changing the way we see wheelchair users.

What Makes Reading Images Difficult?

It's easy to say slow down and take a long look. You might look at an image for quite a while and still feel you don't quite understand it. When reading a text, you can look up unfamiliar words in a dictionary. But what do you do with an unfamiliar sight?

You may see a new **symbol**, a mark or character representing something, on a graph or chart.

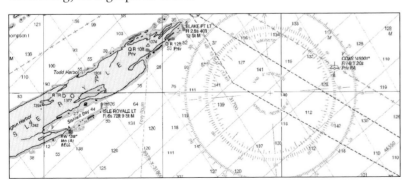

Kate

What do those purple circles represent?

National Oceanic and Atmospheric Administration (NOAA). "Nautical Chart." https://oceanservice.noaa.gov/facts/chart_map.html. Accessed 20 Sept. 2018.

Some images are complex, with many parts, colors, lines, and symbols.

Woah!

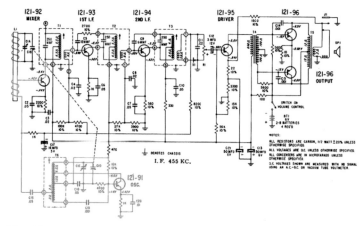

"Signal Flow Transistor AM Radio." *YouTube*, uploaded by AllAmericanFiveRadio, 24 Feb. 2011, www.youtube.com/watch?v=qlx7KRSiPM4. Accessed 17 Jan. 2019.

Some images are deceptively simple.

Okay, I see red. I see black. I see two rectangles. Am I supposed to figure out what this means??!

Rothko, Mark. *Light Red Over Black*. 1957, oil on canvas, Tate, London.

Perhaps you need some background knowledge to understand an image from a distant time or place. You may need to learn something about the purpose and audience of an image in order to understand its message.

Siege of Temesvár, 1552. Turkish miniature, Topkapi Palace, Istanbul.

Anna

Who are these people? Is this a war, or some kind of celebration? Where are they going?

You might need guidance to understand the conventions of an image.

Zach

I see fish? Suns? And a human on the bottom? Who did this? What is it?

Bark cloth (maro), early 20th century. Museum of Fine Arts, Boston.

You might need to look at an image in context, in its setting, to make sense of it.

1. Geospiza magnirostris.   2. Geospiza fortis.   3. Geospiza parvula.   4. Certhidea olivasca.

Gould, John. "Four Types of Finch." *Journal of Researches into the Geology and Natural History of the Various Countries Visited by H.M.S. Beagle* by Charles Darwin. J. Murray, 1845.

Anna

Is this from a book? Why are these heads numbered? What are they illustrating?

Visual Signals

You may need to look for more information—from lecture, class discussion, and assigned reading—when you find an image difficult, but the image itself will also provide clues. A map will often include a **key**, a small reference guide defining symbols, where, for example, you can learn that a dotted line is a road, and a series of ^^^^ are mountains. A graph will often define its numbers, explaining for example that its digits represent millions. Not all images include a key, but many use signals to guide the viewer. Sometimes these signals are overt. Red arrows and flashing lights scream for attention. Sometimes these signals are subtle. The sky shades to black. The typeface changes. We look at a word in ALL CAPS and we think *this is important*, or, why is this person shouting? When studying an image, it is important to watch for overt and subtle signals. It is useful to know some of the specialized names for these signals.

Informational Images: Graphs and Charts

- **Axis,** a reference line used for measuring. In a graph, you will usually find a vertical axis and a horizontal axis
- **Data Point,** a distinct element of information represented by a number or a dot on a graph
- **Cell,** a unit of information in a chart or spreadsheet
- **Legend,** a key to the symbols and units represented in a graph, chart, or map

These are just a few of the important terms that writers use to describe images. Your instructor may suggest other or additional terms.

While viewers use one set of terms to describe the elements of a graph or chart, they use different vocabulary to describe expressive images such as paintings or photographs. Here again, these are just a few of the terms writers use. Your instructor may suggest others.

Expressive Images: Drawings, Paintings, Photographs

- **Medium,** the materials and technology of an image
- **Focal Point,** the spot you see first, the center of attention for the viewer
- **Frame,** the limits for what the artist chooses to include
- **Line,** the path between points, cutting through space or defining a shape
- **Color,** the different hues you see in the work
- **Value,** the relative shades of light and dark
- **Mood,** the emotional impression an image leaves
- **Composition,** the placement and relationship of figures, lines, shapes, colors, and all the elements the artist includes

Rhetorical Appeals of Images

Visual signals guide viewers just as verbal signals guide readers and listeners. It is also true that visual messages rely on rhetorical appeals, just as verbal messages do. Appeals to ethos, pathos, logos, and kairos can work without words.

Look at this poster featuring the big black eyes, fine whiskers, and downy white fur of a young harp seal. The poster was produced by HarpSeals.org, a Canadian nonprofit dedicated to outlawing seal hunting and ending the fur trade.

The image appeals to pathos, attempting to influence the emotions of the viewer, who can't help feeling tender toward this sweet, defenseless baby. Text complements the photo with the words *Baby Harp Seal* in delicate cursive. A big heart surrounds the word *Love*, as the authors of this advertisement hope that viewers will feel the love for harp seals and click to purchase body scrub in support of HarpSeals.org. With its heart and fluffy dark-eyed baby seal, this image plays on the conventions of a tween poster, with the seal standing in for a teen pop star.

Now consider the **infographic** below, a visual representation of information, produced by PETA, People for the Ethical Treatment of Animals. Like the baby harp seal poster, this map conveys the urgent need to save baby seals. However, this infographic makes quite a different rhetorical appeal.

"A Product No One Wants." *PETA*, 18 Mar. 2014, www.peta2.com/news/canadian-seal-slaughter/.
   Accessed 26 Nov. 2018.

This map displays five countries along with the European Union and shows that each has banned the import of seal pelts. An icon of a seal with a line through it connotes a ban on the seal trade. No cute baby seal face here, no big black eyes, but a strong appeal to reason, or logos. The map declares in words and images that worldwide—even in Russia—seals are, to put it boldly, in capital letters, "A PRODUCT NO ONE WANTS." Appealing to reason, this infographic asserts that if all these countries have outlawed seal imports, then it makes little sense to keep slaughtering these animals. The image also appeals subtly to ethos, emphasizing the credibility of its authors. With a stylized map and statistics—"Prior to the ban, Russia was importing 95% of all Canadian seal pelts"—the infographic suggests that PETA has researched this issue and can present the problem—and the rational solution—with authority. The design here looks official with its simple font, and urgent with its bold lettering. The image draws upon conventions of a war map showing casualties and conflict across the world.

One underlying message with two different visual representations. A portrait of a harp seal works well to evoke an emotional response. A bold infographic conveys the illegality of the seal trade around the world and makes a strong claim that the killing of seals is not only wrong but senseless.

Learning to Read Images

In every field and every forum, images transmit arguments, opinions, information, and diverse perspectives. In college you may find yourself analyzing an advertisement in your composition class, reading a graph for economics, studying a painting in art, and examining all of the above for history.

Taking Notes on Images

How do you take notes on what you see? Begin by writing what you see while the image is in front of you. *I see the stick figure of a person using a wheelchair. I see Jordan jumping up to catch a Frisbee.* Don't trust your memory. Write your impressions while you view the image. Your notes will be more accurate and more detailed, because the act of writing forces you to notice more. There are many ways to take notes on images. You could jot down phrases and questions as they occur to you. *Huge horse! Sun setting on the horizon. What's going on with that red spot in the distance?* You could draw your own picture, diagramming the elements you see and working out visually how they fit together.

Kate

I need to discuss a graph that shows the decline in infant mortality in Rwanda.

Jordan

My assignment is to write a brief analysis of a children's book illustration.

Zach

I am writing about an everyday object.

Anna

I am writing a response to a black and white photograph.

Writing a moment-by-moment account of your experience seeing, you begin to slow down, moving beyond first impressions. You look more closely, scrutinizing details you might have overlooked. While writing, you log your experience as a viewer, crafting notes that can serve as a springboard for your written response. Keep a record of your source, as well, documenting the image in the format your instructor prefers. You will use this documentation in your written response. (See Chapter Eight for a discussion of documentation.)

REFLECT on a time you studied visual material, either in or outside class. What did you look at? A graph? Poster? Advertisement? Describe what you were doing when you looked at this material. What were you trying to learn or see? What was your approach? If you wrote about this material, what terms did you use?

From Description to Analysis: An Everyday Object

Zach begins with note-taking as he tackles an assignment to write about an everyday object. He chooses a coffee mug with a funny message printed on it.

Zach

My assignment is to look closely at an everyday object and analyze its appearance. I'm supposed to identify the audience—the users of this object, and the purpose of this object, as well.

Zach identifies the purpose of the mug as a vessel for drinking, and the audience as anyone who drinks coffee. His instructor asks him to be more specific.

Dr. B.

Pretend you're trying to explain this object to a Martian who has never seen one before.

Zach develops his notes.

> Okay, this is an object that people on earth use for drinking. It's made out of thick ceramic because it's designed to insulate hot beverages like tea or coffee. The thick walls and handle also help to protect the user's hand from burning.

Zach has explained the purpose and design of a coffee mug. Now he needs to address the specific qualities of his coffee mug, which has a message printed on it.

https://www.etsy.com/?ref=lgo. Accessed 29 Apr. 2017.

What makes this mug funny? The joke seems obvious. People don't want to have conversations before they drink their coffee. But how does that joke work visually? Zach slows down and begins to write a series of notes on what he sees.

> This is a plain ordinary coffee mug (you can tell by the size and shape). It's got words on it with lines. The words and lines represent three stages in waking up. 1. You want silence. "Shhh." 2. Then you still want silence, but you're "almost" ready to hear someone talk. 3. You're ready to listen.

At this point, Zach stops taking notes. He thinks maybe he's done. Then he remembers that his instructor reminded the class to keep in mind the rhetorical situation, the relationship between speaker, audience, and message.

> The audience for this mug is anyone who needs to be reminded how important coffee is in life. The rhetorical situation is that the coffee drinker is tired and cranky and not ready to communicate with anybody until most of the coffee is gone. The appeal is to pathos. You better watch out. I'm warning you!

At this point Zach looks at the lines on the mug. The lines communicate the coffee drinker's message without words. He concludes his paragraph by considering the overall effect of words and lines on the mug.

The lines on the mug make a funny appeal to logos. It's like they are measuring the amount of coffee you need to speak. There are no units of measurement here, but there is this semi-scientific appeal to exact quantities—as if a mood can be measured by levels of caffeine. Overall, the mug makes the coffee drinker's demands more graphic. The mug is not only telling its message. It is showing the viewer exactly how little coffee should be in the mug if you want to talk. One other thing that makes the mug funny is the change in font of the words. shh is printed unevenly and sleepily. *almost* is in cursive which looks a little bit formal and stand-offish. NOW you may speak is printed with all caps for NOW so the lettering is wide awake and full of authority.

From Description to Analysis: A Photograph

While Zach's instructor asks him to write about an everyday object, Anna's instructor asks for analysis of an artwork, the 1933 photograph "White Angel Breadline, San Francisco" by Dorothea Lange (1895–1965).

Anna looks at the photo and begins taking notes, jotting down what she sees. She organizes her notes using the visual signals her instructor asked the class to study.

Focal Point
At first glance the white hat draws my eye. The hat looks like the focal point because it's white in contrast to all those dark coats surrounding it. My eye travels down to the bright cup in the hands of the man and then to the fence he's leaning on.

Composition
I think the composition is a triangle with the hat at the apex and the fence at the base. Looking more closely I see the composition is two interlocking triangles—a bigger triangle from hat to fence and a smaller triangle formed by the man's arms and his clasped hands.

Lange, Dorothea. *White Angel Breadline, San Francisco*. 1933, gelatin silver print, Museum of Modern Art, San Francisco.

Anna

We are supposed to look closely at this photograph and discuss the mood and possible message of the piece. Our instructor asked us to consider especially the focal point, composition, and frame of this photograph, as well as the historical context of the Depression, which we talked about in class.

Anna stops there and stares at the photograph. Suddenly she begins to see even more triangles!

> If you look even more closely, you can see triangle indentations in the hats of two men with their backs turned. Geometry is very important in the picture.

At first, Anna doesn't know what to say about the frame of the picture. Her instructor said that the frame is important because it defines what the artist chooses to include and exclude from the image. Anna considers why Lange made the choices she did.

Frame
Lange frames her image so the man in the dirty white hat is front and center. She could have stepped back to

photograph a larger scene, or she could have zoomed in on the one man, but she chose to show him standing there in a crowd of other men dressed like him.

Anna finishes her written response with a discussion of the mood of the photograph. As she discusses mood, Anna builds on her close study to support her own conclusions about the image.

Mood

The mood of this picture is very depressing. Lange is making choices to underline this. For example, she chooses to take her picture in black and white, which makes the whole world look sad. It is partly because the man at the focal point looks so hopeless. His cup is empty and you can definitely imagine him not having enough to eat. To make matters worse, he is framed by other men who are dressed like him and probably just as poor.

Anna worked hard on this, and she is surprised by her instructor's written comments, asking for some revisions.

Anna, You really looked closely at the photograph. Just be careful in your last section about jumping to conclusions. Consider the date of the picture. Lange didn't necessarily choose black and white to make the world bleak. Most photographs in 1933 were black and white—even the happy ones. Also, what are your thoughts about the rhetorical appeals this photograph makes?

Rereading her assignment, Anna sees the instruction to draw upon class discussion of the Great Depression (1929–39). Now Anna revises her response, and answers her instructor's question about rhetorical appeals.

The mood of this picture is extremely sad. It is an image taken during the Great Depression, a time of mass unemployment, poverty, and hunger. The man's cup is empty, his shoulders are hunched and his mouth is frowning. He leans against a fence which looks like a barrier. Visually the fence says stay out. No one is looking at him—except the viewer. The composition of the photograph forces you to look at the white hat, the arms, the clasped hands and the empty cup. In real life you might want to turn away from hardship, but Dorothea Lange designs her picture so you have to look.

From Description to Analysis: A Graph

Just as note-taking helps Anna to notice subtle details in a photograph, the process of writing notes helps Kate to interpret a graph. In order to describe the graph, she must study it closely.

Kate's instructor asks the class to analyze a graph demonstrating the decline in infant mortality in Rwanda over a period of 25 years. The assignment reads:

This graph makes a strong claim about public health in Rwanda. How do the authors of the graph support that claim? How do they represent numerical information visually? What questions does this graph raise?

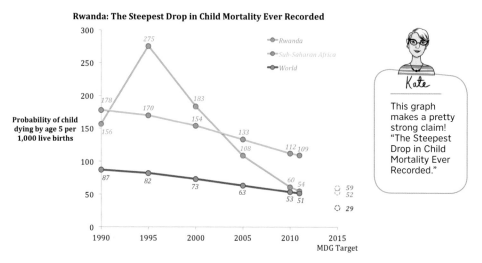

"Paul Farmer's Graph of the Year: Rwanda's Plummeting Child Mortality Rate." *Wonkblog*, 29 Dec. 2013, www.washingtonpost.com/news/wonk/wp/2013/12/29/paul-farmers-graph-of-the-year-rwandas-plummeting-child-mortality-rate/. Accessed 26 Nov. 2018.

Kate begins by documenting the graph. The founder of Partners in Health, Dr. Paul Farmer, along with several co-authors, published their infant mortality data in the *British Medical Journal* in 2013—but this graphic representation of the data appears online in Wonkblog. Therefore, she cites Paul Farmer as author, but Wonkblog as the site she accessed.

Kate looks at the graph, and notes the bold title.

The first thing that catches Kate's eye is the steep downward slope of the line marked Rwanda. Putting this visual information together with the headline "Steepest Drop in Child Mortality Ever Recorded," Kate suspects that this line represents the sudden drop in deaths.

But what is child mortality? And what does this steep drop mean? Kate begins writing notes, describing what she sees in each part of the graph.

> I see that the numbers on the horizontal axis, the line running horizontally across the bottom of the graph, are dates spanning 1990 to 2015. This axis measures the passage of time. Now I look at the vertical axis, the line running vertically along the side of the graph, and I see the words "Probability of child dying by age 5 per 1,000 live births." Aha! This is how the graph defines and records child mortality. Child mortality means the death of a child before the age of five. The vertical axis measures child mortality by showing how many children in 1,000 die before the age of five.

Now the plummeting drop in Rwanda makes more sense. Kate compares the line representing Rwanda to those representing Sub-Saharan Africa and the world.

> The top line representing Rwanda shows infant mortality spiking and then plummeting. The middle line represents child mortality in Sub-Saharan Africa, while the bottom line represents child mortality in the world.

PARAPHRASING VISUAL MATERIAL

Examining these lines together, she describes the graph in detail, crafting what is essentially a verbal paraphrase of visual material.

> This graph represents the number of children dying before the age of five in Rwanda, in Sub-Saharan Africa, and in the world. In 1990, the first year shown, 87 children out of every 1,000 died in the world. The child death rate in Rwanda was much higher than this at 156 out of every 1,000. However, that rate was still lower than that of other African countries. Over the next five years, the death rate in Rwanda increased drastically. By 1995 it had skyrocketed to 275 children out of every 1,000, far higher than any other country, including those in Africa. Then something began to happen. The child death rate in Rwanda went down incredibly fast. From 275 in 1995, the death rate declined to 108 in 2005 and then to only 60 in 2010. The steep downward slope of the orange line on this graph demonstrates this incredible change. Child mortality in Rwanda has decreased so much that it is now lower than that of other African countries, and approaching that of the rest of the world.

After writing the description, Kate feels that she understands what the graph conveys.

Kate

Describing the graph forced me to study it closely and understand it better, but when I was done I felt that the graph did a better job conveying this information than my written text did. I guess that's why they say a picture is worth a thousand words.

Kate understands what the numbers represent, and what the lines on the graph illustrate. Now she considers the questions the graph raises. Why did the death rate spike? Why did it go down? As she answers these questions, she makes the move from description to her own assessment of the graph's limitations.

Seeking a deeper understanding of this graph, Kate looks at the image in context. The graph illustrates a larger argument in a journal article. Kate reads and then documents this paper in her notes.

Farmer, Paul, et al. "Reduced Premature Mortality in Rwanda: Lessons from Success." *BMJ*, Jan. 2013, pp. 346–65.

After reading the journal article, Kate can better judge whether this graph effectively supports the author's claims. Thinking back to class discussion, Kate considers historical context as well. What was it about 1995 that caused the death rate to spike in Rwanda? 1995 was the height of the genocide and civil war in Rwanda. In this year civilians of all ages were slaughtered in racial violence. This graph illustrates a public health triumph in Rwanda, but does not include the vectors of civil war, political, and economic disaster, and recovery. Kate notes:

The numbers in this graph can only tell part of a larger story. By 1995 Rwanda was a death trap. In the years following the war, Rwanda's population recovered dramatically. Better public health played a part, and increasing political stability played a part. How are these connected? And how did these death rates improve so much? This is a question the graph cannot answer.

Building on her description, Kate notes that this graph focuses on just one part of a complex public health crisis. Kate makes the move to analysis by pointing out the limitations of this particular visual representation of data. Can you see where she makes this move? Kate signals her transition to analysis with the sentence "The numbers in this graph can only tell part of a larger story."

Stepping back to look at the larger picture, considering how different elements work together to convey a message—this is what you do when you move from description to analysis. Kate begins by describing and decoding a graph—simply figuring out which line represents what. When she takes a step back to look at the context of the graph and to discuss what the graph does and does not convey, she engages in analysis.

From Description to Analysis: An Illustration

Jordan's instructor has asked students to write a brief analysis of a children's book illustration.

> *Choose an illustration from a children's book and write one to two paragraphs answering the following questions. How does this illustration interpret the accompanying text? What interpretative choices does the artist make? Why do you think the artist chose this particular moment to illustrate? Read the illustrated scene and consider the relationship between text and image.*

Jordan chooses an illustration by Sir John Tenniel (1820–1914) from one of his favorite books, *Alice's Adventures in Wonderland*. At first, he simply looks at the picture online, but his instructor asks him to study the illustration in the book itself, so that he can write about the relationship between image and text.

Jordan studies the image on the page with the text printed under it.

> The Caterpillar and Alice looked at each other for some time in silence: at last the Caterpillar took the hookah out of its mouth ...

Jordan writes:

> This illustration opens Chapter V of the book and it takes up most of the page. Together the illustration and the text

Tenniel, John. Illustration for *Alice's Adventures in Wonderland* by Lewis Carroll. 1865 from facsimile edition. Dover, 1993, p. 44.

create a mysterious mood where the caterpillar and Alice
are looking at each other. It's interesting that there is so
little text included here. The caterpillar takes his pipe out
of his mouth, so you assume he is going to speak, but
you have to turn the page to find out what he says. That
means the layout on the page creates some suspense.

Now Jordan focuses on the illustration itself. How does this
image interpret the text? He begins by writing what he sees as he sees
it, telling the story of the image.

The first thing I notice about this picture is that Alice
is really short. She can barely see over the top of the
mushroom. Actually you can't even see most of her face,
just her eyes. Her eyes are big and dark. She looks like a
four year old with that little body and those huge eyes …

It's interesting that although the caterpillar and his toadstool are
so big, the first thing Jordan notices is little Alice. In his experience of
the illustration, she is the focal point.

The caterpillar is a lot bigger than Alice, but I think I
notice her first because of her eyes. They are so dark
compared to the rest of the picture. The illustration is a
black and white line drawing and most of the lines are
thin and scratchy, but Alice's eyes are black ink—the
darkest points in the composition. The Caterpillar is
bigger and smokes a large pipe, but you can't see his eyes
at all. His body is also sketchy …

As he describes this illustration, Jordan begins to use the
vocabulary his instructor provided in the assignment.

The illustration is a close-up. The focus is very
tight—just Alice and the caterpillar and a few smaller
mushrooms and flowers. You can't see the bigger
world at all. I think that Sir John Tenniel is choosing to

interpret this part of the story by presenting the world
from Alice's miniature point of view. With her big eyes,
she looks pretty confused.

Stopping to think about Alice's confusion, Jordan looks back at
Lewis Carroll's chapter and rereads Alice's words to the caterpillar.
Asked who she is, she answers, "I hardly know, sir...."
    Jordan uses this statement to put the illustration in context,
drawing a connection between verbal and visual texts.

It makes a lot of sense for Alice to look confused, because
as she states in the chapter, she hardly knows who she
is anymore since she has "changed several times" since
getting up that morning.

Describing what he sees as he sees it, Jordan discusses many of
the choices Tenniel makes—his use of line, color, focus. Now Jordan
turns to the larger question in the assignment. Why did Tenniel
choose to illustrate this particular moment?

Sir John Tenniel could have illustrated many other incidents
in the chapter, but he chose this moment where Alice is
talking to the caterpillar in order to show how tiny she is.

Looking again at the illustration, Jordan amends his description to
speculate on what Tenniel might be conveying with Alice's big eyes
and childish body. As he does so, Jordan augments his paragraph and
builds on his description to develop his own response to the image.

It's not just her size—it's her state of mind. This new
world down the rabbit hole is getting weirder by the
minute. This is an illustration that puts the wonder in
Wonderland. If you look really carefully, you can see how
Tenniel makes this point, showing Alice gripping the
toadstool with her little hand. She is just trying to hold on.

Jordan is happy with his analysis, but when he submits it, his
instructor points out an element he may have overlooked.

Jordan, you make some wonderful observations about Alice, but what about the caterpillar? Some people would say that the caterpillar smoking his pipe is really the most provocative aspect of the illustration. What part does the caterpillar play?

Intrigued, Jordan looks again at Tenniel's illustration. Alice and her big eyes still seem like the focal point, but what is she looking at? Suddenly, Jordan begins to see the illustration differently. He starts adding to his description of the image.

> After looking at this image for a while you realize how sexual it is. The long shape of the caterpillar's body is totally male and the open flower just above Alice's head looks female. What exactly is going on here between them? Then there is the question of what the caterpillar might be smoking. Lewis Carroll says the caterpillar speaks to Alice in a "languid, sleepy voice" which sounds like he is on drugs. So here is a girl talking to a stoned caterpillar while grabbing a mushroom. The scene is both sexual and druggy. Tenniel decides to illustrate this moment and embrace the weirdness of Alice's "adventures."

Jordan chooses an illustration of a book he knows well. As he writes about that image, he learns more. Then his instructor's comments challenge him to delve deeper still. Reading closely, taking notes, asking and answering questions, you will uncover more than you thought possible. Persisting past a first glance to look slowly, you will be amazed at what you see.

When writing about visual material, ask yourself:
What do I see?

Rhetorical Situation

- Who is the intended audience for this image?
- What is the purpose of this image?
- What genre or form does this image take?
- What rhetorical appeals does this image make?

Visual Information

- Is there a claim here?
- How is the claim supported?
- Are there elements of a graph or chart?
- Is there a legend or key?

Visual Signals

- What catches your eye first? This is the focal point.
- Where does your eye travel? Write down this progression and you will find clues to the composition or visual structure of the image.
- What visual elements can you identify? Color? Line? Value?
- What mood do they create?

ACTIVITIES

1 Choose an everyday object and describe it to a Martian. Explain the purpose of this object and describe exactly how it works. What materials are used? How do they serve the object's purpose? Who is the intended user (or audience) of this object? Is the object decorated or styled in a certain way? How would you describe this decoration? Does the decoration make the object more useful? More amusing? More attractive?

2 One theme, two very different images. Look carefully at these two images stressing the importance of financial planning. What claims do these images make? What visual signals can you identify? What rhetorical appeals do these images use? Alternatively, choose two different images on the same theme and discuss the claims they make.

"Bold, Modern, Life Insurance Newspaper Ad Design for a Company in Australia." *DesignCrowd*, uploaded by shpaolin, 12 Feb. 2013, www.designcrowd.ca/design/1456620. Accessed 20 Sept. 2018.

PLAN for LIFE

 Every day for the next 20 years, another 8,000 baby boomers will turn 65. That's roughly **one person every 10 seconds**.

 Nine of ten adults aged 65 years and older say they have taken **at least one prescription drug** in the last 30 days.

29% of all American workers have **less than $1,000** saved for retirement.

 American workers are **$6.6 trillion short** of what they need to retire comfortably.

 One out of every six elderly Americans is already living below the federal poverty line, according to the U.S. Census Bureau.

Only about 13% of all Americans are **65 years of age or older**.

 By 2030, that number will **soar to 18%**.

 Between 1991 and 2007, the number of Americans between the ages of 65 and 74 that filed for **bankruptcy increased an astonishing 178%**.

 From a recent survey, **74% of American workers expect to have to work** even though they are "retired."

One out of three working Americans does not have retirement savings beyond Social Security.

As of 2011, the average monthly Social Security benefit was $1,179. Couples who each earn this amount have an **annual retirement income of $28,296**.

 The average American spends **20 years in retirement**.

 To **raise a child** from birth to the age of 18, costs an average of **$241,080**.

 **$326** — The amount parents spend each month on out-of-pocket expenses for their **child with special needs**.

 88% of parents who have children with special needs have **not set up a trust fund** to preserve eligibility for benefits such as Medicaid and Supplemental Social Income.

Through each stage in life, Financial and Estate Planning solutions from Wolters Kluwer can serve as trusted resources for solidifying your client's financial future.

 **Wolters Kluwer**
When you have to be right

Wolters Kluwer Tax and Accounting US. "Plan for Life: Finance and Estate Planning." *SlideShare*, 24 Sept. 2015, www.slideshare.net/WoltersKluwerTAAUS/plan-for-life-finance-and-estate-planning-infographic. Accessed 20 Sept. 2018.

3 Choose one of the following images. Write down what you see. Now use your notes to answer some or all of the following questions. Does the image evoke a certain mood? How so? Consider composition, color choices and values, focal point, and frame. What rhetorical appeals does this image make? Does the image convey a message? How would you characterize that message?

Photograph of girls carrying dolls, by Eudora Welty (1909–2001).

Welty, Eudora. *Dolls*, Jackson. 1936, Mississippi Department of Archives and History.

"Give a hand to wildlife," WWF (World Wildlife Fund).

Daniele, Guido. "WWF Elephant." *guidodaniele.com*, Oct. 2006, www.guidodaniele.com/hand-painting/handpaint-advertising/category/47.html. Accessed 20 Sept. 2018.

Woodblock print, by Utagawa Hiroshige.

Hiroshige, Utagawa. "Driving Rain, Shono." *Fifty-Three Stations of the Tokaido*, 1833–34.

4 Look at the following graphs. Choose one to analyze. Write a short description, explaining the purpose of the graph and how it conveys information. Now consider these questions. What information does the graph include? What does it exclude? What questions does the graph raise? How might you go about answering those questions?

"Largest Bike-Sharing Programs Worldwide, Early 2013." *Permaculture News*, 26 Apr. 2013, www.permaculturenews.org/images/update112_largest.PNG. Accessed 26 Nov. 2018.

Unemployment rates and earnings by educational attainment, 2017

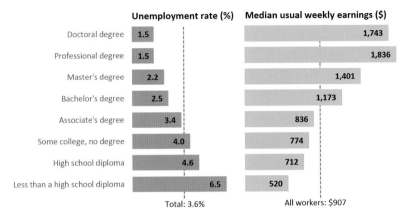

Note: Data are for persons age 25 and over. Earnings are for full-time wage and salary workers.
Source: U.S. Bureau of Labor Statistics, Current Population Survey.

"Unemployment Rates and Earnings by Educational Attainment, 2017." Bureau of Labor Statistics, 27 Mar. 2018,
https://www.bls.gov/emp/chart-unemployment-earnings-education.htm. Accessed 26 Nov. 2018.

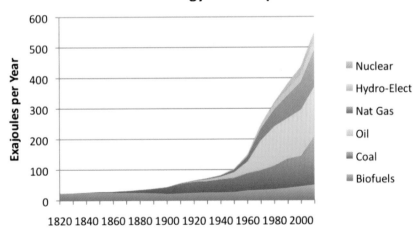

Tverberg, Gail. "World Energy Consumption by Source, Based on Vaclav Smil Estimates from Energy Transitions:
History, Requirements and Prospects Together with BP Statistical Data for 1965 and Subsequent."
www.ourfiniteworld.com/2012/03/12/world-energy-consumption-since-1820-in-charts/. Accessed 26 Nov. 2018.

5 One scene, two images. Look at these illustrations of Alice and the caterpillar. Each interprets the passage Jordan studies. How would you characterize the artists' respective interpretations? Which elements in Lewis Carroll's scene does Rackham choose to emphasize? How about Dalí? How does each artist depict the caterpillar? What about Alice? What is the relationship between Alice and the caterpillar? What do the artists choose to include? What do they leave out? What mood does each image evoke?

Rackham, Arthur. "Advice from a Caterpillar." *Alice's Adventures in Wonderland* by Lewis Carroll. Easton Press, 1907, p. 50.

Dalí, Salvador. *Advice from a Caterpillar*. 1969, lithograph, Dallas Museum of Art.

6   Illustrate a passage from a book or story of your own choosing. You might use pen, pencil, paint, photography, collage, or another medium. Lay out your illustration on the page with the text you are illustrating. Consider how much text you want to include on the page, and where you will put it. Write a commentary about the choices you made when interpreting the text visually.

5

BUILDING AN ARGUMENT: CLAIMS AND SUPPORT

Writing an Opinion Piece.
Writing a Review.

ANNA   I really, really hated that movie.

JORDAN   Why?

ANNA   Because it's the worst movie ever made.

JORDAN   It was hilarious.

ANNA   It was gross.

JORDAN   Exactly! *Attack of the Killer Tomatoes* is one of the best gross out movies of all time.

ANNA   It was terrible. I will never get those 87 minutes back.

JORDAN   How was it terrible? It just wasn't your thing.

ANNA   It was BAD.

JORDAN   That's not an argument!

What Is an Arguable Claim?

Why is Jordan frustrated with Anna? She is telling him exactly how she feels. *Attack of the Killer Tomatoes* was bad because it was terrible and it was terrible because it was gross and it was gross because she hated it. This is her honest response, but Jordan doesn't think she has an argument. What's missing?

An argument begins with a **claim**, or assertion, and then supports that claim. Anna has a claim, all right. *Attack* is the worst thing she has ever seen. However, she does not support that claim. She simply restates it in different words. Seething, Anna does not tell Jordan what was wrong with the movie—or even what went wrong with her experience of the movie. Nor does she provide him with an opening to respond. Anna is an expert on her own feelings, so there is little Jordan can say to engage her on the subject.

An effective claim invites a response—agreement, disagreement, or some of both. If an emotional statement does not invite a response, how about a statement of fact? *We went to a movie last night*. Well, it's hard to argue with that. This statement describes an activity but does not invite debate. *The movie was scheduled for 8:55*. This is a statement easily verified by checking the movie listings. Little to argue about here. A self-evident or purely descriptive statement does not provide a strong claim. What about this statement? *The movie began well but devolved into incoherence in the second half*. This is an arguable claim, a statement that requires support and calls for debate.

How can you tell the difference between a factual statement and an arguable claim? Try to imagine the response to each. Statements of fact, description, or definition invite little in the way of response. *We had popcorn at the movie*. That's nice. *Horror films scare me*. Okay, so what? In contrast, an arguable claim invites the audience to agree or disagree, to demand clarification, retraction, and above all, evidence. *Horror movies glorify the physical and emotional abuse of women*. Hold on! What do you mean by that? What evidence do you have? This is an arguable claim.

Different Kinds of Argument

An argument can begin with strong feelings, but if it begins and ends with emotion, it will devolve quickly into a tirade. There are places for this kind of speech. Many talk radio shows and message boards provide excellent public forums for furious rants. By the same token, personal journals and late-night conversations provide a safe space to vent. The trouble with diatribes is that they are easily dismissed. Anna's feelings about the movie are heartfelt, but they seem to say more about her than about the film. What was it that upset her so much? A particular scene? Emotional manipulation? Poor special effects? If she wants Jordan to take her claims seriously, she needs to support them with evidence.

What kind of claim is appropriate for the situation? And what evidence provides effective support? In part that depends on the genre you choose, the audience you address, and the purpose of your argument.

Speaking to Jordan, Anna can get away with focusing on herself and her own response to the movie. *This movie was terrible. It was like Swiss Cheese; it had so many holes. Half the time I had my eyes closed because the movie was so stupid and gross. The rest of the time I was looking at my watch—like, when will this end?* She claims the movie was terrible and then supports her claim with evidence from her own experience. She had to close her eyes because the film was so gross she couldn't look. She was constantly looking at her watch, because she was so eager for the movie to end. Documenting her own response, Anna provides plenty of evidence for her claim. However, this kind of personal testimony holds up best in conversation.

Let's suppose that Anna is preparing a written response to the movie, a film review for class. She might claim: *This film is an unwatchable mess.* However, her argument will be more effective, more precise and rigorous, if she moves past her own bad experience to support her claim with examples from the movie itself to illustrate poor craftsmanship and an incoherent plot. As evidence that the film is a mess, she might write: *Three plot points remained unresolved at the end of the movie.* As evidence that the film is badly constructed,

Zach

I think the best arguments are very precise. You can follow them point by point. I don't like it when an argument is vague or emotional.

Kate

I think the best arguments allow me time to think and respond. If you come on too strong, I start distrusting you. That's why I shy away from aggressive salespeople. I don't want pressure. I want an argument to make sense to me.

Anna

If you're going to convince me with an argument, you'd better have solid evidence. For example, if you're a politician and you want me to vote for you, show me your voting record. Show me the list of your donors. I'll judge what you say by what you've done.

Jordan

I like arguments with graphs and charts, so I can look at the evidence. Show me your results graphically!

REFLECT: Think about an argument you found convincing, either in writing or in conversation or in graphic form. How would you describe the way that argument worked? What made it so compelling? Now think of an argument that did not convince you. Can you pinpoint the problem? Did you think the claim was weak? Was evidence lacking? How so?

she could mention the slapdash special effects.

As always, it is important to know your audience when you develop an argument. It is important to understand your genre as well. Some arguments take a formal structure. A mathematical proof is a formal argument. Instead of beginning with a claim, a proof often begins by stating assumptions explicitly: *Let ABC be a right-angled triangle ... Let AD be drawn perpendicular ...* After stating assumptions, the proof builds a set of observations about those assumptions and then ends with a general claim. A sonnet can work as an argument as well. The fourteen-line love poem often begins with a claim, *Shall I compare thee to a summer's day?/Thou art more lovely ...* After stating this claim, the sonnet presents possible problems and obstacles. Time corrupts, death intrudes—*rough winds do shake the darling buds of May.* A sonnet often concludes by explaining how to overcome these problems. Love will conquer death, and poetry will outlast time: *So long lives this, and this gives life to thee.* Other arguments take a looser structure. In conversation or private journals, arguments develop casually, without explicit axioms. Arguments can take many forms, and they can succeed—and fail—in many different ways.

Understanding and Avoiding Fallacies

Anna argues poorly when she declares the movie was bad because it was terrible. As she leaves the movie theater she resorts to **circular reasoning**, also known as **begging the question**. Circling back to an unsupported claim leads to what rhetoricians call a **fallacy**, an internal flaw in an argument. The ancient field of rhetoric identifies many such fallacies. For just as rhetoricians devote themselves to identifying the best arguments, they also diagnose problems in the weakest.

If Anna were making her claims in writing, her reader might well accuse her of another fallacy, **overgeneralization**. She declares *Attack* the worst movie ever made, and she can just about get away with this in conversation. However, in a formal paper, this statement might not hold up, because Anna cannot possibly demonstrate that *Attack* is the worst movie ever made. After all, she has not seen every movie ever made.

Fallacies can derail an argument, and it is important to recognize and watch out for them. Many begin with an abuse of rhetorical appeals.

FALLACIES OF PATHOS

Appeals to pathos have their place in genres such as pep talks, advertisements, sermons, and eulogies. The coach who appeals to a losing team's sense of pride may well rouse that team to victory. The speaker who makes us cry may initiate change in a culture or a community. However, appeals to pathos are not always appropriate. Problems develop when emotion takes over. As we have seen, Anna gets a little carried away when she leaves the movie theater. If she gets angry enough, she might speak broadly and resort to **hasty generalizations**: *Violent movies are evil!* Or she might turn on Jordan, insisting *Everybody knows that violent movies are evil.* Such **bandwagon appeals**, assumptions of shared belief and common experience, serve as staples for speakers trying to bring together an audience. In college writing, they look pretty weak. After all, how can you assume everybody shares your opinion? Indeed, Jordan declares that he likes the movie that offended Anna so much. It is dramatic but false to assume that we're all in this together. The fairer course, and the more interesting one, is to admit a plurality of opinions. If Anna were developing a written argument, she would do better to modify her statement. *Many people enjoy violent movies. However, I find them detestable for the following reasons.*

FALLACIES OF ETHOS

Many arguments begin by establishing the speaker's or author's credibility. If you deliver a speech protesting your neighborhood council's recent decision, it makes a lot of sense to start by identifying yourself as a longtime resident. If you write an article arguing against college tuition increases, you would do well to explain that you are a college student. As with pathos, however, appeals to ethos can cause problems when they substitute for reasoned support of your claim. The fact that you are a college student concerned about tuition is not a reason to halt tuition increases.

Kate

I admit it drives me crazy when people say just trust me and don't give any reason.

Zach

How about when they give reasons, but they're all bogus, like look everybody knows this is true?

Anna

Or—you must be a moron if you don't agree with me?

Jordan

That happens all the time online. Insults instead of arguments.

REFLECT: Have you come across a fallacy of pathos or ethos recently? What were the circumstances? What was your response?

Establishing relevant credentials—*I have five years' experience*—can serve you well, but exaggerating those credentials can backfire. Name-dropping and boasting can undermine credibility with an audience. In 1988, 41-year-old vice-presidential candidate Dan Quayle compared himself favorably to a young John F. Kennedy. His opponent, 67-year-old Senator Lloyd Bentsen pounced, exposing and then topping Quayle's appeal to ethos with a strong appeal of his own. Emphasizing his own age and experience, Bentsen declared, "Senator, I served with Jack Kennedy. I knew Jack Kennedy. Jack Kennedy was a friend of mine. Senator, you're no Jack Kennedy."

If you appeal to ethos, consider audience and rhetorical situation. In some cases, you should avoid an appeal to ethos altogether. You wouldn't interject in a mathematical proof—*Trust me on this. I've been studying math for years*. Appealing to ethos in the wrong context can undermine the credibility you want to establish. You also do yourself no favors by establishing your authority at the expense of others. *He just doesn't get it. He's an idiot!* Indulging in personal, or *ad hominem*, attacks, you sound desperate. You make a poor case when you attack the integrity of your opponent or audience.

FALLACIES OF LOGOS

When you develop an argument appealing to logos, you appeal to reason. A true appeal to logos requires respecting the intelligence of your audience. After all, to whose reason do you appeal? Theirs.

Convincing an audience means helping that audience to follow your argument. The best appeals to logos begin with shared principles of rational inquiry and evidence. Ideally, when you develop your argument, you appeal to rational thinking that overrides differences of personality or prejudice.

Many **logical fallacies** take the shape of a rational argument, but do not hold up on examination. A parenting activist declares, *Allow toddlers to play with your phone and you'll hook them on electronics. They'll become gaming addicts before they're five years old*. This is a claim that seems to draw a reasonable connection but collapses under its own weight. The speaker makes an ungrounded assumption that playing with a cell phone leads to obsession with electronics, which leads to gaming addiction, one condition sliding into the next, a fallacy known as **slippery slope**.

If you are checking for fallacies in your own arguments or those of others, stay alert to the connections between cause and effect, claim and conclusion. Consider this statement: *I saw you yesterday. Today I've got a terrible cold. You made me sick!* Or this assertion: *Water usage has steadily increased over the past five years, draining our reservoirs. Because of this, we've got a water shortage*. Do these conclusions follow? Of course it is possible that you got me sick, and it's quite possible that wasting water led to a water shortage, but to insist on a connection without further evidence is to fall into a **fallacy of cause and effect**, or *post hoc ergo propter hoc*, Latin for *after this, therefore because of this*, an assumption that when one event follows another, the first event *caused* the second. Investigators refer to this fallacy when they say **correlation does not imply causation**. You may observe two events or actions or phenomena in close proximity, but that does not necessarily mean one caused the other.

It is natural and often useful to connect the dots between events, drawing conclusions, and synthesizing information. However, when you are building an argument, you need to consider multiple factors. *Stepping back, I have to admit that something or someone else might have caused my cold. In fact, I might have been coming down with it before I saw you.*

Come on too strong and the only readers who will follow you are those who already agree with you. Make a more nuanced statement and neutral or opposing readers may consider some of your ideas.

Even so, it's tempting to oversimplify and overstate your case. There's drama in a stark bold statement, which is why advertisers and public speakers use them. Consider this claim: *Either you conserve water, or you destroy our world.* A passionate assertion, but a **false dilemma,** or artificial choice. After all, water usage alone will not destroy the world. What of greenhouse gases? Toxic waste? Many factors endanger the environment. It's unfair to threaten us with just one. Qualify this statement, give up the stark either/or dilemma, and you'll lose shock appeal, but gain credibility. *Use water carefully because your choice affects our environment.*

Like the rigid tree that will not bend, dramatic claims crack and break under pressure. Perhaps you've heard a statement like this: *If you don't love this video, you don't have a heart.* Or an assertion like this: *Our campus security guards are Nazis.* The energy in each claim comes from a false comparison, or fallacy of **moral equivalence.** Someone who dislikes a particular show is not necessarily heartless. Security guards might be overbearing, but unless they are perpetrating genocide, they have little in common with Nazis. When you make a claim like this in casual conversation, your audience might laugh knowingly. However, in an argument for your instructor, such claims fall short. You need to justify each comparison, and this means you need to avoid overreaching for effect.

Overstatement and oversimplification lead to one kind of fallacy. Unsupported connections lead to another. *Honesty means telling the truth. When he avoided talking about the problem, he was dishonest with me.* Taken separately, each sentence seems reasonable, but when you put them together you wonder, does this follow? The speaker shifts from defining honesty as telling the truth to a new definition of honesty as openness. Using one term, but changing its meaning, this argument sinks into the fallacy of **equivocation.**

You are vulnerable to equivocation if you allow your argument to drift from one idea to the next. If you define honesty as telling the truth, you need to maintain that definition throughout your argument. If you want to include openness as a kind of honesty, you should expand your definition. *Honesty means telling the truth and speaking openly, without hiding information or avoiding certain subjects.* Defining your terms and qualifying your claims, you will bolster your argument.

Another way to strengthen your argument is to entertain possible objections. After developing a complex case, it's all too easy to simplify and caricature claims on the other side. Sketching these claims quickly, only to dismiss them, you raise a **straw man**, conjuring a flimsy opponent, just so you can knock him down. Consider the politician who declares, "There are those who say the economy can't be fixed. They think our best days are behind us...." Rousing the party faithful, the politician characterizes the opposition as defeatist and fatalist—straw men without a plan of their own. The opposite of the straw man is a fair summary, in which you accurately present an opposing viewpoint before explaining why you take a different approach.

JORDAN   So, when you say it was the worst thing you've ever seen, do you mean the worst movie? Or just the worst horror movie?

ANNA   Well, I hate horror movies.

JORDAN   Oh, so you already came in expecting to hate it.

ANNA   No, I went in with an open mind. You said it would be funny.

JORDAN   It WAS funny!

ANNA   No, it was scary.

JORDAN   It's funny and scary at the same time. Why can't those two things go together?

ANNA   People getting squashed by giant vegetables is not funny.

JORDAN   And for you funny is ... people sitting around telling jokes while they're sipping tea?

ANNA   Funny is making people laugh without dying.

Defining Your Terms

In some situations, an impassioned speech or a strong sales pitch makes sense. However, in other contexts, the strongest arguments are not the loudest. In serious debate, or written analysis, you may find that the strongest arguments are more than passionate; they are precise. How do you develop a precise argument? Begin by presenting your reasons for taking a position. This may require you to define your terms, and to spell out your criteria when you make a claim.

As Anna explains what she was expecting, she clarifies what she means by *funny*, explaining that in her mind funny excludes death by tomato. After defining funny, Anna begins to articulate her criteria for comedy, explaining her reasons for hating the movie. It was not funny; it was disturbing. She supports her claim by stating that, in her opinion, horror and comedy do not mix. *This is how I define a funny movie. "Attack" does not fit that definition. Therefore, in my opinion, it is a terrible movie.*

As she clarifies her position, Anna also finds a way to speak about the movie without resorting to the quick fix of fallacy. She explains what she means by funny and why the movie disappointed her. While it is impossible to support the generalization that *Attack* is the worst movie ever made, Anna can develop a reasonable argument that the movie did not live up to her standards and expectations.

Argument and Audience

In a conversation with friends, arguments can be loose and casual. *Hey, we have to go to the beach today. We have no choice. It's gonna rain tomorrow, and Honeycomb Creamery is on the way!* This is a real argument with a claim and plausible support, appealing to logos—*let's go while the weather is good*—and to pathos—*Don't you like ice cream?* However, it's a casual argument depending on the good will of the listener to supply connections the speaker leaves out.

In another rhetorical situation, expectations for argument could be quite different. If a meteorologist claims *Today is the best day this week to go to the beach*, the public expects to hear why this is true. The meteorologist supports forecasts with weather maps, charts, and satellite pictures. If a food critic pronounces a certain ice cream *the best*, we expect to read the criteria used to define the best ice cream, whether it's by price or portion size or quality of fresh ingredients.

Different audiences dictate different standards for claims and support. A student writing a research paper must provide a full citation for every source quoted. However, no one expects in-text citations in conversation. A lawyer arguing before the court is constrained to use specific kinds of evidence. The anonymous author of an online comment is free to use any kind of evidence—or none. If you want to argue effectively, it is crucial to understand the constraints, conventions, and expectations of your rhetorical situation.

Argument Assignments

Many writing assignments require you to develop an argument. Sometimes your instructor will ask explicitly for an argument.

> *Write a cogent, well-supported one-page argument for or against drilling for oil in Alaska. By cogent I mean logical and convincing. I want to see how you get from one point to the next, and I want you to be clear about how each point supports your claim.*

Sometimes instructors do not use the word *argument*. However, their assignments carry an implicit expectation of argument. If your instructor asks for a discussion, an evaluation, a comparison, or an analysis, you will probably need to make a claim and back it up.

Anna

My favorite assignment this semester was a restaurant review. I took my notes from four different dinners at Alonso Cuban Café to write a review with some pros and some cons. The assignment didn't mention argument, but my review argued that the food Is worthwhile despite the restaurant's slow service.

REFLECT: Think about a recent writing assignment. Were you asked explicitly to develop an argument? Or was there an unstated expectation that you prepare an argument? What was the purpose of your argument? What was your claim? How did you support it?

An instructor may ask you to take a position on an important issue. Here again you will need to make a claim and support it, developing an argument.

Jordan

We had to prepare for a debate in class on whether it is ethical to eat animals. We didn't get to choose sides. Our instructor chose for us. Although I'm a carnivore, I had to argue against eating animals. We read several articles on the subject, and in the end our team argued that eating animals is unethical for three reasons: slaughtering causes suffering, processing uses up valuable resources, and breeding and feeding exhausts our land.

Writing an Opinion Piece

UNDERSTANDING THE GENRE

Kate's instructor assigns a two-to-three-page essay in an unfamiliar genre. The assignment reads: *Write an op/ed on a public issue affecting your profession or quality of life.* Kate has never written an op/ed in or out of class. Although she knows that these opinion pieces appear every day in the editorial pages of the newspaper, she does not make a habit of reading them. She begins by looking through some samples her instructor provides. Two catch her eye. The first is an opinion piece by former Supreme Court Justice John Paul Stevens arguing, not only for stricter gun control, but also for a repeal of the Second Amendment, which establishes the right to bear arms. Stevens begins by reflecting on recent protests by schoolchildren who want to find a way to end gun violence.

> Rarely in my lifetime have I seen the type of civic engagement schoolchildren and their supporters demonstrated in Washington and other major cities throughout the country this past Saturday. These demonstrations demand our respect. They reveal the broad public support for legislation to minimize the risk of mass killings of schoolchildren and others in our society.

Stevens declares that student protests show the time is right for stricter gun control laws. He builds on this assertion to make a broader claim. It is time to do away with the Second Amendment altogether.

> That support [for gun control] is a clear sign to lawmakers to enact legislation prohibiting civilian ownership of semiautomatic weapons, increasing the minimum age to buy a gun from 18 to 21 years old, and establishing more comprehensive background checks on all purchasers of firearms. But the demonstrators should seek more effective and more lasting reform. They should demand a repeal of the Second Amendment.
>
> Stevens, John Paul. "Repeal the Second Amendment." *The New York Times*, 27 Mar. 2018, p. A23.

The next paragraphs in Stevens's op/ed develop his argument. He asserts that the Second Amendment is outdated, misinterpreted, and dangerous.

The second op/ed responds directly to Justice Stevens. In fact, it appears the same day, with the title, "What Justice Stevens' Op/Ed Gets Wrong About the Second Amendment." The author, Jay Willis, presents Stevens's argument with summary and quotation, reminds the reader of Stevens's background as a longtime Second Amendment opponent, declares his respect for the justice as "one of the most important jurists in modern history," and then asserts, "But if you believe, as he does, that enacting more robust gun safety legislation would be a good thing, gutting one-tenth of the Bill of Rights isn't the way to do it" (Willis, 2018).

Willis's argument is not directly about the merits or dangers of gun ownership, but about what he perceives to be a threat to the Bill of Rights. He argues that eliminating an entire amendment would be a difficult and perhaps unrealistic legislative goal, and sets a dangerous precedent. If we get rid of the Second Amendment, we might open the door to future abridgement of the Bill of Rights and endanger our civil liberties.

> The Second Amendment, as written, is a *negative* right. It allows you to own a gun if you choose to do so, but it

does not require the federal government to, say, hand every citizen a firearm of their choice.

This means that the Second Amendment's hypothetical disappearance would merely enable Congress to legislate where it has not previously been able to do so (Willis, 2018).

Willis develops his argument further by adding that Stevens's suggestion will only provoke those who want to protect and maintain gun ownership, sparking "easily inflamed passions, shifting public attention from the merits of specific proposals and transforming the gun control debate into a shadow referendum on what it means to be an American" (Willis, 2018).

These op/eds differ greatly in substance, but they have a lot in common when it comes to structure. Each author makes a strong claim. Each supports that claim with examples and analogies. Each author responds directly to a recent event. Stevens responds to recent demonstrations. Willis reacts to Stevens's bold proposal. Responding in this way to a current situation or statement, these authors write with a **sense of urgency**, appealing to kairos (for more on kairos, see Chapter Two). It is this urgency that catches Kate's eye and keeps her reading. These authors write as though the topic matters. Lives are at stake. Freedom itself is on the line. It is this urgency that animates a good opinion piece. In a larger sense, all the writing you do will benefit from an urgent desire to communicate and a strong investment in your message.

Kate's assignment encourages her to write with this sense that the stakes are high and that the question matters.

> *Write about an issue that matters to you, and to others as well. Don't think of this assignment as an academic exercise. Argue for a public audience in the real world.*

COMING UP WITH A CLAIM

Write about an issue that matters to you. Kate begins by thinking about her work as a nurse. *Okay, I worked as a nurse for three years. Something about nursing. But what's the issue?* She cares deeply about her profession, but she is not sure what her argument will be.

She begins with a personal statement, just because she has to start somewhere.

> I've always been drawn to nursing because I love to take care of people.

This is a beautiful statement, and it's also true, but it does not touch upon a public issue. Kate develops her initial idea by generalizing from her personal experience.

> Nurses feel a mission to nurture patients. However, our caseload is such that we do not have time to take care of patients properly.

This is a better claim because it invites discussion. Really? Is it true that nurses take care of so many patients that they can't do their job well? Kate's listeners or readers will pursue this claim, if only to see how she develops it. Kate remembers a survey at her hospital and quickly turns to that survey to support her claim.

> Nurses feel a mission to nurture patients. However, a poll at my hospital revealed that our caseload is so high that often we do not have time to provide essential services. If hospitals cannot ease this burden, patients will die.

Kate sharpens her claim with a strong sense of urgency and a provocative prediction.

SUPPORTING A CLAIM

Kate has a claim. Now she thinks about what kind of argument she wants to develop—an argument about why nurses need a lighter caseload. Keeping this in mind, she builds on her opening sentences, presenting the results of the poll at her hospital.

> Conditions are such that we cannot do our job properly. A poll at my hospital revealed that 70 percent of nurses feel that caseload impacts the quality of care they provide.

This is a start, but Kate is not sure what to do next. She rushes to connect the problem to her prediction that patients will die.

> The result of this is worse outcomes for patients, including death.

ARGUING STEP BY STEP

A mathematical proof falls apart if you leave out a line. A verbal argument falters when you skip a step. Kate skips several steps when she jumps straight from the problem—too many patients—to the result—worse outcomes and death. The reader thinks—wait. The survey talked about how nurses feel. They might perceive a connection between high caseload, quality of care, and worse outcomes, but is there a causal relationship? If there is, Kate needs to spell it out.

Her instructor makes this point when she shows him the opening of her op/ed.

> *This is intriguing, and you make a strong claim. However, you need clearer evidence to support your claim convincingly. The informal survey you mention comes from just one hospital. Maybe that particular hospital has problems. Can you find a published national or statewide survey that draws a connection between high caseloads, patient outcomes, and mortality?*

Kate's instructor makes an important point. It is not enough to make a claim and support it with any evidence that comes to hand. You need to consider what kind of evidence would be convincing. When Kate looks at op/ed pieces, she sees that they often refer to published studies that extend beyond one particular hospital or institution. Kate decides to replace her hospital's survey with results from "The State of Patient Care in Massachusetts Survey" by the Massachusetts Nurses Association.

> 90% of nurses report they do not have enough time to properly care for their patients; 77% report medication errors, 72% report readmission of patients and 64%

report injury or harm attributed to unsafe RN patient
assignments.

"MNA: 'State of Patient Care in Massachusetts' Survey Released for National
    Nurses Week Finds Nurses Sounding the Alarm over Deteriorating
    Conditions for Hospitalized Patients and Need for Safe Patient Limits ."
    CISTON PR Newswire, Massachusetts Nurses Association, 8 May 2018.

Kate also cites a statistic from a previous Massachusetts survey in
which "One in four Bay State nurses says that patient deaths are
'directly attributable' to having too many people in their care at one
time ..." ("One in Four MA RNs"). Kate does not have access to the
raw data in these surveys. She quotes from summaries reported in
the news. Her instructor allows this for the purposes of her op/ed.
However, he tells Kate that if she were writing a research paper, he
would expect her to quote from the surveys themselves. (For more on
research, see Chapter Nine.)

ANTICIPATING POSSIBLE OBJECTIONS

Kate's instructor voices some possible objections when he urges
her to replace what looks like a casual survey with a published
one. When Kate looks at her own work, she can imagine other
objections as well.

> You might argue that nurses simply want a lighter
> caseload, just to make our lives easier. Some critics say
> that our concern about patient safety is really a thinly
> disguised union initiative to argue for better working
> conditions. You could also argue that these surveys are
> biased, because the nurses responding want to tilt the
> outcome in their favor.

The best arguments anticipate possible objections and engage
them. You might think it's better to ignore counter-arguments.
However, you will write with more authority if you show that
you have considered other points of view. In college you want to
sound balanced, fair, and knowledgeable. Showing that you are
aware of potential objections or problems with your reasoning, you
demonstrate the depth of your thinking. Also, you can answer those

objections early, on your own terms. Kate revises her work along these lines.

> It is true that the survey of nurses was administered by the Massachusetts Nursing Association together with National Nurses United, which are both professional organizations. Admittedly, these organizations advocate for better working conditions for nurses, and it is always important to look at the source of a survey before accepting its findings. By the same token, however, it is important to look at the source of statements criticizing the nurses' surveys. Many of the sharpest critics are hospital administrators, who are concerned about keeping down costs. Lightening caseloads might mean hiring more staff, which would affect the bottom line. Granted, this is a complex problem, and the financial aspect is important—but nurses are not willing to place hospital financials above patient care.

Kate

It was actually helpful to bring up possible objections to my ideas, because this is a controversial subject and not all my readers are going to be sympathetic to my point of view. If I am going to win them over, I need to show that I have thought about other perspectives, and that I am developing a reasonable argument. I don't want my reader to dismiss me as emotional or to say I'm biased, just because this issue means a lot to me as a nurse.

Zach

When I'm reading an argument, I will trust the writer who seems balanced and fair. If all I hear is one side of the question, I start thinking, wait, what is he trying to sell me? Or I think, why is she lecturing me on this? Treat me like an adult.

Kate signals to her reader that she is introducing an objection or possible obstacle to her claim with the words *it is true that* ... and *admittedly* ... Then she signals her answer with the phrase, *by the same token, however* ... She introduces a second possible objection with the word *granted* ... and then introduces her answer with the word *but.* This pattern of acknowledgement and response reflects the give and take of formal debate or respectful conversation.

REFLECT on a time you thought of a possible objection to your own argument. Did you address the objection? If so, how?

You could argue ... but I believe ...
Granted ... nevertheless ...
It's true that ... but ...
Admittedly ... but I think ...

CONCLUDING THE ARGUMENT

In her conclusion, Kate sums up and extends her argument, emphasizing what is at stake, not only for patients, but for nurses themselves.

> There are only so many hours in the day and only so many tasks each person can do. Because of understaffing by hospital officials who care more about the bottom line than about patient safety, nurses are currently stretched to the limit and beyond. Our concern is not cynical or selfish but based on our mission as caregivers. We went into this profession to serve our patients. How ironic, then, that because of high caseload, we end up hurting those we want to heal.

After proofreading her op/ed, Kate sends it to her instructor, but she also posts it online for her class to read. Her classmates will comment on her work, and she will have a chance to respond.

Writing a Review

Jordan's instructor asks her students to write a review.

> *Write a review of a book, a movie, a restaurant, or a recent purchase. Please use evidence to support your claim. Feel free to include quotations, photographs, or video clips. Evaluate your experience and support your critical judgment with concrete details.*

UNDERSTANDING THE GENRE

Jordan looks at some reviews online. Most of them start with an evaluation. A review of a vacuum cleaner begins *Excellent suction, great buy.* A review of a restaurant begins *Not for the hungry or the faint of heart.* Jordan realizes that his claim will be evaluative. Is this a good book? Is this restaurant worthwhile?

COMING UP WITH A CLAIM

Recalling his conversation with Anna, Jordan decides to review *Attack of the Killer Tomatoes*. Awarding the movie five stars, he makes a bold claim:

> *Attack of the Killer Tomatoes* is a priceless classic of modern cinema.

Now all Jordan has to do is back this up!

QUALIFYING A CLAIM

At first, Jordan is happy with his claim. He likes it because it's strong and it will grab the reader right away. However, when he rereads his statement, he remembers Anna's response to the movie. He has to admit that some readers might not sympathize with his assertion of the movie's greatness. They might even think he's joking. After all, *Attack of the Killer Tomatoes* is not an award-winning, critically acclaimed film. It's a low-budget flick from 1978 that became a cult classic as one of those movies so bad that it's good. Jordan decides to **qualify** his claim, modifying and tempering his broad generalization to make a specific and defensible statement.

Jordan

Qualifying my claim made it easier to support and also more interesting to argue, because I could delve into the genre of the low-budget horror-comedy, which is something I know a lot about, and can write about in detail.

Anna

Reading Jordan's intro I was like okay fine, I am willing to believe this movie is a great example of the genre. It happens to be a genre I hate, but yes, it can be a classic of its kind.

> *Attack of the Killer Tomatoes* is a priceless classic of the low-budget horror-comedy genre.

REFLECT: Can you think of an example of a broad claim? Something you've read? Heard? Said yourself? Is such a broad claim supportable? Why or why not? How might you qualify that claim?

Maybe it's a stretch to argue that this movie is a classic of modern cinema as a whole. However, it's quite reasonable to argue that the film is a masterpiece of its kind. Qualifying his claim helps Jordan to set the parameters of his argument. Instead of comparing this movie to all others, he can compare it to others in its class. We're not talking Ingmar Bergman here. We're talking *Killer Clowns from Outer Space*. Jordan develops this idea in his first paragraph.

> *Attack of the Killer Tomatoes* is a priceless classic of the low-budget horror-comedy genre. While it did not

win many awards (actually, it won no awards) and it did
not receive many good reviews, it is an innovative movie
pioneering the concept of the killer vegetable. It is also
highly enjoyable for its crazed style and over-the-top yet
delightfully fake-looking special effects.

ARGUING STEP BY STEP

Now Jordan has a fairly precise claim and two points he will need to
support. First, the movie is innovative. Second, it is enjoyable for its
crazed style and its special effects. He takes each point in turn.

Jordan draws upon his knowledge of other movies to support his
claim that *Attack* is innovative. Comparing *Attack* to other movies is
another way for Jordan to define his terms. He is spelling out what
he means by innovative.

> The killer tomatoes in this movie are ridiculous but also
> strangely terrifying. Subsequent movie-makers were
> fascinated by this effect, as you can see in *Creepshow* (1982)
> and *Little Shop of Horrors* (1986). Setting *Killer Tomatoes*
> apart is the stunning similarity of tomato juice to blood,
> as you can see in this movie trailer: www.youtube.com/
> watch?v=aX0Wch1UNuw. Tomatoes are ridiculous and at the
> same time gory. They are naturally raw, pulpy, and explosive,
> so they are the perfect vegetable for comedy-horror.

After explaining why he thinks the artistic choices in this movie
work so well, Jordan moves on to his own experience of the movie.
He supports his point that the movie is enjoyable for its crazed
performances and special effects.

> The movie is entertaining because of the total commit-
> ment of its cast. There is something amazing about
> actors giving 110% to an entirely ridiculous scenario.
> The level of belief here, along with the driving score, is
> awesome. The cheesy special effects only heighten the
> insanity. A lot of the tomatoes look like papier-mâché as
> they roll along—yet everyone is screaming in terror. The
> movie dares you to laugh and you do!

Jordan acknowledges the weaknesses of the movie, admitting that the special effects are cheesy. Because he does not pretend that the movie is flawless and brilliant, he sounds rational rather than delusional. He admits that the movie is ridiculous and then claims that this is part of its charm.

ANTICIPATING POSSIBLE OBJECTIONS

Even as Jordan writes, he remembers an inconvenient truth. Anna wasn't laughing. Once again, he qualifies his argument to address possible objections. After all, he cannot reasonably claim that everyone laughs at this movie or finds it as delightful as he does.

> Admittedly, not everybody enjoys watching obviously fake giant tomatoes roll down a street. Understanding the greatness of this movie may require some knowledge of film history and artists like H.G. Wells and Alfred Hitchcock that the movie spoofs so well.

CONCLUDING THE REVIEW

Jordan answers these objections by reminding his reader that this is a particular kind of movie, excellent in its own way.

> However, if you love the absurd, this movie is for you. As a killer-vegetable-alien invasion flick, it is, in my opinion, the best of its kind.

Jordan's argument is stronger and more precise because he qualifies it and acknowledges an opposing point of view. Like Kate, he develops a reasonable argument by refining his initial claim and supporting his points with concrete details. Personal judgment motivates his argument, but he does not pass off opinion as absolute truth. He makes a strong statement, demonstrating why he awards *Attack* five stars. At the same time, he acknowledges that others may feel differently, or come to the movie less informed. His argument allows room for the reader to reply.

Effective arguments do not banish personal opinion or strong feeling. On the contrary, arguments often begin with passion and concern. *The situation is not working, and this is why. Here's what I think. Let me show you what I mean. I know you're convinced I'm wrong, but here's why you should change your mind.* These are the appeals you hear in conversation and on street corners. *Do you have a minute to hear about our petition?* You hear these appeals on the radio when politicians argue *This is why you should elect me,* and online where consumers comment on their purchases, sometimes to praise—*This is the best vacuum cleaner I have ever used*—and sometimes to blame—*What? Are you kidding me? It's a total waste of money.* We hear passionate arguments every day, but the most thoughtful define their terms and support their claims. These are the arguments your instructors want you to practice writing, because they will earn you a hearing. When you define your terms, you establish a common vocabulary with your listener or reader. This is what I mean by *funny.* This is what I mean by *fair.* When you support your claims, you show that your statements and judgments are not arbitrary. Even if you cannot convince your reader, you will deliver your message with clarity, nuance, and cogent reasoning.

To begin an effective argument:

- You need a claim
- That claim should invite a response
- That claim should require support
- Keep your audience in mind
- Consider what kind of support will be appropriate

To develop an effective argument:

- Qualify your claim if necessary
- Define your terms
- Consider possible objections
- Support each point
- Write with a sense of investment and urgency

ACTIVITIES

1 Look at the following brief arguments. Can you identify one or more fallacies? First, name the fallacies you find. Then choose one argument and rewrite it. Is there a way to modify the language so that you can avoid fallacy?

1. You skip your workout on Monday and you'll end up skipping Tuesday as well. The next thing you know your gym membership lapses and you'll be so obese and out of shape, you'll have trouble walking up the stairs.

2. Stereotyping is refusing to look at people as individuals. It's hurtful and unfair. That's why prejudice is wrong.

3. Downloading music and movies off the internet isn't really illegal. Everybody does it!

4. If you drive a car, you don't care about our planet's future.

5. Only psychos campaign for animal rights.

6. The World Wide Web isn't just a great invention; it's the greatest invention in the history of humankind.

7. My back went out when I got pregnant the first time, and I've never been the same. It's terrible to say, but in my case having kids caused chronic pain.

2 Read these three film reviews. Identify and describe the claim in each of the following passages. Does the author qualify that claim? What kind of support do you think such a claim requires? What rhetorical appeals does the author make? Who do you think the intended audience might be?

Understatement has its uses too, so this morning's report on the event of last night will begin with the casual notation that it was a great show. It ran, and will continue to run, for about 3 hours and 45 minutes, which still is a few days and hours less than its reading time and is a period the spine may protest sooner than the eye or ear. It is pure narrative, as the novel was, rather than great drama, as the novel was not. By that we would imply you will leave it, not with the feeling you have undergone a profound emotional experience, but with the warm and grateful remembrance of an interesting story beautifully told. Is it the greatest motion picture ever made? Probably not, although it is the greatest motion mural we have seen and the most ambitious film-making venture in Hollywood's spectacular history.

It — as you must be aware — is *Gone with the Wind*, the gargantuan Selznick edition of the Margaret Mitchell novel which swept the country like Charlie McCarthy, the "Music Goes 'Round" and similar inexplicable phenomena; which created the national emergency over the selection of a Scarlett O'Hara and which, ultimately, led to the $4,000,000 production that faced the New York public on two Times Square fronts last night, the Astor and the Capitol. It is the picture for which Mr. Gallup's American Institute of Public Opinion has reported a palpitantly waiting audience of 56,500,000 persons, a few of whom may find encouragement in our opinion that they won't be disappointed in Vivien Leigh's Scarlett, Clark Gable's Rhett Butler or, for that matter, in Mr. Selznick's Miss Mitchell.

For, by any and all standards, Mr. Selznick's film is a handsome, scrupulous and unstinting version of the 1,037-page novel, matching it almost scene for scene with a literalness that not even Shakespeare or Dickens were accorded in Hollywood, casting it so brilliantly one would have to know the history of the production not to suspect that Miss Mitchell had written her story just to provide a vehicle for the stars already assembled under Mr. Selznick's hospitable roof....

Nugent, Frank S. "David Selznick's 'Gone with the Wind' Has Its Long-Awaited Premiere at Astor and Capitol, Recalling Civil War and Plantation Days of South — seen as Treating Book With Great Fidelity." *The New York Times*, 20 Dec. 1939, p. 31.

Gone with the Wind presents a sentimental view of the Civil War, in which the "Old South" takes the place of Camelot and the war was fought not so much to defeat the Confederacy and free the slaves as to give Miss Scarlett O'Hara her comeuppance. But we've known that for years; the tainted nostalgia comes with the territory. Yet as *GWTW* approaches its 60th anniversary, it is still a towering landmark of film, quite simply because it tells a good story, and tells it wonderfully well.

For the story it wanted to tell, it was the right film at the right time. Scarlett O'Hara is not a creature of the 1860s but of the 1930s: a free-spirited, willful modern woman. The way was prepared for her by the flappers of Fitzgerald's jazz age, by the bold movie actresses of the period, and by the economic reality of the Depression, which for the first time put lots of women to work outside their homes.

Ebert, Roger. "Gone with the Wind." Rev. of *Gone with the Wind*, dir. David O. Selznick, 21 June 1998, www.rogerebert.com. Accessed 9 Sept. 2015.

If the Confederate flag is finally going to be consigned to museums as an ugly symbol of racism, what about the beloved film offering the most iconic glimpse of that flag in American culture?

I'm talking, of course, about *Gone with the Wind*, which won a then-record eight Academy Awards, including Best Picture of 1939, and still ranks as the all-time North American box-office champ with $1.6 billion worth of tickets sold here when adjusted for inflation.

True, *Gone with the Wind* isn't as blatantly and virulently racist as D.W. Griffith's *Birth of a Nation,* which was considered one of the greatest American movies as late as the early 1960s, but is now rarely screened, even in museums.

The more subtle racism of *Gone with the Wind* is in some ways more insidious, going to great lengths to enshrine the myth that the Civil War wasn't fought over slavery—an institution the film unabashedly romanticizes …

Lumenick, Lou. "'Gone with the Wind' Should Go the Way of the Confederate Flag." *New York Post*, 24 June 2015, nypost.com/2015/06/24/gone-with-the-wind-should-go-the-way-of-the-confederate-flag/. Accessed 9 Sept. 2015.

3 Write a one-to-two-page review of a book, a movie, a restaurant, or a recent purchase. Evaluate your experience and support your critical judgment with concrete details.

4 Identify and describe the claim in each of the following opinion pieces. Does the author qualify that claim? What kind of support does the author offer? Does the author introduce other possible points of view? How? Do you think the argument is effective? Why or why not?

Save Us from the SAT.

The SAT is a mind-numbing, stress-inducing ritual of torture. The College Board can change the test all it likes, but no single exam, given on a single day, should determine anyone's fate. The fact that we have been using this test to perform exactly this function for generations now is a national scandal.

The problems with the test are well known. It measures memorization, not intelligence. It favors the rich, who can afford preparatory crash courses. It freaks students out so completely that they cannot even think.

As the mother of two former SAT takers (one a sophomore in college, the other a senior in high school awaiting the result of his applications), I can also point out another problem with the test: It usually starts around 8:30 in the morning. I don't know if the members of the College Board have ever met a 17-year-old at that hour, but I can tell you this is not the time of day I would choose to test their ability to do anything, except perhaps make orangutan sounds.

I sympathize with college-admissions deans who want a simple, accurate measurement of student potential. But no such measurement exists, as I can attest from 25 years as an English professor. Students flower or diminish unexpectedly, in ways unpredictable and strange. One of the great joys of teaching is that moment when a student makes a leap and creates something new. The possibility of that leap is unlikely to be measured by a test involving bubble sheets. The only way to measure students' potential is to look at the complex portrait of their lives: what their schools are like; how they've done in their courses; what they've chosen to study; what progress they've made over time; how they've reacted to adversity. Of course colleges try to take these nuanced portraits into account, but too often they're overshadowed by the SAT. Our children, precious, brilliant, frustrating, confused souls that they are, are more than a set of scores.

Boylan, Jennifer Finney. "Save Us from the SAT." *The New York Times*, 6 Mar. 2014, p. A25.

In S.F., It's B.Y.O.B: "Bring Your Own (Water) Bottle."

If you're going to San Francisco, be sure to carry a water bottle there. Why? Because the Board of Supervisors voted this week to ban the sale of single-use bottles of water in city buildings and parks and at city-permitted events, making San Francisco the largest municipality in the country to phase out plastic water bottles. The ban will cover indoor events starting Oct. 1, and will be extended to all events by 2016. There would be exceptions for some sports outings, such as foot races, and planners could apply for waivers if they can't secure a water supply.

There are good reasons to banish small, single-use plastic bottles. They leave a huge environmental footprint. Producing bottles for American consumption takes about 17 million barrels of oil annually, enough to fuel 1.3 million cars for a year, according to the Pacific Institute. Plus there's the oil consumed in transporting the containers from bottler to seller. The average American goes through 167 water bottles in a year, but only recycles about 38. San Francisco leaders estimate that tens of millions of empty bottles end up in local landfills each year.

But now that San Francisco has banned the bottle, is the city prepared to quench its citizens' thirst with plentiful, clean public water? Many cities across the country have failed to maintain or neglected to install adequate drinking fountains. While some consumers choose bottled water because they believe that it is unsafe, or that it tastes bad, others buy it for convenience. They are out and they are thirsty. If the city doesn't have an adequate system of public fountains, those consumers may end up buying soda or other high-calorie beverages, which would not be affected by the ban. That's not exactly the best public policy outcome.

So go ahead, San Francisco and other cities: Ban the bottle. But only after you have invested in building and restoring a network of free public water.

"In S.F., It's B.Y.O.B: 'Bring Your Own (Water) Bottle.'" *Los Angeles Times*, 6 Mar. 2014, www.latimes.com/opinion/editorials/la-ed-bottled-water-ban-san-francisco-20140306-story.html. Accessed 9 Sept. 2015.

5 Write a two-to-three-page op/ed about a public issue that concerns you.

6 Each of the following makes a claim that trees are important, but each argument takes a different form. Identify the genre in each case. Now describe how the author or artist builds an argument. Why are trees important, and what do we lose when we destroy them? How does each author support his or her claim? How does genre shape argument in each case?

John Muir (1838–1914) was a naturalist and environmental activist who founded the Sierra Club. This passage comes from his 1897 essay, "The American Forests," in The Atlantic.

Notwithstanding all the waste and use which have been going on unchecked like a storm for more than two centuries, it is not yet too late, though it is high time, for the government to begin a rational administration of its forests. About seventy million acres it still owns, — enough for all the country, if wisely used. These residual forests are generally on mountain slopes, just where they are doing the most good, and where their removal would be followed by the greatest number of evils; the lands they cover are too rocky and high for agriculture, and can never be made as valuable for any other crop as for the present crop of trees. It has been shown over and over again that if these mountains were to be stripped of their trees and underbrush, and kept bare and sodless by hordes of sheep and the innumerable fires the shepherds set, besides those of the millmen, prospectors, shake-makers, and all sorts of adventurers, both lowlands and mountains would speedily become little better than deserts, compared with their present beneficent fertility. During heavy rainfalls and while the winter accumulations of snow were melting, the larger streams would swell into destructive torrents; cutting deep, rugged-edged gullies, carrying away the fertile humus and soil as well as sand and rocks, filling up and overflowing their lower channels, and covering the lowland fields with raw detritus. Drought and barrenness would follow.

Muir, John. "The American Forests." *The Atlantic*, 1 Aug. 1897, pp. 145–57.

Gerard Manley Hopkins (1884–89) was an English poet known for his delicate wordplay and his interest in religion and the natural world. He wrote this poem to commemorate a grove of poplar trees chopped down in 1879.

Binsey Poplars

felled 1879

My aspens dear, whose airy cages quelled,
Quelled or quenched in leaves the leaping sun,
All felled, felled, are all felled;
   Of a fresh and following folded rank
      Not spared, not one
     That dandled a sandalled
    Shadow that swam or sank
On meadow & river & wind-wandering weed-winding bank.

   O if we but knew what we do
     When we delve or hew—
Hack and rack the growing green!
    Since country is so tender
To touch, her being só slender,
That, like this sleek and seeing ball
But a prick will make no eye at all,
Where we, even where we mean
     To mend her we end her,
   When we hew or delve:
After-comers cannot guess the beauty been.
   Ten or twelve, only ten or twelve
    Strokes of havoc unselve
    The sweet especial scene,
  Rural scene, a rural scene,
  Sweet especial rural scene.

Hopkins, Gerard Manley. "Binsey Poplars." 1879. *Gerard Manley Hopkins: Poems and Prose*, Penguin Classics, 1985.

"Protect Trees." *Thomson Multiwood*, www.multiwood.in/blog/protect-trees. Accessed 26 Nov. 2018.

6

ACADEMIC ARGUMENT: THESIS AND ORGANIZATION

Writing a Thesis and Introduction.

ANNA   What now?

ZACH   We had to submit the introduction for our papers taking a stand on a public issue.

ANNA   Okay ...

ZACH   Look at what my instructor said!

ANNA   "You do an excellent job describing the state lottery system. What's missing is a thesis statement."

ZACH   But I DO have a thesis.

ANNA   Where?

ZACH   I underlined it right there. *The lottery is an important form of revenue for the state government because sadly so many people buy tickets paying good money for an incredibly small chance to win an incredibly big prize.* How is that not a thesis statement?

ANNA   I think maybe you were supposed to take a stand and say what *you* think about the lotteries?

ZACH   I did! That's why I used the word sadly.

What Is a Thesis?

What is Zach missing? He tells his reader that his paper is about the lottery. This is his **topic**—the subject of his paper. He also hints at his point of view when he uses the word *sadly*. However, his instructor is not satisfied. She wants Zach to come up with a **thesis statement**—a formal claim stating the writer's position concisely and precisely in one or two sentences. As we saw in Chapter Five, claims come in all shapes and sizes. A thesis is a claim with the following attributes:

- A thesis takes a position on a subject.
- A thesis invites discussion.
- A thesis requires support.
- A thesis usually appears in the first paragraph of a paper.
- A thesis is concise—usually one or two sentences.

Some rhetorical situations do not require a thesis statement. In conversation with friends, you might declare *I'm in a bad mood and I hate the world right now*. By the same token, there are genres of writing that do not require a thesis statement. A story for creative writing class: *When I stepped off the plane I felt alone*. A report on a recent event: *The student protest began at noon*. A personal narrative: *This is the story of my first ski trip*. An instruction manual: *Take out the four screws in the large bag*. Note that each of these statements carries a strong purpose—to emote, to narrate, to inform. These statements work well in their genres. However, none qualifies as a thesis.

In many college writing assignments, your instructors will expect the formal claim of a thesis statement. Your assignment may not say this explicitly, but any time you are asked to argue, to evaluate, to compare, to persuade, or to respond to material, there's a good chance you'll need to come up with a thesis.

Consider the following sentences by students. Note the factors that set the thesis statement apart.

Statement in conversation: Fast food is disgusting.
This is one person's opinion. You could respond—why do you think that? But in the end, the speaker is the expert on his own feelings about food. Not much to discuss here.

Statement in short story for creative writing class: The greasy fried food depressed Bob even more, as he kept eating himself into oblivion.
This is a fine description of binge-eating and contributes to the larger story of Bob. However, the statement does not invite debate or require evidence. The author of the story created Bob, and remains the expert on his behavior and feelings.

Statement in report for nutrition class: The total calories of the "Happy Meal" is 405.
This is a statement of fact and works well as a point of information, but the writer does not take a position on the information provided.

Statement in report for sociology class: The prevalence of fast food in poor urban neighborhoods and the scarcity of stores selling fresh fruit and vegetables lead to what is called food deserts.
This statement defines a food desert as a place where nutritious food is scarce. The term desert suggests a bleak, life-threatening place, but the author does not comment on this here. The observation that food deserts crop up in poor urban neighborhoods suggests that nutritious food might be out of reach for poor people in more ways than one. This is a provocative idea that could serve as the basis for a thesis statement, but it is not a thesis yet.

Often nutritious food is out of reach, not only because of price, but because of geography.
This thesis invites discussion. Is geography such an important factor? The thesis requires support, as well. The reader thinks, show me a map. Show me the grocery stores in each neighborhood and give me a sense of what is available. Show me the prices, as well. How does nutritious food compare to fast food?

While this thesis sheds light on the problem of food deserts, another thesis could focus on possible solutions.

A partnership between business and government agencies could prevent food deserts in the poorest urban neighborhoods.

This statement invites discussion. The reader thinks—*really? What kind of partnership are you proposing? How would this partnership work? Is such a partnership possible?* This statement also requires evidence. The reader wonders—*How do you know that such a partnership would prevent food deserts? What examples can you show me?* The writer takes a position, venturing that a partnership could prevent food deserts. Inviting discussion and requiring evidence, this sentence looks like a promising thesis statement.

The thesis could be even stronger if the author sets it up with the definition of food deserts above. Consider the two statements together. We have underlined the thesis.

The prevalence of fast food in poor urban neighborhoods and the scarcity of stores selling fresh fruit and vegetables leads to what is called food deserts. A partnership between business and government agencies could prevent food deserts in the poorest urban neighborhoods.

Often a thesis statement is most effective when its author introduces it with a sentence or two. The introduction to a thesis could define terms, for example explaining what a food desert means and why it is detrimental. In other cases, the introduction to a thesis could frame a problem the thesis will address, or provide background and context for the author's assertion. Defining your topic is a great way to set up your thesis. However, it is essential to understand that a topic is not a thesis.

What Is the Difference between Topic and Thesis?

A topic denotes an area you will explore, a problem you might address, a question you might answer. A thesis tells your reader what you want to say about your topic. Defining the topic of a paper is an important task. Zach spends a lot of time developing a cogent definition of the state lottery system that will be the subject of his

Zach

Okay, here goes. The lottery is an important form of revenue for the state government because sadly so many people buy tickets paying good money for an incredibly small chance to win an incredibly big prize. Do I take a position? Well, I thought I was saying lotteries are sad because they are almost impossible to win, but I guess my position isn't coming through. Does my thesis invite discussion? Um. Not really, because I am mostly stating facts. Does my thesis require support? Not a lot of support, because what I'm saying is well known. People aren't going to question my assertion that state governments make a lot of money from lotteries, because it's common knowledge. I guess this is more of a topic than a thesis statement.

Kate

Here's a statement from an op/ed I wrote on nursing. Human contact is what nurses value, and this is why they choose their profession. Do I take a position? Yes! I take a strong position that human contact motivates people to choose nursing. Does my thesis invite discussion? Yes. Not everyone will necessarily agree with my interpretation of the motivation of nurses. Does my thesis require support? Yes. My thesis requires a lot of support. My reader will ask how do you know why nurses choose their profession? This is definitely a thesis statement.

paper. He ends up with a good explanation of his topic, and he is surprised when his instructor tells him he is missing a thesis.

If you feel you have written a sentence that could serve as your thesis, try testing your statement with three questions:

- Does my thesis take a position?
- Does my thesis invite discussion?
- Does my thesis require support?

Moving from Topic to Thesis

Kate is taking a course on American culture in the 1950s. Her instructor hands out the following assignment.

> In the 1950s, new home appliances revolutionized domestic life. Choose one appliance and put together a presentation, in a form of your choosing, to help your audience understand its impact on the family and society as a whole.

Kate looks at her class notes and recalls discussions of new technology in the home. In the 1950s the garbage disposal became popular, as did the electric washing machine and dryer,

REFLECT: Think about a past or current writing assignment requiring a thesis. Look at your thesis statement and test it. Do you take a position? Does your thesis invite discussion? Does it require support? If you cannot say yes to each of these questions, do you think you might have a topic instead? How might you modify your topic statement to craft an arguable thesis?

the dishwasher, and the refrigerator. Kate's instructor showed the class 1950s print ads for the refrigerator, and she remembers how surprised she was at the hype about an appliance she had always taken for granted. She decides to write about the refrigerator.

This is a topic, and a broad one at that. Kate could read for days about the invention of the refrigerator, the early marketing of this product, the commercial as well as domestic use of refrigerators, the way the refrigerator revolutionized industry. But where should she focus her energy? What part of this information will be relevant for this assignment?

WHAT IS THE SCOPE OF YOUR TOPIC? CONSIDER PURPOSE, GENRE, AND AUDIENCE

Much of the time, your assignment will give you a sense of the **scope,** the extent, and limits of the work you need to do. A writing assignment may specify a page or word limit. An oral assignment may specify a time limit for your presentation. In one sense, your scope involves the time you will put in and the length of your project. In another sense, scope involves your thinking. If you are writing about an appliance, do you want to discuss its invention and sales history, or just the way we use this appliance in everyday life? How much background material do you want to include? Do you want to discuss the way people in other countries use this appliance, or will you focus only on the United States? These are the kinds of questions you need to answer in order to define the scope of your project. Your assignment can guide you here.

Kate's assignment asks her to discuss the *impact* of an appliance on families and society. If she is writing about impact, that means she needs to focus on what the refrigerator did for people. The technology of refrigeration is fascinating, but not relevant here. The history of the appliance is not central. Her **purpose** is to discuss how the refrigerator changed lives.

As she thinks about the work ahead, Kate considers the **genre** she has chosen—a ten-minute oral presentation with slides. She will not have time to discuss every facet of the refrigerator's impact. She needs to focus her presentation on a few important points.

Finally, Kate thinks about her **audience**—her classmates and instructor. Her course focuses on social and domestic history, and her presentation will build on class discussions about the impact of technology on the family. With all this in mind, Kate chooses to focus on how the refrigerator made life easier for families.

She writes this initial statement:

> The refrigerator enabled families to store food for much longer than they could on a shelf.

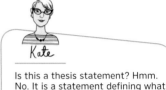

Is this a thesis statement? Hmm. No. It is a statement defining what a refrigerator does.

As we saw in the last chapter, a cogent argument often begins with defining terms, and describing something that happened. However, definition and description are not enough. How might Kate take this descriptive statement and build a thesis?

CONSIDER THE SIGNIFICANCE OF YOUR TOPIC

Thinking about the significance of your topic is one way to move beyond definition. Kate thinks about the fact that refrigeration allowed people to keep food fresh for a much longer time. Then she recalls class discussions about the ways that technology liberated people from daily chores. Synthesizing information from her class notes and her own experience, she begins to think along these lines. Without a refrigerator, people—no, not just people, *women*—must have gone shopping every day. To have a refrigerator meant freedom from that daily chore. It also meant that the stores themselves could keep their food fresh longer. Building on these ideas, Kate comes up with a new statement.

> The refrigerator not only revolutionized food storage, but contributed to the changing role of women in and outside the home.

This is a strong claim for the significance of the refrigerator. Does it invite discussion? Yes. The reader wonders—how could one new appliance change the role of women in society? Does this statement require support? Yes. Kate will have to provide evidence that the refrigerator changed women's lives—not only in, but outside the home. She will look for articles and books that discuss the way appliances like the refrigerator changed the shopping and cooking habits of women and freed them to pursue new work and leisure activities. Kate has a thesis, and she built it from her topic. She began by defining the refrigerator as a device to keep a family's food cold. Then she expanded her definition to consider what this technology might do for many families. Finally, she came up with a thesis while considering the refrigerator in a larger social context.

ASSERT YOUR OWN VIEW IN CONTRAST TO OTHERS

Another natural way to develop a thesis statement is to consider the way others view your topic and then to assert your own view. In class, Kate's instructor reminds students to draw upon course readings on technology and social change in post-war America when writing their papers. Kate looks at these readings and finds that many authors believe refrigeration is a big step forward, because families did not have to buy fresh food every day. This line of reasoning makes sense, because it is not always convenient to shop every day. However, as she thinks about her own diet and her own family, Kate reflects that she would prefer to buy fresh local ingredients more often, rather than stock up on a lot of processed food. With this perspective, Kate can take a position of her own. We underline her thesis below.

> Many consider refrigeration a huge improvement in our standard of living because the refrigerator allows us to store food safely for days or even weeks. However, <u>the refrigerator did not necessarily change lives for the better. Shopping habits changed, and diets changed as well, from local seasonal produce to processed food.</u>

Notice the way Kate signals her move from other views to her own idea. The phrase *Many consider* introduces the established view that the refrigerator was an innovation that improved our quality of life. The word *However* signals that Kate maintains a different view. Kate could choose a different formula. She could write, *While X argues that the refrigerator improves quality of life, I believe ...* Or she could assert, *I agree with X that the refrigerator changed life for the better. However ...* In each case, she uses signal phrases to establish what others think and then stake her own position.

Where is the thesis statement here? Where Kate asserts "However, the refrigerator did not necessarily change lives for the better. Shopping habits changed, and diets changed as well, from local seasonal produce to processed food." This thesis asserts Kate's perspective, and provides a provocative critical judgment on the ways in which this technology affects shopping and eating habits.

ASK A THOUGHT-PROVOKING QUESTION

Considering the significance of a topic is one way to come up with a thesis. Considering other viewpoints and then asserting your own is another fine way to develop a thesis. A third way to build a thesis is to answer a question about your topic. Sometimes your instructor will provide the question in your assignment. At other times, you might think of a question on your own. Reviewing her class notes, Kate recalls a moment when another student pointed out that large numbers of women were homemakers in the 1950s. When technology changed domestic life, it changed the life of women and mothers. Course readings emphasize this point as well. Kate thinks about this and reflects on the title of her course: American Culture in the 1950s. At one lecture her instructor asked the class, "How does technology change culture?" As she considers this question, along with her class notes and course readings, Kate comes up with an interesting question about refrigeration. If refrigeration changed the lives of mothers, did it change cultural views of motherhood as well? This question could provide Kate with another opportunity for a thesis statement, because she could answer her own question with a formal claim which looks like this. We underline her thesis.

> Historians believe that the introduction of the refrigerator changed the shopping and cooking habits of housewives. Did refrigeration change cultural views of motherhood as well? <u>I believe that even though the refrigerator made the lives of women easier, it became a symbol for maternal shortcuts, cold efficiency and alienation.</u> In the 1950s the term "refrigerator mother" came into use to describe mothers who did not bond well with their babies.

This thesis draws a connection between changing technology and changing views of motherhood. Kate's assertion invites debate. How does she know that people associated the refrigerator with cold efficiency? Is she talking about a backlash against innovation? Is she suggesting that the cold refrigerator replaced the warm fireplace at the heart of the home? Where is her evidence for this? Kate's thesis will require support. In order to show how the refrigerator became an important metaphor for changing views of motherhood in the 1950s, she will need to look at examples from the popular press and from psychologists. Her instructor suggests that she look up the work of psychologist Leo Kanner, who discussed cold mothers.

An observation, an assertion, or a question—each can provide material for a thesis statement. Do you have some idea of what you want to say, or the position you want to take? Now consider *how* you want to take your stand or write your thesis. What kind of assignment is this? Who is your audience? And what are your instructor's expectations?

The Style of a Thesis: First or Third Person? Position? Format?

When you take a position in a thesis statement, it is natural to write in the first person. A thesis statement beginning *I argue* or *I believe* will serve you well in assignments where you are asked to write a personal response or to take a stand on a question. Zach's assignment is to take a stand on a public issue. His instructor makes it clear that the first person is fine. Zach will state his claim in a direct and personal fashion. However, not all assignments welcome a first-person assertion.

Differentiating her view of refrigeration from that of others, it's natural for Kate to use the word I.

> Many consider refrigeration a huge improvement in our standard of living because the refrigerator allows us to store food safely for days or even weeks. However, I question whether the refrigerator actually changed lives for the better. While in the past, families had shopped

> daily for local seasonal produce, the refrigerator caused them to shift to buying a great deal of processed food at large chain stores. In my opinion, this move actually changed diets and quality of life for the worse.

Using the word I, and referring to her opinion, Kate prepares the reader for a thoughtful personal essay. However, Kate's instructor assigned a historical analysis, which requires a more formal tone. The instructor asked students to write in the style of course readings, all of which are in the third person. Therefore, she will need to frame her thesis differently.

> Many consider refrigeration a huge improvement in our standard of living, because the refrigerator allows us to store food safely for days or even weeks. However, some economists and food historians question whether the refrigerator is such a blessing. By the 1950s, the refrigerator enabled families to shift from daily, local, seasonal shopping to increased reliance on big chain supermarkets and processed food. This paper argues that the refrigerator saved time, but damaged overall nutrition.

Instead of focusing on the writer's personal views of refrigeration, this thesis focuses on a debate among scholars. Using the third person, Kate presents the debate on refrigeration and discusses the strengths and weaknesses of each side of the argument. Then, without using the word I, she asserts her own viewpoint. *This paper argues that the refrigerator saved time, but damaged overall nutrition.*

If you are unsure about whether to use "I" in your thesis statement, it is important to look at your assignment and to ask for guidance, if necessary. Think about where your thesis will appear, as well. What are your instructor's expectations? And what will work best in the genre you have chosen? Does your instructor want your thesis right up front as the first sentence of a presentation, or as the last sentence of your first paragraph? Some instructors ask students to signal a thesis by underlining it. Others ask students to signal a thesis with the phrase *I argue*. Still others ask for no special format.

Formats may vary and styles may differ, but in every case, your thesis should invite discussion and require support.

What Signal Does Your Thesis Send?

With a thesis, a writer not only makes a claim, but signals the kind of argument that will follow. Consider the following passages and note the different message each thesis sends the reader. We have underlined the thesis in each.

> I hate "classical music": not the thing but the name. It traps a tenaciously living art in a theme park of the past. It cancels out the possibility that music in the spirit of Beethoven could still be created today. It banishes into limbo the work of thousands of active composers who have to explain to otherwise well-informed people what it is they do for a living. The phrase is a masterpiece of negative publicity, a tour de force of anti-hype. I wish there were another name. I envy jazz people who speak simply of "the music." Some jazz aficionados also call their art "America's classical music," and I propose a trade: they can have "classical," I'll take "the music."
>
> Ross, Alex. "Listen to This." *The New Yorker*, 16 Feb. 2004, pp. 146–55.

Beginning with the word I, music critic Alex Ross makes a passionate statement with his thesis. He hates the term classical music, because it relegates the music he loves to the past. Ross's first person thesis sets the tone for a personal essay. Ross certainly takes a position with his thesis, and his position invites discussion. The reader wonders—is the term classical music really so dangerous? Is it actually scaring people away? Ross's thesis will require support. He needs to demonstrate that the term classical is detrimental. Writing about music, Ross takes the role of scholar and listener. In the genre of the personal essay, he feels free to express his feelings about his subject. His strong opening "I hate" would look out of place in an academic essay on Beethoven.

Alex Ross himself writes quite differently about Beethoven on another occasion. In the following essay, published 10 years after the essay above, Ross uses his thesis to set up a historical argument. Notice the long lead up to the thesis here, and the careful presentation of facts introducing the thesis.

> Beethoven is a singularity in the history of art — a phenomenon of dazzling and disconcerting force. He not only left his mark on all subsequent composers but also molded entire institutions. The professional orchestra arose, in large measure, as a vehicle for the incessant performance of Beethoven's symphonies. The art of conducting emerged in his wake. The modern piano bears the imprint of his demand for a more resonant and flexible instrument. Recording technology evolved with Beethoven in mind: the first commercial 33⅓ r.p.m. LP, in 1931, contained the Fifth Symphony, and the duration of first-generation compact disks was fixed at seventy-five minutes so that the Ninth Symphony could unfurl without interruption. After Beethoven, the concert hall came to be seen not as a venue for diverse, meandering entertainments but as an austere memorial to artistic majesty. Listening underwent a fundamental change. To follow Beethoven's dense, driving narratives, one had to lean forward and pay close attention. The musicians' platform became the stage of an invisible drama, the temple of a sonic revelation.
>
> Above all, Beethoven shaped the identity of what came to be known as classical music. In the course of the nineteenth century, dead composers began to crowd out the living on concert programs, and a canon of masterpieces materialized, with Beethoven front and center.
>
> Ross, Alex. "Beethoven's Bad Influence." *The New Yorker*, 20 Oct. 2014, pp. 44–49.

In his thesis asserting the impact of Beethoven, Ross does not use the word I, nor does he include any reference to personal feeling—hate, envy, or wishing. Ross writes that listeners have come to associate classical music with dead composers and the past. This is the same topic he addresses in his personal essay about hating the term "classical." However, in the Beethoven essay, Ross uses his thesis to identify the worship of a single great composer as the cause of this dismaying trend. He takes the position that once listeners began to idolize Beethoven, they lost interest in living composers. This thesis invites discussion. Was it really love of Beethoven that inspired this trend? Or were other factors involved? The thesis also requires support. Historical accounts, analysis of concert programs, perhaps even interviews with living composers and teachers could provide Ross with evidence. Writing in the third person, Ross prepares readers for a dispassionate argument tying the stuffy stereotypes of classical music—the hushed concert hall, the worship of the past—to reverence for Beethoven.

A thesis based on fact and appealing to logos is highly prized in many academic disciplines. A thesis like this takes a stand and presents the author's interpretation, but does so without overt reference to emotion or personal convictions. Avoiding appeals to pathos, academic theses make strong appeals to logos and ethos, emphasizing the reasoning and research that inform the author's formal claim.

Consider the following abstract for a journal article by anthropologists danah boyd and Alice Marwick. We underline the thesis.

While teenage conflict is nothing new, today's gossip, jokes, and arguments often play out through social media like Formspring, Twitter, and Facebook. Although adults often refer to these practices with the language of "bullying," teens are more likely to refer to the resultant skirmishes and their digital traces as "drama." Drama is a performative set of actions distinct from bullying, gossip, and relational aggression, incorporating elements of them but also operating quite distinctly. While drama is not particularly new, networked dynamics reconfigure how drama plays out and what it means to teens in new ways. In this paper, we examine how American teens conceptualize drama, its key components, participant motivations for engaging in it, and its relationship to networked technologies. Drawing on six years of ethnographic fieldwork, we examine what drama means to teenagers and its relationship to visibility and privacy. <u>We argue that the emic [insider] use of "drama" allows teens to distance themselves from practices which adults may conceptualize as bullying. As such, they can retain agency—and save face—rather than positioning themselves in a victim narrative.</u> Drama is a gendered process that perpetrates conventional gender norms. It also reflects discourses of celebrity, particularly the mundane interpersonal conflict found on soap operas and reality television. For teens, sites like Facebook allow for similar performances in front of engaged audiences. Understanding how "drama" operates is necessary to recognize teens' own defenses against the realities of aggression, gossip, and bullying in networked publics.

Marwick, Alice E., and danah boyd. "The Drama! Teen Conflict, Gossip, and Bullying in Networked Publics." *A Decade in Internet Time: Symposium on the Dynamics of the Internet and Society, University of Oxford, Sept. 2011. SSRN*, Sept. 2011, http://ssrn.com/abstract=1926349.

The authors make a strong claim to ethos when they refer to their six years of fieldwork, interviewing teens and observing their behavior on the internet. The authors do not use the word *I* to make their claim; nor do they use the third person. They use the word *we* to take a position: "we argue." Papers in the sciences and social sciences often have multiple authors. The word *we* conveys that joint effort, along with a sense of consensus and scientific process. Presumably, the investigators discussed the evidence and checked with each other before presenting their idea that teens use the term drama to describe and contain online behavior that adults might term bullying.

boyd and Marwick take a strong position, asserting that adults view online activity by teens in one way, while teens view their online behavior quite differently. The thesis invites discussion. How are the authors so confident that teens differentiate drama from bullying? Could it be that one teen's drama is another teen's tragedy? This thesis also requires support. The reader expects the authors to bolster their claim with detailed discussion and analysis of field notes, interviews, and surveys.

Anna

A lot of times the question my instructor asks helps me figure out a position that turns into a thesis statement. For example, I got this assignment last week: *Write an essay addressing the following: Why did the Nazis come to power in 1933?* I looked at my lecture notes and I found these factors—runaway economic distress, effective propaganda of Hitler, Anti-Semitism, and increasing nationalism. The purpose of the assignment is for us to gather what we had learned into one argument, so I used these notes to come up with a thesis.

Anna's thesis
Four major factors—effective propaganda, economic distress, Anti-Semitism, and nationalism—created a perfect storm bringing Hitler to power in 1933.

Jordan

I look at my data and take notes on important trends. In my economics class we're studying college attendance. While looking at data from the long form of the census, I noticed that students are more likely to graduate when at least one parent has graduated from college. When I looked more closely, I saw that the numbers are even better if the students' *mother* was the college graduate. I used this observation to come up with a thesis for my class project.

Jordan's thesis
A student whose mother has a college degree is more likely to graduate from college.

REFLECT: Consider a writing assignment in which you need to craft a thesis statement. How did you go about it? If you are currently working on a writing assignment requiring a thesis statement, how is that thesis coming? Are you drawing upon course materials to come up with your thesis? How so?

Your instructor will not expect you to base your thesis on six years of fieldwork, or to draw upon a lifetime of music listening. Usually, in college you write in response to questions, course material, and discussions in class. Coming up with a thesis could involve synthesizing information from lectures with assigned readings. Or, it could involve studying course material in depth and coming up with your own interpretation.

Understanding your assignment and the expectations of your instructor will help immensely as you work to come up with a thesis. Ask yourself—would it be appropriate to take a position with the word "I?" Or does my instructor expect a third person thesis? Should my thesis refer to my personal convictions? Or should my thesis refer to facts and data? Interpretation and analysis of texts? Graphs? Historical events?

Developing a Thesis

You may feel some pressure to come up with a thesis statement right away. Your instructor might ask you to turn in your thesis, or to exchange your thesis with a classmate's for discussion before you start writing your paper. Coming up with a thesis can be difficult; you may not feel ready. However, instructors understand that a thesis can change during the writing process. Turning in your thesis statement first allows you to take suggestions before you commit to writing your whole paper. Submitting the thesis alone, you launch a trial balloon. In the sciences, a trial balloon thesis has a technical term, a **hypothesis**. However, you don't have to be a scientist to test and improve your thesis during the writing process. Ask yourself the following questions:

- Does this thesis move beyond stating or defining my topic?
- What style does my thesis take? Is this the style my instructor expects?
- What rhetorical claims does my thesis make? Are these claims appropriate for this assignment?
- What kind of evidence will my thesis require?
- Do I need to adjust my thesis after looking at the evidence?

When you submit your thesis, your instructor can check your work quickly, and you can make adjustments if necessary. Even if your instructor does not require you to submit your thesis for approval, it makes sense to test and discuss your thesis statement before committing to it.

ZACH   Okay, listen to this. Since the dawn of history, gambling has been a part of the human experience with lotteries playing a large role in society elevating the poor to the very rich with just a stroke of chance. Captivating the imagination, the lottery has become an irrational obsession to millions in the present day who end up contributing to a hugely powerful revenue stream for the state.

ANNA   Huh?

ZACH   You don't like it?

ANNA   I don't get it! Which part is the thesis?

Zach is supposed to take a stand on a public issue. His essay will benefit from an introduction in which he states his own point of view quickly. His instructor expects to see Zach taking that stand, so when Anna says *Huh?* Zach realizes his thesis is not coming through clearly.

ZACH   Okay, how's this? The lottery is a huge source of revenue for the state government. In fact lottery earnings exceed income tax in some states.

ANNA   That's a lot shorter. But I'm still not sure what YOU have to say about the state lottery.

Even a sympathetic reader cannot read Zach's mind. A critical reader won't even try. If his thesis only hints at a direction, then it is not doing its job. Taking a position means Zach must lay his cards on the table.

ZACH   Okay, try this. State lotteries provide a huge revenue stream to the government. This is because people are obsessed with winning and so they continue to play, despite the odds. Essentially lotteries tax people who don't understand probability. Lotteries take advantage of the poor and uneducated.

ANNA   Whoa!

ZACH   Was it that bad?

ANNA   Lotteries are a hidden tax on the poor and uneducated. I think you have a thesis!

How a Thesis Sets the Parameters of Your Work

Your thesis stakes your claim and announces what you will discuss. Your thesis also allows you to exclude what you will not discuss. Anna's instructor asked for a three-to-five-page discussion of Hitler's rise to power. Historians have written whole books on this subject, but Anna knows she has at most five pages and one week to write her paper. Therefore, she limits herself to a brief treatment of four factors leading to Hitler's rise—clever use of propaganda, growing anti-Semitism, increasing nationalism, and economic misery.

Indeed, Anna uses her thesis statement to limit the scope of her paper. Anna's thesis commits her to talking about these four factors and no others. Limiting her scope, Anna also makes an interpretive decision. She is singling out these four factors as the most significant because she thinks that together they created a perfect storm. Although her thesis begins as a descriptive statement, itemizing factors, she moves beyond synthesizing information from class discussion and reading notes to analysis of that information. Her thesis reflects that move.

Jordan: My economics of education paper is supposed to be five to seven pages. I have two weeks to write it. I won't deal with every aspect of higher education in the census. I will focus on the educational history of mothers and fathers and try to correlate these with college matriculation of their children.

Zach: My instructor assigned a three page essay. I have three days left to put it together. I won't have time to talk about every aspect of the lottery system. I am going to focus on the long odds of winning and the studies showing how many low-income citizens buy lottery tickets.

REFLECT: Consider a current writing assignment that requires a thesis statement. What is the page limit? What are your time constraints? Can you narrow your thesis to limit the scope of your paper?

Using a Thesis to Outline Your Paper

An effective thesis sets the stage for the argument to come, and it can do even more than that. It can help organize your paper as well.

Sometimes a thesis statement contains a **game plan** for the rest of your paper. Consider Anna's claim:

> Four major factors brought Hitler to power—clever use of propaganda, growing anti-Semitism, increasing nation-alism, and economic misery. Together, these created a perfect storm in 1933.

Because Anna is writing a short essay, she will devote one or two paragraphs to each of the four major factors and then write her conclusion. If she were writing a longer paper, she could, of course, write much more about each point. In both cases, however, she can use her thesis to organize her work. She will write about each of her four factors in turn. But which should she discuss first? Each seems important.

Anna

I think I'm going to start by discussing economic misery, because it seems like this caused so much anger. That anger created a climate for growing anti-Semitism and nationalism, so I'll write about those next. I'll finish with propaganda, because I feel like Hitler used propaganda to take advantage of the population. Oh wait! Maybe I need to add something to my thesis!

As she thinks about how to order the four factors leading to Hitler's rise to power, Anna starts thinking about the relationship among them, and she concludes that each led to the next. This is a new claim that she can use to focus her thesis. Instead of merely listing four factors that created a perfect storm, Anna writes:

> Economic misery led to increased anti-Semitism and nationalism in Germany, and Hitler capitalized on this with clever propaganda to seize power. Conditions were bad, but he had the skill and the desire to turn them to his advantage.

Deciding how to order her four factors leads Anna to make an interpretive statement about their relationship. In the process, she makes a bolder and more focused claim.

This thesis suggests a game plan for completing the paper. She writes down this plan in the form of a loose **outline**, or list of points. Look at the way Anna develops an outline from ideas in her thesis.

Anna's Outline

- Introduce thesis: Economic misery led to increased anti-Semitism and nationalism in Germany, and Hitler capitalized on this with clever propaganda to seize power. Conditions were bad, but he had the skill and the desire to turn them to his advantage.
- Discuss economic misery.
- How misery led to a rise in anti-Semitism.
- How misery led to the rise of nationalism.
- How Hitler capitalized on the situation with clever propaganda.
- Conclusion—Hitler took advantage of a terrible situation. He couldn't have done it alone. At the same time, miserable conditions weren't enough to bring him to power. He was opportunistic.

In contrast, Zach's thesis statement does not contain an obvious game plan. He asserts:

> Essentially, the lottery taxes people who don't understand probability. Lotteries take advantage of the poor and uneducated.

Does this thesis suggest any kind of organization for the paragraphs to follow? Zach looks at his thesis and he thinks about his audience. His writing seminar does not include many math majors, and chances are they don't know a lot about probability. Then Zach's instructor points out that it might be a stretch to say that lotteries are a kind of tax. After all, taxes are mandatory. Lotteries are not.

Zach's instructor explains that if Zach is going to support his thesis that lotteries take advantage of the poor and uneducated, he needs to define these terms. It seems like a lot of work—but the good news is, defining each term could be a useful way to organize the essay. Zach might begin by discussing how the lottery system works and how the money provides important revenue to state governments. After talking to his instructor, he decides that he will explain how lottery revenue is different from tax revenue. Then he can discuss the slim chance that ticket buyers will actually win. Finally, he can explore the irony that people who don't understand probability are imposing an unnecessary tax on themselves.

Zach's Outline
- Introduce thesis: Lotteries take advantage of the poor and uneducated.
- Explain how the lottery system works.
- Discuss how much money state governments make from lotteries.
- Explain the basic principles of probability.
- Spell out the terrible odds of winning a lottery. (You are more likely to be struck by lightning.)
- Discuss the tragedy that people waste money on lotteries because they don't know their math. Cite statistic that many are poor and uneducated.
- Conclusion: Advocate for better oversight of lotteries. Propose that all high schools teach probability!

In the sciences and social sciences, a thesis statement often points to the investigative work that led to it. Jordan introduces his thesis with a reference to data gathered in a study of graduation rates. Looking at the data, Jordan notices something striking. Students with a mother who went to college are themselves more likely to go to college! Jordan uses this observation as his thesis statement:

> Analysis of college matriculation suggests that a student whose mother has a college degree is more likely to go to college.

This thesis prepares the reader for an extensive discussion of the graduation rates among different student cohorts. Jordan's thesis is descriptive in the sense that he is recording what he sees in the data. However, the thesis interprets as well, identifying a trend and proposing a causal connection. In the context of this economics assignment, Jordan is asserting his own point of view.

Jordan realizes that in his economics paper he will need to convince a reader with a clear rational argument. He is writing for an audience interested in statistics, and he will have to appeal to logos, introducing and explaining the data he uses and building his analysis of that data step by step. Therefore, Jordan sets up his thesis with the words "analysis of graduation rates suggests ..." His thesis does not spring from personal conviction—*I believe*—but from analysis of data. When Jordan outlines his paper, he itemizes and expands on the elements of his thesis statement. After stating his thesis, he will present his supporting data. Then he will analyze that data. Finally, he will show that the numbers support his thesis.

REFLECT: Consider your thesis statement in a recent or current writing assignment. Does the thesis suggest a structure for the paragraphs to follow? Can you use your thesis to develop an outline for your paper?

Jordan's Outline

- Introduce thesis: Analysis of graduation rates suggests that a student whose mother has a college degree is more likely to graduate from college.
- Present graduation rates of all students in the United States.
- Present and discuss the set of students who have one or more parents with college degrees.
- Contrast this group with students whose parents do not have a college degree.
- Present and discuss the subset of students who have a mother with a college degree.
- Conclusion: A mother with a college degree is a more significant factor than a father with a college degree.

Consider purpose, audience, and genre when you think about the style and format of a thesis.

What is a thesis?

- Not all genres require thesis statements.
- Academic genres often do.
- A topic is not a thesis.
- A thesis establishes what you want to say and excludes what you will not say.
- You can use your thesis to organize and outline your paper or presentation.

Tests of an effective thesis

- Does my thesis take a position?
- Does my thesis invite discussion?
- Does my thesis require support?

Refining and developing your thesis

- You can develop your thesis from your topic, building from a descriptive statement or definition to make a claim of your own.
  - consider the significance of your topic
  - develop a thesis in contrast to the ideas of others
  - consider a question rising from your topic.

ACTIVITIES

1 Test each of the following statements with three questions: Does this statement take a position? Does it invite discussion? Does it require support? Which statements qualify as an effective thesis? Which do not? How might you develop a thesis from those that do not qualify?

Student statements in Anna's geography class.

- One major factor responsible for rising sea levels is the melting of polar ice.
- Rising sea levels threaten the existence of several island nations, including Kiribati, Maldives, Palau, and parts of Fiji and Micronesia.
- I am fearful for future generations, when it comes to climate change.
- According to studies by the National Center for Atmospheric Research (NCAR), reducing car emissions cannot stop the rise of sea levels. Even so, reducing emissions remains a worthwhile goal, because lower emissions will slow the rise of the oceans, buying time for future generations who must adapt to a new landscape.
- In the 1930s, Americans did not want to believe that our farming practices depleted the soil and led to the dust bowl. In the 1980s, we did not want to admit that climate change was real. We have a long history of denial when it comes to environmental change, and when it comes to awareness, we lag far behind other countries.

Student statements in Kate's public health class.

- New strains of tuberculosis are a problem in developing countries.
- Tuberculosis-resisting treatment is more common in those countries which have received some aid. Patients have received antibiotics inconsistently, which allows the disease to come back even stronger.
- According to the World Health Organization (WHO), nearly 10 percent of tuberculosis patients suffer from drug-resistant TB. Without increased funding for treatment, the number of TB cases will continue to grow, and the disease will be much more difficult to treat.
- TB is rare in the United States, but for humanitarian reasons and for our own self-interest, Americans should be concerned about outbreaks in other countries.

Student statements in Jordan's film class.

- A screwball comedy is a movie that makes fun of traditional love stories. It often contains competitive banter between a man and woman who don't want to admit they are attracted to each other.
- The screwball comedies of the 1930s and 40s reflect an uneasiness about the changing role of women in the workplace.
- Screwball comedies were extremely popular in the 1930s and 40s.
- There is no such thing as a screwball comedy anymore. The workplace relationships and the snappy comebacks of that genre can be found on television now—not in the movie theater.
- People wanted to escape their hard lives during the Great Depression, and this was why they enjoyed screwball comedies.

2 Study the following texts, identify a thesis statement, and state that thesis in your own words. Answer the following questions for each. Who is the probable audience? What kind of support do you think each thesis requires?

From the 10 October, 2012 press release of the United States Anti-Doping Agency (USADA).

Today, we are sending the 'Reasoned Decision' in the Lance Armstrong case and supporting information to the Union Cycliste Internationale (UCI), the World Anti-Doping Agency (WADA), and the World Triathlon Corporation (WTC). The evidence shows beyond any doubt that the US Postal Service Pro Cycling Team ran the most sophisticated, professionalized and successful doping program that sport has ever seen ...

US Anti-Doping Agency (USADA). Statement Regarding the U.S. Postal Service Pro Cycling Team Doping Conspiracy, 10 Oct. 2012, www.cyclinginvestigation.usada.org. Accessed 20 Sept. 2018.

From "Capitalism and Freedom" by Milton Friedman (1912–2006), a Nobel Prize-winning economist who advocated for free markets, school choice, and deregulation of industries.

The free man will ask neither what his country can do for him nor what he can do for his country. He will ask rather "What can I and my compatriots do through government" to help us discharge our individual responsibilities, to achieve our several goals and purposes, and above all, to protect our freedom? And he will accompany this question with another: How can we keep the government we create from becoming a Frankenstein that will destroy the very freedom we establish it to protect? Freedom is a rare and delicate plant. Our minds tell us, and history confirms, that the great threat to freedom is the concentration of power. Government is necessary to preserve our freedom, it is an instrument through which we can exercise our freedom; yet by concentrating power in political hands, it is also a threat to freedom.

Friedman, Milton. *Capitalism and Freedom*. University of Chicago Press, 1962, p. 2.

Slide from TED Talk on Original Thinkers by Adam Grant.

Grant, Adam. Slide from TED Talk on Original Thinkers. *YouTube*, www.youtube.com/watch?v=fxbCHn6gE3U. Accessed 28 Jan. 2019.

From "Why Our Future Depends on Libraries, Reading, and Daydreaming" by Neil Gaiman (b. 1960), an English writer whose work includes the comic book series The Sandman *and the novels* American Gods, Coraline, Stardust, *and* The Graveyard Book.

We all—adults and children, writers and readers—have an obligation to daydream. We have an obligation to imagine. It is easy to pretend that nobody can change anything, that we are in a world in which society is huge and the individual is less than nothing: an atom in a wall, a grain of rice in a rice field. But the truth is, individuals change their world over and over, individuals make the future, and they do it by imagining that things can be different.

Look around you: I mean it. Pause for a moment and look around the room that you are in. I'm going to point out something so obvious that it tends to be forgotten. It's this: that everything you can see, including the walls, was, at some point, imagined. Someone decided it was easier to sit on a chair than on the ground and imagined the chair. Someone had to imagine a way that I could talk to you in London right now without us all getting rained on. This room and the things in it, and all the other things in this building, this city, exist because, over and over and over, people imagined things.

Gaiman, Neil. "Why Our Future Depends on Libraries, Reading, and Daydreaming." *The Guardian*, 15 Oct. 2013, www.theguardian.com/books/2013/oct/15/neil-gaiman-future-libraries-reading-daydreaming. Accessed 26 Nov. 2018.

From Notes on Nursing *by Florence Nightingale (1820–1910), a social reformer, statistician, and founder of the fields of nursing and public health.*

In watching diseases, both in private houses and in public hospitals, the thing which strikes the experienced observer most forcibly is this, that the symptoms or the sufferings generally considered to be inevitable and incident to the disease are very often not symptoms of the disease at all, but of something quite different— of the want of fresh air, or of light, or of warmth, or of quiet, or of cleanliness, or of punctuality and care in the administration of diet, of each or of all of these. And this quite as much in private as in hospital nursing.

The reparative process which nature has instituted and which we call disease, has been hindered by some want of knowledge or attention, in one or in all of these things, and pain, suffering, or interruption of the whole process sets in. If a patient is cold, if a patient is feverish, if a patient is sick after taking food, if he has a bed-sore, it is generally the fault not of the disease, but of the nursing.

Nightingale, Florence. *Notes on Nursing: What It Is and What It Is Not.* D. Appleton and Company, 1860, p. 8.

3 Study the following thesis statements. Identify the kind of support you think the thesis will require. What kind of argument does each thesis suggest? Write a brief outline for one or more. If the thesis does not suggest an obvious argument, write a couple of sentences speculating on where the paper might go from here.

- President Lincoln's views on slavery evolved over his political life, as he moved from opposing slavery in new states to a position opposing slavery in all states; he was principled, but also pragmatic.
- A campus poll of 50 pairs of randomly paired freshmen demonstrates that roommates develop similar study schedules, similar eating habits, and end up with similar grades as well.
- Cutting down on medical screenings for breast cancer will save money, but could cost some patients their lives.
- The British Empire dominated its colonies, but those colonies influenced the Empire as well, forever changing England's culture, diet, and population.
- I believe better math education for girls is the key to increasing the number of women engineers.

4 Select a thesis statement from one of your previous papers or a current assignment. Answer the three questions:

- Does my thesis take a position?
- Does my thesis invite discussion?
- Does my thesis require support?

If the answer to any of the questions is no, how would you modify your thesis?

7

DRAFT AND REVISION

Writing a Comparison Paper.

Zach sitting in the library. Typing frantically on his computer.

ANNA   How long have you been here?

ZACH   I don't know.

ANNA   Do you plan to sleep at all?

ZACH   No negativity!

ANNA   *Studying his wild hair and crazed eyes.* You are not looking good.

ZACH   I'M FINISHING THIS THING IF IT TAKES ALL NIGHT.

Draft: Where Do I Start?

Zach's paper is due in the morning, so he must write three to five pages in one night. This is a stressful situation because he is pressuring himself to develop an argument, gather and organize evidence, and write his draft all at once.

How might you avoid this kind of stress? One answer is to start writing earlier—but like most good advice, this is easier said than done. It's not always possible to finish with time to spare. However, it helps to view the work as a multi-step process. Depending on your assignment, those steps might include reading, gathering information, taking notes, and building a draft. In the best case, you would revise your work as well. Without revision, you will be submitting a rough draft, which will never read as smoothly as a final draft.

You will notice that we include revision in this chapter on writing a draft. We could have saved revision for the next chapter, but we believe that revision is essential to every step of the writing process. When you refine a thesis statement, you engage in a kind of revision. When you add concrete details to a literacy narrative, you are revising. You revise every time you develop an idea, add a new piece of evidence, or clarify a thought. It is important to review and revise your work once you have finished a draft, but, ideally, you will also revise while drafting.

Zach

No matter how late it gets, I always read through and spell-check my work.

It's great to **proofread**, reviewing and correcting sentence-level problems, such as typos, and errors in spelling, grammar, and punctuation. However, proofreading cannot substitute for **revision**, which involves testing and developing ideas, refining your thesis, reviewing and improving the structure of your argument and your writing as a whole. You will work on many writing assignments in college, but these rules will hold true for all of them:

- Writing projects require multiple steps.
- First draft ≠ final draft.
- Proofreading ≠ revision.

EXAMINE YOUR ASSIGNMENT

Zach, Kate, Anna, and Jordan each work in their own way. However, no matter what your process looks like, it makes sense to take some time to consider your instructor's expectations before you start working. What kind of writing will you be doing? What preparation will you need to do before you start? Your assignment may require you to take a stand or develop an argument. What kind of claim will you be making? Will you need to develop a formal thesis statement? What kind of support will that thesis require? (For more information on the thesis, see Chapter Six.) Your assignment may require you to analyze a text or image, interpret data, or present an informational report. If so, how might you focus your discussion? For each assignment, consider the steps you will need to take. These could include reading, viewing, or listening to material, taking notes, identifying a topic, developing a thesis, gathering evidence, and writing a provisional outline.

Zach's composition instructor assigns a three-to-five-page essay addressing a contemporary problem. The instructor emphasizes, *I want to hear why YOU think this problem is important.* He writes:

> *Write about a contemporary problem that affects you. The problem could be financial, environmental, ethical, even political—but I want to hear why YOU think this problem is important. Your essay should answer these questions. Where does the problem come from? How does the problem impact your life? How might we solve this problem?*

Searching for a topic, Zach writes down the first words that come to mind. *I have so many other things to do besides writing this*

Zach

I guess I usually end up pulling all-nighters.

Kate

I try to do some thinking early on and write some notes. Then even if I end up writing my paper the night before, I have something to work with.

Jordan

I just start writing whatever comes to mind for my first draft. I like to keep it spontaneous and then revise later.

Anna

Writing a big messy first draft would be very stressful for me! I like to plan everything and allow plenty of time, because I write slowly and carefully.

REFLECT: Consider a recent writing assignment. What steps did you take to begin it? Did you stay up later than you wanted the night before it was due? How would you characterize your writing process? Do you allow time for revision?

paper. I need more time! I wish I could be more productive. At first, he shrugs this off. Then he begins thinking more seriously about his own statement. Lack of productivity really is a huge problem in his life. Zach sends a quick message to his instructor, Dr. T. *Could I do productivity as my topic?* Zach checks his calendar and then glances at the messages on his phone. Soon he is looking something up on the internet. That search leads to another, and an hour passes before he notices his instructor's reply. *That's a VERY broad topic. Can you narrow it down? What is it about productivity that interests you? How is productivity a problem?*

Zach writes back, *I mean lack of productivity.*

Dr. T. writes, *Hmmm. Tell me more. Is lack of productivity becoming a serious issue for you? How so?*

Zach writes, *Sometimes, my computer is like a black hole for me.*

Dr. T. *Interesting! So, you're talking about technology interfering with productivity. Now, that could be promising.*

Zach. *My computer is, like, my greatest tool and my greatest downfall.*

Dr. T. *Ah ha!*

Ah ha? Zach thinks, after Dr. T signs off. He rereads this exchange and then he says *Yeah*, and he writes down the following sentence.

> Technology, which is supposed to help us, is actually hurting productivity.

Is this an effective thesis? Zach asks himself: *Does this thesis invite discussion? Yes. People are going to say—why do you blame technology for lack of productivity? Does this thesis require support? Yes. I am going to have to find some evidence that technology is distracting me, and maybe others, but how am I going to do all that? And when?*

DEVELOP A GAME PLAN

A to-do list provides you with an agenda for the day. A game plan for your paper breaks the job into a set of smaller tasks. A game plan is not an outline listing the points you will make. You may not have figured out all those points yet, and you may not have come up with all your evidence. Your game plan simply lists the tasks you must complete to finish your draft. Ideally, you will also estimate how long each task will take.

Initially, Zach tries a simple plan: *Sit in the library until I type enough to make it onto page three.* However, the library closes before he gets that far. Zach takes a walk and begins to rethink his strategy.

Okay, what have I actually done here? I've got a thesis statement: Technology, which is supposed to help us, is actually hurting productivity. But what do I actually have to write in the body of my paper? I need to describe the kind of technology people use. Then I need to explain how all those devices and apps prevent people from getting work done. I will ask the question—how can this problem be solved? And then I will come up with some ideas. Or if I can't think of any, I will just say we are all doomed. THE END.

With these thoughts in mind, Zach goes to the Atomic Bean and types a game plan on his phone.

1. Write down thesis. Technology we use to save time is actually harming productivity.
2. Explain what technology I'm talking about.
3. Find examples of how devices and apps eat time. Look for articles? Scientific studies? Talk about my own personal experience?
4. Discuss whether the problem can be solved or whether we're hopelessly addicted to technology.
5. Write a conclusion making this problem sound significant!

Zach's game plan only took a few minutes to write. His essay will take a lot longer. He looks at each item in his game plan and thinks—how much work will each step take?

- Writing down the thesis. 1 sentence.
- Explain what technology I'm talking about—probably just a paragraph, which would be maybe 15 minutes.

- Examples ... 4–6 paragraphs. Look for articles? Scientific studies? But wait. This assignment is not a research paper. The genre is personal essay, so I don't need external sources. I can focus on my own experience, which will hopefully take one night.
- Conclusion—??? One paragraph. I'll figure it out when I get there.

GATHER AND TAKE NOTES ON YOUR MATERIAL

After you devise a game plan, consider what kind of material you will need to support each point. Sometimes that material will take the form of examples. Zach plans to write first about technology we use to save time. He lists examples in his game plan.

1. Explain what technology I'm talking about.
   Examples: phones to access information, social media to connect with friends.

Next, Zach's game plan calls for an argument that this technology saps productivity.

2. Find examples of how devices and apps eat time.

Because this is a personal essay presenting Zach's opinion, he gathers and notes examples from his own experience.

1. Technology I use to save time.
   My phone is probably my most important tool. I use it to keep track of my assignments and my appointments, to stay in touch with friends, to find places, for shopping, banking, etc.

2. Technology that eats productivity.
   My phone is incredibly useful, and I would be lost without it. However, it also means that I am constantly distracted by games, shopping, friends. I don't even want to know how much of my time I am spending on my phone.

> My computer is a place I can type up my assign-
> ments but at the same time listen to music, chat with
> friends, look for bargains, play games, watch movies....

As Zach gathers material and prepares notes, he does not worry about writing polished prose. Zach is just writing questions and comments as they occur to him. Once he has gathered material to support each of his points, his game plan has grown from a simple list into an outline with several paragraphs of notes under each heading.

BUILD YOUR DRAFT FROM NOTES

It is comforting to write from notes. With even a brief list of points or examples, you will not feel pressured to conjure three to five pages out of thin air. Think of your notes as building blocks for your draft as you develop each example into a paragraph. The more detailed your notes and your game plan, the better prepared you will feel when you sit down to write.

Zach takes his notes on wasting time with technology and builds the following paragraphs from them. Because he is writing a personal essay, he begins with an example from personal experience.

> My phone is incredibly useful and I would be lost without
> it. My phone saves me a lot of time. I can quickly get in
> touch, plan my schedule, and find out information and
> directions. At the same time whenever I take out my
> phone (which is constantly) all my favorite methods of
> procrastination are there staring me in the face.
>
> I have a similar problem with my computer when I sit
> down to work. I plug in my headphones and start listening
> to music, open tabs and chat with friends, not to mention
> keep track of football games, and it's like the news and
> the scores and the people I know are all calling to me.

He finishes the draft and submits it for his instructor's comments.

ZACH   What does *awk* mean?

ANNA   Awkward. That's when you should look for a different way to express your idea.

ZACH   Less awkwardly?

ANNA   Yeah.

ZACH   What about *w.c.*?

ANNA   I think that's word choice, as in look for a different word because the one you used doesn't fit here.

ZACH   What about *you may need to unpack this paragraph*?

ANNA   You have too many ideas going on at once, and you need to separate them out.

ZACH   But her final comment is *This is a solid first draft with lots of potential!*

ANNA   Oh, that means you have to rewrite the whole thing.

ZACH   What???? Hey, Jordan!

ANNA   Now you're asking him?

ZACH   I'm getting a second opinion!

REVISION

Most written work benefits from revision. Even the most experienced writers can improve a draft by rereading and reconsidering the choices they have made. Indeed, the best writers are the biggest fans of revision. They read their own paragraphs critically, making large and small adjustments, sometimes cutting them altogether and replacing them with new material. Why do this extra work? Writers revise because they know that with more thought, their writing will improve. Revision requires careful attention to detail *and* serious reflection on your writing as a whole. When you revise, you reflect on the entire concept of the piece, its central idea, organization, logic, and transitions from one idea to the next.

When revising, it is enormously helpful to show your work to others for comments and questions. Sometimes, your instructor will ask you to turn in a draft, or exchange drafts with classmates for comments. If you do not have this opportunity, you can show your draft to a friend, or make an appointment with a tutor at the writing center or learning center on campus. Your reader can say—*this makes sense, but over here I don't follow you. This part is interesting, but you're losing me here. Could you explain?* Friends or roommates might know little about your topic, and that is a great advantage, because they won't understand you without clear and coherent writing.

While it is useful to respond to readers' questions and comments, the best revisions begin and end with your own reading and reflection. When you review your work, ask yourself the following questions.

Revision Checklist

DOES MY WRITING RESPOND TO MY ASSIGNMENT?

If my assignment asks me to address a question, do I address it? If the assignment asks for a certain format or genre, does my writing take that form? If the assignment requires three examples, do I provide them? Check to make sure you have done the writing required in the expected form. If you have not, then revise to satisfy those expectations.

DO I NEED A THESIS? IF SO, DO I HAVE ONE?

If you are developing an argument with a thesis statement, it is helpful to check that thesis. First of all, does your thesis fulfill the requirements we outlined in Chapter Six? Does your thesis take a position? Does it invite discussion? Does it require support? If your thesis does not satisfy these requirements, consider qualifying or modifying your statement. It's good to start revision with a hard look at your thesis, but it's even better to test your thesis early, when you are starting to draft your work. This is a case where draft and revision intertwine. A solid thesis will support you as you write. Check your thesis early in your draft, and then check it again during revision.

DO I DEFINE MY TERMS WHERE NECESSARY?

Assignments such as personal reflections might not require rigorous definitions of the terms you use. The reader of your literacy narrative knows what you mean when you use the word childhood. For other assignments in more formal genres such as academic essays, it is important to establish exactly what you mean when you talk about childhood, or poverty, or plant genetics, or technology, or state's rights. In Zach's case, it's easy for him to assume his reader knows what he's talking about when he says technology is taking up all his time. But what is the real culprit here? His phone? His social media apps? The internet itself? Or the games he plays? He needs to pinpoint the problem. Defining your terms clarifies your assumptions for the reader, and also establishes the scale and scope of your argument.

DOES MY EVIDENCE SUPPORT MY THESIS?

When you are satisfied with your thesis, take a look at the way you support it in your paper. First of all, consider what kind of evidence your thesis requires. Is your evidence relevant? Do you explain that evidence adequately? Remember, in addition to introducing evidence, you need to help your reader understand how that evidence relates to your argument or larger purpose. Second, ask yourself whether you provide sufficient evidence to make a convincing case. Kate is writing a paper about motherhood in the *Narrative of the Life of Frederick Douglass*. Her thesis is that Douglass's mother inspired him to reject slavery, seeking freedom for himself and others. Kate is happy with her thesis, but as she finishes her draft, she begins to worry that her paper is too short. The fact is that Douglass only mentions his mother three times in the entire book, and so Kate does not find many opportunities to bolster her thesis. Kate can't find supporting evidence where there is none. Then she remembers a scene in Douglass's autobiography when the wife of his owner teaches him to read. She decides to modify her thesis, writing that two women, Douglass's biological mother and his early teacher, inspired him. This new thesis allows Kate to expand her evidence, drawing upon Douglass's recollections of the woman who taught him to read and write. Like a scientist, Kate modifies her hypothesis, as she follows where the evidence leads. Kate's willingness to modify her thesis opens a new avenue of inquiry for her, and enriches her written work.

An argument can drift away from its thesis. In a history paper Jordan presents this thesis:

> The stock market crash of 1929 has been overrated as the cause of the Great Depression. It was just one factor in a larger economic downturn.

Then in the body of his essay, he focused on the Dust Bowl. As his instructor points out in comments, Jordan becomes so interested in the Dust Bowl that he forgets to write about the stock market crash and neglected to explain what he meant when he asserted that the crash was overrated. In revision, Jordan trims his long discussion of the Dust Bowl and adds paragraphs on the failure of the banks and the worldwide economic downturn as two other factors contributing to the Depression.

DO I SHOW HOW MY EVIDENCE SUPPORTS MY THESIS?

Sometimes supporting material seems self-explanatory. However, your reader may not be familiar with the graphs or the texts or the events you discuss. What is obvious to you may not be obvious to others. It helps to check your work to make sure that you tie each piece of evidence to your thesis statement. In his paper on time-wasting technology, Zach provides an example from his own experience:

> I can easily spend over an hour on my phone without even noticing.

However, as his instructor points out, it is not enough to provide an example. Zach needs to show how that example supports his thesis. *How does that hour on your phone relate to the claim that time-saving technology actually wastes time?* In revision, Zach adds sentences spelling out the connection between his example and his thesis.

> My phone has my calendar, my contacts, and my course info on it, but it's also got games and unlimited media. The device I use to manage my time is also the thing I use to waste my time!

DO I ADDRESS POSSIBLE OBJECTIONS?

Students sometimes think that the strongest arguments cannot risk acknowledging objections or other points of view. However, as we saw in Chapter Five, your argument becomes stronger, more nuanced, and ultimately more convincing when you address possible objections and acknowledge other interpretations. You make a strong appeal to ethos when you present yourself as a fair-minded and rational writer. In an essay on genetically modified organisms for her public health class, Kate argues strongly that GMOs are dangerous. However, her instructor points out that her paper would be more convincing if she addressed arguments on the other side of the issue as well. In her revision Kate acknowledges possible benefits of GMOs:

> Admittedly plant breeding can save lives by averting crop failure and famine. It is also true that plants can be engineered to withstand insects, which could cut down on the use of toxic pesticides. The question is—what trade-offs do we want to make?

DO I DEVELOP MY IDEAS?

While writing her essay on GMOs, Kate mentions in passing, *Some GMOs would surprise you.* But she does not develop this observation. Which GMOs are surprising? Why? To whom? Why is this significant? Her instructor comments: *Unclear what your point is here.* In her second draft, Kate develops her point and weaves it into her larger argument:

It is surprising how many fruits and vegetables are genetically modified. Many consumers are unaware that fruit like papaya, squash and zucchini have been genetically engineered. GMOs are extensive in the grocery store, but public awareness is not.

DO I GUIDE THE READER WITH STEP BY STEP PARAGRAPHS AND SMOOTH TRANSITIONS?

Sometimes students skip steps in an argument. Kate ran into this problem when she wrote an op/ed on nursing in Chapter Five. At other times, students overload their paragraphs, jamming ideas together. Zach runs into this problem as he writes his essay on the way technology steals our time. One of his paragraphs looks like this:

It's ridiculous how much people depend on technology to save us time. For example I can't live without my phone which is where I keep all my contacts, my calendar, my social media, and all the apps I can't do without. My fitness app that tracks my steps is something that I look at constantly and I've been known to take extra steps to get up to my target numbers even when I have better things to do. I am constantly wasting time tracking my own data which my computer is supposed to track for me.

Zach's paragraph drifts from depending on technology to how he wastes time on technology. Jamming these separate points together, he doesn't have much space for either. His instructor comments *unpack this paragraph.* In response, Zach decides to divide his material into two paragraphs.

It's ridiculous how much people depend on technology to save us time. For example, I can't live without my phone which is where I keep all my contacts, my calendar, my social media, and all the apps I can't do without. I can't get through the day without checking my email, my social media, and all my news feeds and blogs. I crave information, and the more I get, the more I want.

It should be convenient to have information at my fingertips 24/7, but this does not save me any time. In fact, it causes me to waste huge amounts of time. My fitness app that tracks my steps is something that I look at constantly and I've been known to take extra steps to get up to my target numbers even when I have better things to do. I am constantly wasting time tracking my own data which my computer is supposed to track for me.

Notice that now each of Zach's paragraphs develops just one main idea. Instead of throwing all his information at the reader in one paragraph, Zach metes out his material one idea at a time. He allows each point its own paragraph and leads his reader gradually from one point to the next.

In revision, Zach also adds a **transition**, one or more sentences to prepare his reader for the move from one point to the next. Notice how Zach begins his second paragraph above. *It should be convenient to have information at my fingertips 24/7, but this does not save me any time.* What makes this sentence a transition? It glances back at the first paragraph, referring to the convenience of technology, and then looks ahead at Zach's new point: technology does not save him any time.

DOES MY CONCLUSION ADD VALUE?

A conclusion that simply repeats your initial claim or summarizes your argument is not doing enough work. Zach discovers this when he turns in his technology paper with a conclusion recapitulating his introduction.

The bottom line is that technology designed to save time actually causes people to waste a lot of time. I am not sure this problem can be solved.

Zach's instructor comments *This seems like a recap of your intro. Do not just repeat what you already said.*

An effective conclusion explains the significance of the paragraphs that come before, effectively answering the question *So what?* In the sciences and social sciences, a strong conclusion may also suggest paths for future inquiry. Zach expands his conclusion, adding the following lines:

> People depend on their technology to get things done and at the same time they depend on tech for entertainment. Some experts suggest turning off phones at a certain time each night or disconnecting while working. It would be interesting to run an experiment to see whether these actions improve grades, sleep, and even relationships.

The Importance of Proofreading

In addition to testing and strengthening the structure of a paper, effective writers look closely at each sentence to correct grammatical errors, spelling mistakes, and such issues as awkward phrasing or word choice. A computer can check for some of these errors, but cannot catch all of them. You mean to write *wrap* but you type *warp*. An automated spell check will not catch this error, because both words are spelled correctly. Or you mean to say *principle*, meaning a belief, but you type *principal*, which means the head of a school. Only you know which word is correct, because only you as the author understand the context.

Just as you check your work on a math problem set for careless errors, you will benefit from proofreading your writing before you hand it in. Remember as well to check your writing when you get your paper back from your instructor. Comments on your paper can provide valuable information, not just on big structural issues, but on sentence-level problems as well. Study your instructor's comments in the margins and look for patterns. Does your instructor keep writing *Word choice? Comma problem? Run-on sentence?* These may be the areas to study. If you see corrections that you don't understand, ask your instructor for an explanation, consult a grammar handbook or an online guide, such as the Purdue O.W.L., an excellent free website providing information on every aspect of the writing process. If you prefer to get help in person, go to your college writing center. Tutors will not edit your writing for you, but they can strategize with you about your assignment as a whole. They

Jordan

I always get *transition?* in the margins of my papers. I've learned that it means I need to add a transition linking one paragraph to another. So now I try to check for that before I turn in my work.

Zach

When I got back my response to an interview of the writer Chinua Achebe, my instructor said I had a good understanding of the themes, but I needed to move past summary and add more of my own ideas. I revised to add my own thoughts on "how writing affects my purpose in life."

Anna

For the past few years my teachers have complimented my English, but sometimes they point out errors that remain. This was very frustrating, because the mistakes were small and hard to catch! Now I go to the writing center just to go over my work with a tutor to try to catch any problems I didn't see.

Kate

In my op/ed on nursing, I started by referring to an informal poll someone did at my hospital. My instructor asked for a published poll by a national or statewide organization. Using the "State of Patient Care in Massachusetts," I was able to write with better evidence and more authority.

can also help with specific grammar and punctuation issues—explaining what a semicolon means, how to avoid run-on sentences, where to use commas and why.

Keep in mind that every time you revise, you need to proofread. Even as you develop and improve your writing, you introduce the possibility of more small errors. With a quick proofreading, you can address them. Treat yourself and your reader to this last finishing touch.

Draft and Revision throughout College

REFLECT on a time you revised your work, either on your own, or in response to a reader's suggestions. What kind of revisions did you make? Did you add transitions? Develop your thesis statement? Add new evidence? Or did you end up making other changes? Looking back, how would you compare your first draft to your revised draft?

In college you must adjust to writing requirements in courses in many different disciplines. You may find yourself putting together a multi-modal portfolio for your gender studies class (see Chapter Nine), an annotated sketchbook for art history, and a traditional essay for your government course. Your assignments will vary, but in each case, it helps to break down an assignment into step-by-step tasks. Many composition instructors do this for their students, in order to prepare them for writing in other classes. Your instructor might ask for a thesis statement first, and then set a deadline for a provisional draft before the final draft is due. Anna's writing class focuses on history and culture. Her instructor breaks down a major paper in this way.

Drafting a Comparison Essay

Assignment: In a three-to-five-page paper, compare images of childhood from two different historical periods. What does each image tell us about the period's definition of childhood? How has our conception of childhood changed?

Friday: Submit images and thesis statement.
Wednesday: Rough draft due.

Take a look at the way Anna drafts her paper, step by step.

EXAMINE YOUR ASSIGNMENT

Anna's assignment asks her to compare two images in order to answer a question about how views of childhood have changed. The word compare suggests that Anna will need to look closely at two images. She will also have to decide how she wants to structure her comparison. In class, Anna's instructor, Dr. C., presents two options. She can discuss one image first and then the other. Alternatively, she can compare the images point by point, once she decides which points of comparison are important.

Anna's instructor does not request a personal narrative. Nor does he ask her to take a stand about childhood or to offer her opinions up front. As Anna thinks about possible thesis statements, she knows that this assignment does not call for first person claims, such as, *I think people treat children differently now than they did in the old days* or *I believe children have a lot more freedom now than they used to.* On the contrary, the expectation here is for careful analysis grounded in selection and evaluation of two specific pictures of childhood.

NARROWING YOUR TOPIC

Anna spends some time thinking about which images to choose. Her course focuses on the history of childhood, so her instructor has presented many images of babies and young children from different time periods and different cultures. Anna decides she would like to use images from different countries in

DR. C.

Historians look at many examples before they generalize about cultural change. You are looking at just two images. Don't **overstate your case** with exaggerated claims. Show your reader that you are aware that you are using limited evidence.

different centuries. When Anna sees a magazine with a picture of a twenty-first-century prince, George of England (b. 2013), she decides to find another royal picture, and settles on a portrait of another prince the same age. Searching online she discovers a seventeenth-century prince, Cosimo de' Medici III of Italy (1642–1723).

Sustermans, Justus. *Portrait of Cosimo de' Medici III*. 17th century. Private collection.

Stillwell, John. *Prince George of Cambridge First Birthday*. 2014, Getty Images.

DEVELOPING A THESIS

Anna chooses these images because they depict children of the same gender, the same age, and the same rank in different historical periods. Initially she had chosen one picture of a girl and one of a boy, but in a conference, her instructor pointed out that when you are comparing two images or two texts or two objects, it is more effective to look for a pair with several factors in common. Keeping the variables of gender, age, and rank the same, Anna lays the groundwork for a clear focus on historical differences. Indeed, her thesis statement reflects this focus.

Two portraits of royal one-year-olds reveal how our conception of childhood has changed over the centuries from emphasizing preciousness to activity.

After Anna turns in her thesis statement, her instructor comments, *Interesting! Excellent images, but what do you mean by preciousness? And what do you mean by activity? Clarify.*

Anna thinks this over. She knows exactly what she means by preciousness, but she concedes that someone else might not. She takes the word out and revises her thesis, searching for another way to clarify her point.

Two portraits of royal one-year-olds reveal how our conception of childhood has changed over the centuries from an emphasis on beauty to an emphasis on active play.

Anna's instructor writes—*Okay! Send me your rough draft.*

Anna looks at her calendar and quickly concludes that she doesn't have time to work on this paper for the full five days before the due date. She has a problem set due in her math class, and a midterm approaching in psychology. However, she decides she can work on drafting on Monday and Tuesday. To prepare for drafting the paper, she spends an hour on Sunday typing up notes on each image.

DEVISING A GAME PLAN

Reviewing these notes, Anna studies the images again and asks herself—what am I looking at here? One prince is formally dressed; the other wears play clothes. One child stands inside, the other in a playground. One prince is standing still, while the other is taking his first steps. How do these observations support her thesis about changing ideas of childhood?

Anna decides that her paper will focus on a change in children's clothing from formal to informal, a change in setting from interior to playground, a change in behavior from stillness to movement, and a change in genre from oil painting to photograph. (For more on analysis of images, see Chapter Four). She develops a game plan, for a point-by-point comparison.

Topic: Changing Ideas of Childhood

Thesis: Two portraits of royal one-year-olds reveal how our conception of childhood has changed over the centuries from an emphasis on beauty to an emphasis on active play.

1. Clothing—one to two paragraphs
2. Setting—one to two paragraphs
3. Behavior—one to two paragraphs
4. Genre—one to two paragraphs
5. Conclusion—one paragraph

GATHERING MATERIAL AND TAKING NOTES

Anna looks closely at each image, and takes detailed notes under each heading of her game plan. Of course, Anna has her own initial impressions of each picture. She could write her notes in the form of a running commentary of what she sees, and these notes would be useful in their own way. However, taking notes with a game plan helps her to search systematically for certain aspects of each image. The game plan focuses her search.

Anna's game plan looks like this when she adds her notes to each section. As you can see, she comes up with comments and questions while gathering material.

Thesis: Two portraits of royal one-year-olds reveal how our conception of childhood has changed over the centuries from an emphasis on beauty to an emphasis on active play.

1. Clothing
Cosimo looks like a girl. He's wearing a dress. Clothes so fancy, expensive looking material, embroidery, lace, etc. Shoes with ruffles, hat in his hand. What one-year-old wears this kind of outfit and stands still in it??

George is wearing normal toddler play clothes—denim overalls, shoes like regular kids wear.

2. Setting

Cosimo is indoors in some dark fancy room.

George is outside, possibly at a playground. Is that a climbing structure in the background?

3. Behavior

Cosimo is standing still. Can he even move in so many clothes? He would probably ruin them.

George is taking a step. The photo shows him in motion and it looks like he's an active kid.

4. Genre

Cosimo is in a formal oil painting probably hanging on the palace wall (Check this?).

George is in a photo published in a magazine. Obviously a lot more regular people are going to see the photo in the magazine and online.

BUILDING A DRAFT FROM NOTES

Introduction

Anna begins her paper with an introduction that states her thesis and prepares the reader for the kind of support she will use.

A Tale of Two Princes

Two portraits of royal one-year-olds reveal how our conception of childhood has changed over the centuries from an emphasis on beauty to an emphasis on active play. Clothing, setting, behavior of the children, and genre of the images all contribute to a contrasting idea of what childhood is like in each era.

Supporting Paragraphs

After explaining the kind of evidence she will use to support her thesis, Anna builds her supporting paragraphs from her notes. Following her game plan, she begins by discussing the clothing of each prince.

> The oil painting of a one-year-old Prince Cosimo de' Medici III (1642–1723) "after" Justus Sustermans is a very formal picture, which shows this toddler in a silk dress covered with embroidery and lace. Even the shoes are covered with white ruffles. He is holding a fancy hat in his hand, which adds to the high fashion. These clothes are stiff so it is probably hard to move. In contrast, the photograph of one-year-old Prince George (b. 2013) shows a prince in rugged play clothes—overalls. Cosimo's clothes cover his body, while George's clothes allow him to explore. This reflects two very different perspectives of childhood.

After two paragraphs on clothing, Anna turns to setting, the behavior of each prince, and the contrasting genres of the pictures, the one a formal oil painting, the other a casual photo. She devotes two paragraphs to each of these points.

Conclusion

Finally, on Tuesday night, she writes her conclusion. Ideally, a conclusion adds value to an argument. It should do more than recapitulate Anna's thesis and supporting points. It should touch on the significance of these points, or extend these points a little further, providing the reader with something new to think about. Anna does not have much time left, so her conclusion is brief, but she tries to add a little more to the discussion.

> In these two pictures it is becoming clear how much ideas of childhood have changed over centuries. From the seventeenth century to now people have changed from thinking of children as beautiful little things who just stand there to kids who need activity to play in order to

learn and grow. It is also clear that the ideal of royalty is changing as well. Centuries ago a royal family presented its prince dressed to impress. Now the English royal family is trying to present its prince as a typical kid, just like everybody else.

Revision is important, but difficult to manage entirely on your own. You may know what you want to say, but will your message come across to someone else? Ultimately, only another reader can tell you. This is why professional writers work with editors, and composition instructors encourage students to share their work, exchanging papers with classmates in a process called peer review.

Peer Review

When Anna exchanges her work with her classmate Meghan, their instructor provides a simple worksheet with space for comments on the different parts of the paper.

TOPIC: Is it clear what the essay will be about?

THESIS: Can you find the thesis easily, and does it work as a claim that will guide a comparative analysis?

SUPPORT: Does the evidence support the thesis? Does the author link evidence to the thesis with clear explanation?

ORGANIZATION: Does the essay move coherently from point to point, from beginning to end? Do transitions guide the reader?

CONCLUSION: Does the final paragraph remind the reader of the main argument and then move beyond simple repetition to add interest and value to the paper?

Meghan fills out her comment sheet like this.

> TOPIC: Two portraits of one-year-old princes. These pictures are so cute, also very relevant to childhood.
>
> THESIS: Makes sense to me!
>
> SUPPORT: Lots of good supporting details — very detailed analysis of both images.
>
> ORGANIZATION: Sometimes the organization seemed like too much of a list: clothing, setting, behavior, etc.
>
> CONCLUSION: It makes sense to me that people think kids should be more active now, but how do you know these kids are typical of changing attitudes if they are royal? Wouldn't they be special cases if they live in a castle?

Anna wonders what to do about Meghan's question. Should she ignore it, because bringing it up might be distracting or weaken her argument? She remembers what her instructor said about developing arguments. You build your reader's trust when you address possible objections openly. After some thought, she decides to address her classmate's question in her conclusion.

> In these two pictures it is clear how much ideas of childhood have changed over centuries. It is true these are not ordinary kids they are royal however as princes they also set the fashion and could be thought of as representative of changing ideas of childhood. From the seventeenth century to now people have changed from thinking of children as beautiful little things who just stand there to active kids who need to play in order to learn and grow. You can see this in clothing, setting, behavior and the genre of each image.

Now Anna turns in her essay and waits to hear what her instructor has to say.

Responding to Instructor's Comments

When Anna gets her essay back, she finds a mix of small comments and larger questions in the margins throughout her draft. The comments on her conclusion look like this.

In these two pictures you can see how much ideas of childhood have changed over the centuries. It's true that these are not ordinary kids they are royal however as princes they also set the fashion and could be thought of as representative of changing ideas of childhood. From the seventeenth century to now people have changed from thinking of children as beautiful little things who just stand there to active kids who need to play in order to learn and grow. You can see this in clothing, setting, behavior and the genre of each image.

Watch out! Run-on sentence!

Is this recap necessary?

Do you think it's important to address another change going on here—i.e., a change in conception of royalty over time? What does it mean to dress a prince in overalls, which are not only play clothes but working clothes? What does that say about a twenty-first-century royal family? Following from that, have you considered the rhetorical situation of each image? Who might the intended audience be?

Anna finds Dr. C.'s comments frustrating. She tries to think of a way to answer her instructor's questions, but she is afraid that if she starts talking about changing ideas of royalty she will be writing a completely new paper. Her topic was childhood! Even so, she worries that her instructor will mark her down if she doesn't talk about these issues. She isn't sure how to manage all this. She decides to visit her instructor during office hours.

DR. C.   Is someone lurking out there?

ANNA   Um.

DR. C.   Hey, Anna, come on in.
Sit down and stay a while.

ANNA   I just had some questions about your questions. I don't understand how I can start talking about changes in conceptions of royalty when my topic is childhood. I feel like I'm going to end up going off on a whole other tangent if I start doing that. Or maybe even write a whole new paper which I don't have time to do right now since I have midterms coming up on Thursday!

DR. C.   Hold on, hold on. You don't have to go off and write a whole new paper. I'm asking you to consider another dimension. Think about the audience for these pictures, and think about what each royal family is saying to that audience.

After speaking to her instructor, Anna returns to her draft and takes a long look at the pictures of the two princes. She concedes that Dr. C. makes a good point. The pictures show a huge change in conceptions of childhood, but they show a change in the presentation of the royal family as well. These are public images. The formal portrait of Cosimo presents him in all his regal trappings. The photo of George is casual, but she notices something when she looks at the caption in the magazine. *Buckingham Palace releases new pictures of Prince George.* How did she miss this before? The photo was approved by the royal family for distribution to the public. She thinks about how she can touch on this more complex idea, without distracting or detracting from her argument. Just as she decides to address objections openly in her paper, she decides to make a secondary point about the image of royalty. She will not write a new argument; she will augment the one she has with a richer reading of each image.

She begins by developing and extending her first paragraph. We underline her additions.

Two portraits of royal one-year-olds reveal how our conception of childhood has changed over the centuries from an emphasis on beauty to an emphasis on active play. <u>Royal portraits are an interesting lens for viewing childhood because they depict the highest ranking and most famous child in society. Princes are the ones people look up to. They set the fashion for the ideal child. These two pictures show how the ideal changes. They also show how the public image of an ideal child changes from that of a perfect miniature adult covered in jewels to that of a kid who looks on the surface just like any other cute toddler.</u> Clothing, setting, behavior of the children, and genre of the images all contribute to a contrasting idea of what childhood is like in each era.

With this revision, Anna looks critically at the images she will use to discuss changing views of childhood. She shows her reader that she is aware that princes are not average children. She also explains that these images have an agenda of their own—as representations of royalty. Then she makes a claim about the significance of these images. They are important cultural symbols of childhood. A royal child is exceptional, but Anna suggests that he or she is also representative of the ideals and aspirations of society.

Draft and revision take time. You will not always have a lot of time for your writing. Even so, if you break down your work into smaller tasks and if you test your work at the structural and sentence level, your writing will improve. How do we know? As authors of this very chapter, we developed and adjusted our ideas, gathered information, and built our draft from notes. Then, in response to comments from readers, and each other, we rewrote our chapter, reorganizing our material in a major structural revision. In conjunction with this structural work, we caught and corrected many sentence-level errors, including missing words, vague phrases, fragments, and incorrect comma use. At the end of this process our chapter conveyed our ideas more effectively. We speak from experience when we urge you to build a draft step by step and then revise your work.

Drafting a paper is a multi-step process.

- Study your assignment
- Write a game plan
- Use your game plan to build an outline
- Gather and take notes on your material
- Use your notes to build a draft
- Proofread
- Show your work to a classmate or friend
- Revise to address comments
- Proofread again

Revision questions.

- Does my writing fulfill my assignment?
- Do I need a thesis? And if so, do I have one?
- Do I define my terms?
- Do I have enough evidence to support my thesis? If not, do I need to modify my thesis?
- If my evidence is sufficient, do I show *how* my evidence supports my thesis?
- Do I address possible objections?
- Do I develop my ideas?
- Do I provide transitions?
- Does my conclusion add value?
- Did I remember to proofread?

ACTIVITIES

1 Each of the following paragraphs has a problem identified by the instructor's comments. Respond to the instructor by rewriting the paragraph so that it makes sense and communicates clearly. Feel free to move or add sentences if necessary.

Sleep deprivation is a serious problem. Sleep specialists believe that it is actually dangerous to try to function when you are severely sleep deprived. Driving and operating machinery get to be very dangerous. Accidents can and do happen. Lack of sleep is also a symptom of depression. When people feel depressed they may sit around and get less exercise which in turn leads to an inability to sleep which makes people tired so that the cycle starts all over again.

You make two good points but you jam them together, jumping from the dangers of sleep deprivation to one of the causes. Please revise to unpack this over-loaded paragraph. Try presenting this material in two paragraphs.

Droughts are a major problem right now not only for farmers, but for shoppers facing high food prices, for ranchers lacking water for their animals, for boats which cannot navigate dry rivers, for health reasons that result when people lack a clean water supply, and for the environment which is subject to wildfires. Desalinization is the answer.

You start out talking about droughts and you end up talking about desalinization. Transition needed! Please revise, adding a transition from the problem to your proposed solution.

The attempt to organize a protest was unsuccessful for three reasons — bad publicity, lack of organization, and student apathy. The forecast was supposed to be sunny but thunderstorms prevented most people from coming out to march. The people who did come got soaked and did not stay long. Others who had talked about coming lost interest when they saw the sparse crowds on the news. In fact the big news story was that only a handful of protesters showed up. The mud was so bad that without rubber boots there was barely any way to march through it.

You mention three major reasons that the protest was unsuccessful, but you focus on the weather. Please adjust your initial claim so that it matches the body of your paragraph.

2   Anna completes an assignment typical of many college courses — comparing two texts, or images, or accounts, or charts. Choose one of the assignments below and write a game plan or an essay comparing one of the following pairs of micro-readings. Alternatively, choose your own material to compare.

A.   Compare the following accounts of the Great Fire of Chicago, October 8–10, 1871. How do the recollections of Bessie Bradwell compare to the reporting in a contemporary newspaper account? Consider the purpose, genre, and timing of each account, as well as its intended audience. How does each writer characterize the fire? What kind of language does each writer use — and to what effect? How do the writers situate themselves as participant-observers experiencing the fire?

1926 account of the Great Fire of Chicago by Bessie Bradwell. Bradwell wrote this memoir 55 years after the fire for a collection of eye-witness accounts compiled by historians in honor of the anniversary of the fire. She recalls her experience as a girl of 13 escaping the flames with her family.

On the street it was confusion worse confounded with people crowding you on all sides. It was like a snow storm only the flakes were red instead of white. On one side I was jostled by a man shrieking, "Oh the poor prisoners, they will be burned alive, locked up in their cells." On the other side I was hit by a burly negro carrying on top of his head a crate of live chickens. By chance, I met a gentleman and his wife, friends of my father and mother. They said "Come right along with us," and we proceeded down Washington St. toward the Lake. When we got to State St. the State St. bridge was burning. They said "Come, come with us, we must get over this bridge at once." I hesitated whether I should go down to the Lake or go with them but concluded to go with them across the bridge. Never shall I forget the sight as I looked back on the burning City. On the bridge, a man hurrying along, said "This is the end of Chicago" but with all assurance the thirteen-year-old replied, "No, no she will rise again." My coat had been on fire two or three times. People would run up to me and smother the flames with their hands. Then we hurried on, the fire madly pursuing us. After going a long way, we finally concluded it would be best for us to turn and go west, and early in the morning we crossed to the west side. Proceeding on the west side toward the south we finally found a restaurant. It was crowded and we were all relating our thrilling experiences. After breakfast I left my good friends, telling them I would keep on the west side going south until I got up to 12th St., when I would turn east and go to Mich. Ave.

where I would try to find my father and mother. I told them if I did not find them I would go on the west side where we used to live to some old neighbors. When I finally reached Mich. Ave., a policeman stopped me saying they were blowing up the buildings and I could not go on. After I left my father he kept on carrying his valuable books downstairs, and they were then beginning to blow up the buildings. No expressman was in sight. He concluded his life was more valuable than his law books and ran down Washington St. to the Lake. There he found my mother and brother. His first words were "Where is Bessie?" Mother said "Why, I thought she was with you." My father was sure I was dead. My mother, who was always an optimist, said "No, I'd trust that girl to go the ends of the earth—she'll come out all right, don't you worry." The Lake front was covered with dry goods that had been taken out of the stores and placed in the park. My father concluded that the fire would sweep all over the park and that the only way to save the trunk was to bury it. He went to a neighbor's house and got a shovel and proceeded to dig a hole in the park to bury the trunk. The park was used as the City's baseball grounds. Up walked a policeman and showed his star. "Sir, you are defacing the ball grounds." My father raised his shovel to strike the policeman if he tried to stop him. "You go on or I'll make you see more stars than you ever saw in your life." Evidently this powerful 6 ft. 3 man with a shovel ready to strike was more than the policeman bargained for and he said "Oh, go on, Captain, go on." My mother told me many thrilling tales of the sights she saw there on the Lake front. The church of the Rev. Mr. Patterson caught fire first from the tower and swept down. A bystander said "Oh what a pity, the church is going." A man nearby laughed and said "If the Lord won't save his own church, let her go." As the fire burned all inflammable goods up to the Lake front, my family were obliged to go down to the very edge of the Lake and bathe their faces to keep from burning up. About ten o'clock Monday morning October 9th father dug up his precious trunk, the only thing which was saved on the Lake front.

Bradwell, Bessie. "1926 Account of the Great Fire of Chicago." *Great Chicago Fire*, www.greatchicagofire.org/eyewitnesses/anthology-of-fire-narratives. Accessed 26 Nov. 2018.

This account of the fire appeared in the Chicago Evening Post, 17 October 1871.

The people were mad. Despite the police—indeed, the police were powerless—they crowded upon frail coigns of vantage [perches where you could view the scene], as fences and high sidewalks propped on rotten piles, which fell beneath their weight, and hurled them, bruised and bleeding, into the dust. They stumbled over broken furniture and fell, and were trampled under foot. Seized with wild and causeless panics, they surged together, backwards and forwards, in the narrow streets, cursing, threatening, imploring, fighting to get free. Liquor flowed like water—for the saloons were broken open and despoiled, and men on all sides were seen to be frenzied with drink. Fourth Avenue and Griswold Street had emptied their denizens into the throng. Ill-omened and obscene birds of night were they—villainous, debauched, pinched with misery, flitted through the crowd, ragged, dirty, unkempt, those negroes with stolid faces and white men who fatten on the wages of shame, glided through the masses like vultures in search of prey. They smashed windows reckless of the severe wounds inflicted on their naked hands, and with bloody fingers impartially rifled till, shelf and cellar, fighting viciously for the spoils of their forays. Women, hollow-eyed and brazen-faced, with foul drapery tied over their heads, their dresses half torn from their skinny bosoms, and their feet thrust into trodden down slippers, moved here and there,—scolding, stealing, scolding shrilly, and laughing with one another at some particularly "splendid" gush of flame or "beautiful" falling-in of a roof. One woman on Adams Street was drawn out of a burning house three times, and rushed back wildly into the blazing ruin each time, insane for the moment. Everywhere, dust, smoke, flame, heat, thunder of falling walls, crackle of fire, hissing of water, panting of engines, shouts, braying of trumpets, roar of wind, tumult, and uproar.

From the roof of a tall stable and warehouse to which the writer clambered the sight was one of unparalleled sublimity and terror. He was above almost the whole fire, for the buildings in the locality were all small wooden structures. The crowds directly under him could not be distinguished, because of the curling volumes of crimsoned smoke through which an occasional scarlet rift could be seen. He could feel the heat and smoke and hear the maddened Babel of sounds, and it required little imagination to believe one's self looking over the adamantine bulwarks of hell into the bottomless pit. On the left, where two tall buildings were in a blaze, the flame piled up high over our heads, making a lurid background, against which were limned in strong relief the people on the roofs between. Fire was a strong painter and dealt in weird effects, using only black and red, and laying them boldly on. We could note the very smallest actions of these figures—a branch-man wiping the sweat from his brow and resettling his helmet; a spectator shading his eyes with his hand to peer into the fiery sea. Another gesticulating wildly with clenched fist brought down on the palm of his hand, as he pointed toward some unseen thing. To the right the faces in the crowd could be seen, but not their bodies. All were white and upturned, and every feature was strongly marked as if it had been part of an alabaster mask. Far away, indeed for miles around, could be seen, ringed by a circle of red light, the sea of housetops, broken by spires and tall chimneys, and the black and angry lake on which were a few pale, white sails....

"Account of the Great Fire." *Chicago Evening Post*, 17 Oct. 1871. www.greatchicagofire.org/eyewitnesses/anthology-of-fire-narratives. Accessed 26 Nov. 2018.

B. Compare the paintings of two doctors at work. The first is by Dutch artist Rembrandt van Rijn (1606–69). The second is by American artist Thomas Eakins (1844–1916). As you take notes and consider your answer, you may want to reflect on some of the following questions: How does the role of the doctor change? How do these artists picture the human body in the hands of the physician? What are the roles of the people surrounding the doctor? Do you see similarities in the groupings here? Differences? How would you describe the atmosphere in each painting? How does the artist evoke that atmosphere? When you have completed your draft, exchange it with a classmate for peer review. Revise your draft. Alternatively, choose two other images to compare.

The Anatomy Lesson of Dr. Nicholas Tulp, 1632 oil painting by Rembrandt, The doctor dissects a corpse for his colleagues.

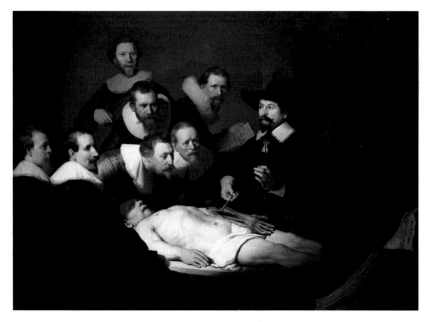

Rembrandt. *The Anatomy Lesson of Dr. Nicolaes Tulp*, 1632. Mauritshuis Museum.

The Agnew Clinic, 1889, shows a doctor performing a partial mastectomy on a woman patient.

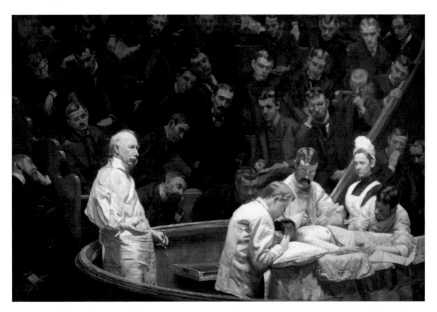

Eakins, Thomas. *The Agnew Clinic*, 1889. Philadelphia Museum of Art.

C. Compare the following passages advising women with alcoholic husbands. The first selection comes from an eighteenth-century guidebook intended to teach women how to behave. The second selection comes from a twenty-first-century website dedicated to helping women who are either struggling with their own substance abuse or that of a loved one. How does advice about alcoholic husbands change from the eighteenth to the twenty-first century? As you answer, you may want to consider some of the following questions. What kind of advice do you find in each passage? What differences do you see? Do you notice any similarities? What is the rhetorical situation of each passage? What might these passages suggest about the changing roles and responsibilities of women in their families and in the larger world? Pay close attention to language, audience, and genre.

From **The Whole Duty of a Woman, Or, an Infallible Guide to the Fair Sex, Containing Rules, Directions, and Observations for Their Conduct and Behaviour through All Ages and Circumstances of Life as Virgin, Wives, or Widows,** *1733.*

Thus in Case a Drunken Husband falls to a Woman's Lot, if she will be wise and patient, his Wine shall of her side; it will throw a Veil over her Mistakes, and will set out and improve every thing she does, that he is pleased with. Others will like him less, and by that Means he may, perhaps, like his Wife the more. When after having dined too well, he is received at home without a Storm, or as much as a reproachful Look, the Wine will naturally work out all in Kindness, which a Wife must encourage, let it be wrapped up in never so much impertinence. On the other Side, it [his temper] would boil up into Rage, if the mistaken Wife should treat him roughly, like a certain thing called, a kind Shrew, then which the World with all its Plenty cannot shew a more senseless, ill-bred, forbidding creature.

The Whole Duty of a Woman, Or, an Infallible Guide to the Fair Sex. London: T. Read, 1737, p. 125.

From **How to Deal with an Alcoholic Husband,** *a blog post at* **Clean and Sober Live.**

Your Options

There's no "one size fits all" advice for dealing with an alcoholic husband. Every situation is different, but you really only have 3 options:

1. Leave
At a certain point, you have to look out for your own well-being, and the well-being of your children—**especially** the well-being of your children.

Most people don't see leaving as an option. Obviously you shouldn't consider leaving the second you realize "my husband is an alcoholic," but at some point it becomes the only right choice. You may not be at this stage yet, but do know that this is an option that you may one day have to take in order to protect yourself and your children.

If your husband is getting physical or violent, even if he hasn't hit you or the kids (yet), then it's time to leave. Perhaps it's just temporary, or perhaps you should be hitting the road and never looking back, but you definitely need to remove yourself and your kids from the threat of physical harm.

2. Stay and Do Nothing

Unfortunately, many with alcoholic spouses choose this option.

Unfortunately, suffering in silence and hoping for the problem to go away won't lead anywhere, except maybe towards misery and depression.

3. Educate Yourself & Get Support

If you're living with an alcoholic, you probably already realize that confronting an alcoholic rarely results in immediate change, or even an acknowledgement of the problem.

If you're not ready to leave, and your husband won't come to terms with his addiction, you can either do nothing and wait for his alcoholism to ruin your family, or you can educate yourself and reach out to others for support.

Josh. "How to Deal with an Alcoholic Husband," *Clean and Sober Live*, www.cleanandsoberlive.com/how-to-deal-with-an-alcoholic-husband/. Accessed 20 Sept. 2018.

8

RESPONDING TO OTHER VOICES/OTHER SOURCES

Practicing Quotation.

ZACH   Okay, finally! I've revised my essay on the Greek urn. It's so much better now. Listen. *When I saw the Greek urn I thought about history because the thing is so incredibly old ...*

ANNA   How old was it?

ZACH   I don't remember. Like thousands of years old. I forgot to copy the date. But listen: *This ancient art form at once so simple and elegant still speaks to me today.*

ANNA   Really?! When did it start speaking to you?

ZACH   When I rented the museum audio guide.

ANNA   Wait, were you just writing down what you heard?

ZACH   No! I was putting it in my own words. That's why I said the art form speaks to *me*, instead of speaks to us. I personalized it.

Why Is It Important to Cite Sources?

Many of your college assignments will involve responding to the words, ideas, images, and voices of others. Whenever you refer to those, you need to cite your sources, telling your reader exactly where you found your material and who authored it. Citing sources constitutes a strong appeal to ethos. You are showing your reader that you have done your homework and therefore can write with authority. Citing sources is also an act of generosity. Scholars document sources carefully so that readers can follow their lead and make their own research contributions. The better the documentation, the easier it will be for others to build on their work. Productive writers and thinkers share sources openly, inviting others to debate and interpret their material.

If Zach listens to an audio guide about Greek urns, he should cite his source, just as he would if he read a book. What about a film? Or a piece of music? In each case, he needs to signal to his reader that he is using the work of others.

If Zach starts to copy down language from an audio guide, he should introduce his source, set off that language with quotation marks, and name the author and title of the guide. *As the museum audio guide states: "This ancient art form, so simple and elegant ..."* (Papdimitrious). If Zach chooses to paraphrase that language he should introduce and document his paraphrase. *The museum audio guide emphasizes the timeless quality of Greek urns.* After the paraphrase he should cite his source: (Papdimitrious). At the end of his essay, he will provide a full citation, using the format his teacher requires. In this case, his teacher requires the MLA documentation format, which, for an audio guide, looks like this.

Papdimitrious, Michael. Audio Guide, Museum of Fine
   Arts, Boston, MA, 20 Sept. 2015.

If Zach's instructor does not specify a particular kind of documentation, Zach should ask for advice on citation. Even for an informal writing assignment, it's important to identify and credit the words and ideas of others. Let's say Zach is simply writing notes during his museum visit. He could add a header: Notes on the museum audio guide. Then he can jot down the documentation information. If he does this the moment he encounters the guide, he will not need to hunt down this source later, when drafting and revising his essay.

Can Zach retell material in his own words for an essay on the Greek urn? Yes, as long as he cites his source. When Zach paraphrases the audio guide and begins passing off what he has heard as his own, he veers dangerously close to plagiarism, appropriating the work of others without attribution. The best way to avoid this problem would be to introduce the inspiring audio guide up front. *According to the museum audio guide, this urn is, "simple, elegant, and timeless."*

Citation and the Rhetorical Situation

In everyday communications we acknowledge the words and thoughts of others, but we don't stop to document them fully. We share ideas online. We share music, and send each other news stories, photos, videos. Cut and paste, post and pin, tweet and retweet. Jordan sends Anna a link to a video with a three-word introduction: *Check this out.* In a quick text, it's enough to provide a link or a casual citation.

We make authoritative statements all the time in conversation. *You can still get the flu even after you have a flu shot.* Well, how do you know? Few people stop to explain and cite their sources while talking to friends. A friendly conversation assumes a certain fluidity and trust. We are all reasonable people here—well, okay, sometimes we're not so reasonable, but we understand each other.

Adopting a conversational style, writers in certain genres do not document sources. A gossip columnist may quote unnamed insiders for juicy details about celebrities. *A source close to the couple says that they had been unhappy for some time before they decided to take a break.* Who is this source? And what does *close* mean? A longstanding friend? A neighbor who lives seven houses away? A recently fired gardener? The conventions of gossip writing encourage anonymity to allow sources to speak freely and to allow for unfettered speculation.

You won't find a bibliography in a blog post about the latest celebrity divorce. Nor will you find footnotes on a fashion magazine's photo spread showing new trends for fall. What you will find at the end of that photo spread is a detailed and accurate list of items pictured. Here in small print, the magazine provides the price and purchase information for each article of clothing. In this rhetorical situation, the magazine documents the work of designers and advertisers for an audience of potential shoppers.

It is crucial for writers—and speakers, and all communicators—to understand the expectations of their audience in each rhetorical situation and the conventions of the genre they choose. The conventions of the gossip column do not match those of a history essay, and you might provoke several pointed questions from your instructor if you write *Sources close to the colonists say that they had been unhappy for some time before they decided to rebel against England*. By the same token, a friendly conversation might grind to a halt if you begin documenting every assertion. *You can still get the flu after vaccination, as you can see in* The New England Journal of Medicine, *pages 112–23.*

Forms of Documentation: Examples from MLA, APA, and Chicago

In most college writing, sources require **attribution**, identification of the origin of the language and ideas you use. The way you document your sources will depend on purpose, audience, and genre. The genre of a formal research paper might require a full bibliography, as we discuss in Chapter Nine. A shorter essay with a few quotes may require brief notes with page references. Your assignment will often specify the style you should use when citing sources. Again, if it does not, you should ask your instructor.

Anna's instructor
I require MLA (Modern Language Association) style for all citations. If you are citing a book, you should document your source like this:

Greenberg, Cynthia. *Summer Leadership Opportunity: Invest in the Future*. Nonprofit Press, 2015.

If you are citing an article, you should document your source like this:

Luo, Baozhen. "China Will Get Rich Before It Gets Old." *Foreign Affairs*, vol. 94, no. 3, 2015, pp. 19–24.

For citation of other sources in the MLA format see Modern Language Association, *MLA Handbook, Eighth Edition*, Modern Language Association, 2016.

Jordan's instructor

I require APA (American Psychological Association) style for all citations. If you are citing a book, you should document your source like this:

Greenberg, C. (2015). *Summer leadership opportunity: Invest in the future*. New York, NY: Nonprofit Press.

If you are citing an article, you should document your source like this:

Luo, B. (2015). China will get rich before it gets old. *Foreign Affairs*, 94(3), 19–24.

For citation of other sources in the APA format see American Psychological Association, *Manual of the American Psychological Association*, New York: American Psychological Association, 2009. Print.

Zach's instructor

I require Chicago style for all citations. If you are citing a book, you should document your source like this:

Greenberg, Cynthia. *Summer Leadership Opportunity: Invest in the Future*. New York: Nonprofit Press, 2015.

If you are citing an article, you should document your source like this:

Luo, Baozhen. "China Will Get Rich Before It Gets Old." *Foreign Affairs* 94, no. 3 (2015): 19–24.

For citation of other sources in the Chicago style, see University of Chicago Press Staff, ed., *The Chicago Manual of Style*, Chicago: University of Chicago Press, 2010.

REFLECT on a recent or current assignment. What citation format does your instructor require? Where have you found models for this format? Did your instructor provide them? Have you found accurate models online? Have you ever run into problems or come up with questions about citing sources? How did you resolve them?

Please note that documentation styles change every few years. The MLA, the APA, and the University of Chicago Press all regularly update their handbooks and modify their guidelines for documentation. It is essential to check with your instructor to make sure you are using the correct, up-to-date format. For an excellent online reference to all these citation styles and others as well, see Purdue O.W.L.: Purdue Online Writing Lab. There are also many citation generators online. You fill in bibliographic information, specify a style, and the online tool then presents you with a formatted citation. While these are useful, we recommend familiarizing yourself with the standards and formats you will be using. With practice, they become easier and easier to implement.

A Good IDEA

It is important to document a source, but a full response to that source requires more than proper quotation and accurate citation. It is your responsibility to **introduce** your source, to **document** that source, to **explain** how this material is relevant, and to **assess** the significance of your source. Four essential steps. You can remember them by the acronym **IDEA**:

- Introduce
- Document
- Explain
- Assess

Avoiding Dropped Quotes, Missing Documentation, and Unexplained Evidence

Using IDEA as a guide, you will avoid some major problems. First of all, if you introduce your quoted material, you will avoid dropping a quote into the middle of your text without preparing the reader. Instructors often flag what they call "dropped quotes" to point out that you have suddenly inserted a text or image or weblink without warning. As with any new idea or material, you need to provide a transition. When you introduce your quote, you pave the way for your reader. Kate is writing about the Declaration of Independence. In her first draft, she drops a quote right into the middle of her paragraph.

> The Declaration of Independence expresses the belief that all (white men) should have equal rights. "We hold these truths to be self-evident, that all men are created equal" (billofrightsinstitute.org). At the time, this was a revolutionary statement.

Kate's instructor writes *DROPPED QUOTE!* in the margin. Kate revises her paragraph to look like this.

> The Declaration of Independence expresses the belief that all (white men) should have equal rights. In this document Thomas Jefferson sets the stage for his argument by declaring, "We hold these truths to be self-evident, that all men are created equal" (billofrightsinstitute.org). At the time, this was a revolutionary statement.

Introducing the passage provides the reader with the author and context for the quote. We know that Kate is talking about Thomas Jefferson's document and that this quote is setting the stage for the argument to come.

When introducing a quotation, try to guide your reader without boring her by repeating the same phrases again and again. Good introductory phrases for quoted material include: *She argues ... He asserts ... The authors contend ...* If you are writing about a character in a novel or play, you might introduce a quote with such phrases as, *She says ... He declares ... She protests ... She insists ... She thinks to herself ...*

Documenting her passage, Kate avoids another pitfall. She provides the source for her quoted material and meets her instructor's expectations for this class assignment. In her discussion of *The Declaration of Independence*, note the way she punctuates her quoted material, setting it off with a comma, using appropriate quotation marks, and then waiting to place her period *after* her source in parentheses.

X declares, "quoted material" (documentation).

Explaining your material, you break it down for the reader. You might clarify difficult ideas or remind your reader of the context of this statement. You want to shed light on your text.

Assessing your material, you show the reader how your quote is relevant to your argument. Assessment provides you with an opportunity for analysis. When Kate writes, "At the time, this was a revolutionary idea," her instructor writes in the margin, *How so?*

Kate revises to add an assessment of her quote.

> In 1776, when inherited rank and wealth were paramount, it was revolutionary to say men were born equal, and it was particularly dramatic to say this in a declaration listing the offenses of the King of England, who was the living symbol of a system where some were born to rule over others.

Kate's revision enriches her quotation from Jefferson, taking into account the date and socio-historical context of the *Declaration of Independence*. Instead of simply dropping her quotation into her paper, she uses IDEA to make that quote work for her as evidence and inspiration for analysis.

Using IDEA to Document a Text

Although Jordan's psychology instructor requests APA style, his first-year writing instructor asks for MLA formatting. You will often be asked to shift from style to style. Each rhetorical situation of source-based writing assumes a purpose, an audience, and a genre. These in turn carry conventions of "correct" documentation style.

Let's look at the way Jordan uses IDEA for an assignment in his first-year writing course.

> Analyze a speech in which the speaker calls the audience to action. What is the speaker's message? What is the rhetorical situation here? What rhetorical appeals does the speaker use? Do you think this speech is effective? Why or why not? Be sure to document your source, using MLA style.

Jordan chooses John F. Kennedy's inaugural address and quotes the president's famous call to action near the end. However, he does not simply cut and paste the quote into his own text. First he **introduces** Kennedy and the rhetorical situation of the speech, in order to set the stage for the quotation.

> In his inaugural address, President John F. Kennedy spoke outside the White House to a large crowd of people, and also to millions listening on the radio and watching T.V. At this time, he challenges Americans. "And so, my fellow Americans, ask not what your country can do for you; ask what you can do for your country" (Kennedy).

Notice that Jordan sets off Kennedy's language in quotation marks. If he chooses to quote three or more lines, he should set off the quotation in a block of text.

> In his inaugural address, President John F. Kennedy spoke outside the White House to a large crowd of people, and also to millions listening on the radio and watching T.V. At this time, he challenges Americans:

> In the long history of the world, only a few generations
> have been granted the role of defending freedom in
> its hour of maximum danger. I do not shrink from this
> responsibility — I welcome it. I do not believe that any
> of us would exchange places with any other people
> or any other generation. The energy, the faith, the
> devotion which we bring to this endeavor will light our
> country and all who serve it. And the glow from that
> fire can truly light the world (Kennedy).

Jordan does not need quotation marks for block quotation unless they appear in what he quotes. He insets his passage with margins on each side, and these margins serve instead of quotation marks.

Correct documentation style extends to the way your work appears on page or screen. Some instructors will insist that you use Times New Roman 12 point font, while others will ask for a different font, or say nothing about this at all. Most instructors ask for one-inch margins all around, and you can run into trouble trying to jam 600 words onto two pages by expanding the margins and shrinking the font. If you plan to insert a chart or graph into your essay, find out which style your instructor recommends. As always, consider your audience, purpose and genre.

Directly after the quotation, Jordan **documents** his source (Kennedy). At the end of his essay, he will provide a full citation.

> Kennedy, John F. "Inaugural Address." 20 Jan. 1961,
> *American Rhetoric,* www.americanrhetoric.com/
> speeches/jfkinaugural.htm. Accessed 29 Jan. 2016.

Jordan doesn't stop there. He **explains** the language in the speech, distilling Kennedy's message for the reader.

> Kennedy is saying each citizen has a responsibility to
> serve in some way. Instead of feeling entitled, we the
> people should step up and ask what can we do to help.

Finally, Jordan **assesses** Kennedy's call to action, spelling out how and why he thinks it is effective.

> John F. Kennedy makes a very effective appeal to pathos, stirring up emotions of pride, responsibility, and patriotism in his audience. He also appeals to logos. Up until this point in the speech he has been explaining that the world is troubled and there is a lot of work to be done. His logical conclusion is that everybody needs to pitch in and do that work. The appeal is very effective because it reminds people not to think so much about themselves and urges them to turn their thinking around to what people can do for their country.

Using IDEA to Document a Video

You can use IDEA to document material in other media as well. In her communications class, Kate received an assignment similar to Jordan's. *Analyze a speech in which the speaker calls the audience to action.* Instead of quoting from the written transcript of a speech, Kate watches the video of a motivational speech by football player Ray Lewis. Kate prepares her own transcript of a dramatic moment in the speech as she watches online.

Then she **introduces** Lewis and the rhetorical situation of the pep talk in order to set the stage for the key idea in Lewis's speech.

> When football star Ray Lewis returned to his alma mater, the University of Miami, he spoke to the players on the college football team and told them: "There is not a person on my team who has consistently beat me to the ball. That ain't got nothing to do with talent. It's just got everything to do with effort" (Lewis).

Next, Kate **documents** her material in MLA style: (Lewis). At the end of her essay she includes a full citation.

Lewis, Ray. "Ray Lewis Addresses the University of Miami
Football Team." 2 Sept. 2011, *YouTube*, www.youtube.
com/watch?v=uu4aVQ-qR8U. Accessed 26 Nov. 2018.

Kate doesn't stop after documenting the speech. She **explains** her material, identifying the core of Lewis's message.

For Lewis, the work ethic of a player is more important
than that player's innate talent. He feels that effort got
him where he is today.

After explaining why she thinks Lewis's words are significant, Kate **assesses** his argument.

I think Lewis makes a good point. All the talent in the
world won't help if you don't put in good effort. However,
he is speaking as a world class athlete. What about those
football players who work incredibly hard, but lack the skills
of a superstar? Effort only gets you so far if you are not
gifted with exceptional talents, not to mention size. His
argument appeals to ethos because he is saying this is who
I am. This is what I stand for. He is also saying — this is who
you should be too. After listening to this speech several
times, I would also say that Lewis appeals more to pathos
than to logos. It makes sense emotionally to keep on trying
and never give up. However, Lewis ignores the reality that
sometimes you can try hard and give your all and fail.

Using IDEA to Document an Image

Texts in every form require documentation. Images do too. Anna follows the IDEA process in her history class to write about western expansion in North America. Anna chooses to study advertisements encouraging settlement in the west. Beginning with an analysis of a Canadian poster from the turn of the twentieth century, Anna introduces the image, documents it, explains it, and then provides her own assessment.

A Canadian poster circa 1890–1920 paints a beautiful picture of the Canadian west. The landscape comes across as peaceful with open fields and blue skies. The color scheme is blue, green, and gold. Flat prairie stretches out to the horizon. The dark brown soil looks rich and ready for planting. The poster makes the west look like a great place to live.

Using IDEA to Integrate Quotations

There are times when writers quote just a few words from a text and weave this language into their own paragraphs. This technique can work beautifully to enrich an argument. Instead of inserting a long block quotation, the writer integrates quotations and maintains the flow of the essay. Anna uses this technique in her essay on westward expansion.

> Gold print and a gorgeous landscape depict "WESTERN CANADA" in a nineteenth century Canadian poster ("Western Canada"). This advertisement for farmers declares that the untouched west is "THE NEW ELDORADO." Spanish explorers once searched for El Dorado, a mythical city of gold. Here the words refer to prairie just waiting for farmers to cultivate with golden wheat. There is gold (wealth) in the "rich virgin soil" of this vast land—which belongs to Indigenous peoples who are not mentioned! There is also room for expansion with "HOMES FOR EVERYBODY." Spanish explorers of the sixteenth century built an empire in the New World. Now, in Canada, farmers are told that "WESTWARD THE STAR OF EMPIRE TAKES ITS WAY." The message here is that the west is golden, open, and safe, "PROTECTED BY THE GOVERNMENT" from Indigenous peoples who might object to giving up their land. The poster is an advertisement for empire.

Introducing brief quotations, Anna's paragraph moves quickly. However, she uses IDEA in this case as well. She **introduces** both the text and the image on the poster. Then she weaves brief quotations from the text into her paragraph, discussing the poster in its own words. Anna **documents** her source ("Western Canada"). She **explains** text and image, showing how words and pictures advertise the golden west and the riches to be found there. *There is gold (wealth) ... There is also room for expansion ...* Finally, she **assesses** her material. *The poster is an advertisement for empire.*

At the end of her essay, Anna includes a full citation of the poster in MLA format.

"Western Canada: The New Eldorado." ca. 1890–1920. *Library and Archives Canada,* www.collectionscanada. gc.ca/posters-broadsides/026023-4000-e.html. Accessed 24 Apr. 2019.

Responding to Other Voices

As a writer, you enter into conversation with your reader, real or imagined, present or future. You also join an ongoing conversation with those who have pondered the questions you explore. Imagine yourself watching friends in heated debate. You're fascinated, and you have something to say, as well. You could push your way into the center of the crowd and interrupt the conversation, talking over everyone else—but you probably won't. You wait for an opening to make your point. The same rules hold for a constructive meeting. First you listen. Then you introduce your own point of view in response. I agree with you about X, but I would take it a step further. I see what you mean, but I come to a different conclusion. You think Y, and she thinks X. What if we draw upon both ideas to develop Plan Z?

At a meeting, you are communicating with your audience in person. While writing, you cannot see your audience, so it is import-ant to keep your reader in mind as you introduce sources. How familiar is your reader with the sources you use? When writing for your composition instructor, you do not have to write about *To Kill*

A Mockingbird by Harper Lee. You can introduce this famous book more elegantly with the title alone, or by writing In Harper Lee's *To Kill a Mockingbird* ... By the same token, it is unnecessary to begin a history paper *At the battle of Gettysburg during the American Civil War* ... Your instructor knows the battle of Gettysburg took place during the Civil War. She wants to find out what you and your sources have to say about the conflict. In contrast, if you are citing and responding to a little known source or more difficult text, your reader may need more of an introduction and explanation. *A little-known work of fiction, the anonymous* Letters Writ by a Turkish Spy, *was the first of the so-called oriental spy novels published in English.*

ZACH Okay, fine, I'm not going to use the audio guide. Now what?

ANNA Why don't you start by describing the urn?

ZACH Nah.

ANNA Then you could write about how at first you didn't like it, but it grew on you.

ZACH Eh.

ANNA Okay, just discuss the foreignness of this ancient object and how it represents a culture that perhaps no one in modern times can completely understand.

ZACH Yeah! That's good!! That's exactly what I think!

ANNA And you can write about the gulf between the modern and the ancient world ...

ZACH Sh! Stop talking! If you say it first, then I'll be copying you.

Working Collaboratively and Working Alone

Many instructors encourage collaboration. In your writing class you might work in a small group to devise a presentation. In biology you work with a lab partner. In math your instructor might encourage you to work with others to tackle problem sets. Many stages of the writing process benefit from group work. When you have trouble starting a project, it helps to brainstorm, free associating ideas in class or with friends. When you finish a draft, it makes a lot of sense to engage in peer review, exchanging your work with a classmate to read closely, ask questions, identify problems, and make suggestions. Some assignments are designed as collaborative exercises. Your instructor may explicitly ask you to work with a partner or a small group to write up a report or draft a presentation. Just as the rhetorical situation determines whether and how to document sources, so the specific requirements of a classroom assignment will determine what kind of collaboration is appropriate. An assignment such as a lab report may require you to list all collaborators. Other assignments take a more relaxed approach to documenting collaboration or advice you have received from classmates or tutors. Here you should err on the side of caution. When in doubt, ask your instructor whether it is okay to work with others, and, if so, how you should acknowledge such help.

Although you will work with peers on many occasions, there are times in college when you need to work independently. Writing assignments often require independent work. In fact, you should assume instructors expect to see your own writing, unless they specifically ask you to collaborate with other students.

Understanding and Avoiding Plagiarism

What do you imagine when you hear the word plagiarism? Stealing? Copying? Buying a paper online certainly counts as plagiarism in college. Alex has to write an essay about Martin Luther King, Jr. He finds one online and passes it off as his own. His instructor uses a computer program to compare Alex's text with those on the internet and quickly discovers what Alex has done. She charges Alex with plagiarism. Alex appears before his college disciplinary board. Asked why he copied the essay, Alex says, "I ran out of time. I panicked. I got scared." The board asks Alex to withdraw from school. Perhaps he can return after a year. Perhaps not.

A story like this makes plagiarism sound simple. Turn in essays you find online and you'll get kicked out of college. Don't go down that road and you'll be fine. However, plagiarism takes other forms as well. Asking a parent to revise—or rewrite—a paper can lead to serious problems, because you may end up turning in work that is not your own. Repurposing your own work from another class is problematic as well. Your instructor almost always expects you to produce new work address-ing the themes, questions, and material in *this* class. Plagiarism doesn't always involve lying. Often it begins when writers attempt shortcuts—recycling old work, outsourcing draft and revision, or skipping steps in the writing process.

Mia is writing a paper about Thomas Jefferson, so she starts reading about him. As she reads, Mia types detailed notes on her computer, cutting and pasting particularly insightful comments found online. In fact, Mia gets so caught up in note-taking that when it comes time to write her paper, she can't tell the difference between her own language and that of others writing about Jefferson. Mia loses track of her sources, and their words get mixed up with her own.

When Mia's instructor reads her paper, he finds passages that don't sound like student work—certainly not like the Mia he knows from previous assignments. He starts googling phrases from her paper and discovers that they come from other writers. At this point, he calls her into his office and asks, "Is this all your own work?"

Mia says yes. Then she says, "I'm not sure."

Jordan

I have definitely felt rushed enough to start—not exactly copying—but taking published writing and putting it in my own words without attribution. At one point in high school I did this, but my teacher was like, "Hey, Jordan. This doesn't sound like you. Where did this come from?" I was like, "um." He said, "You realize this could be plagiarism, right?"

Zach

I know some students in a class that encouraged working in groups of three to four people. For the final project the students were supposed to turn in their own work, but about half the class continued to collaborate—and got busted. The students protested to the disciplinary board that their professor had not been clear about working alone on the final project, but in the end, they got disciplined anyway.

Anna

I had a friend who asked me to help her write a short paper. She was having a lot of trouble, and I spent two hours with her, but even after all that time, she was still stuck. I realized it would be faster to write a few paragraphs for her—so I did! I thought, this is sort of a gray area. It's just a couple of paragraphs, and she is right here with me telling her what she wants to say. Then I felt guilty.

Kate

The whole idea of plagiarism is strange to me. Maybe it's because I'm working and paying my own tuition. Why would I even think about breaking rules when I'm trying to learn this material and get my degree? I don't even have time for this discussion.

REFLECT: Have you known anyone who was accused of plagiarism? Do you think the accusations were fair? Have you ever taken a class where your instructor encouraged collaboration? Was it clear when you could collaborate and when you could not?

Mia's instructor says he is afraid she has been using sources dishonestly. Mia argues that she didn't mean to deceive, insisting that she made an honest mistake while taking notes. Even so, Mia has appropriated the ideas and words of others, and this is plagiarism. The paper does express Mia's ideas, but it patches in other work as well. If Mia is to avoid this kind of plagiarism, she needs to change her method of reading, note-taking, and writing. She can't just cut and paste a good source and then plan to document it later. She must document each source immediately in her notes so that she'll know where her material comes from when she starts writing. (See Chapter Three for a discussion of note-taking.)

Many colleges distribute their own guidelines or codes of academic conduct. These spell out the institution's policies on plagiarism. Such codes may also list different kinds of plagiarism to guard against. These may include inappropriate collaboration and patching together sources without acknowledgement, as well as handing in purchased or recycled work. Such lists are helpful, but no list can cover every situation when it comes to writing and research. If your assignment is ambiguous about whether you can work with others or whether you must work alone, then ask your instructor for clarification. By the same token, if you find yourself overwhelmed, it's far better to go to your instructor and ask for an extension than to plagiarize. It is also crucial to ask for advice if you find yourself in a murky situation. If you aren't sure whether your instructor sanctions collaboration, ask. If you find your assignment's expectations confusing, request clarification. Remember that college is a community. That community offers students support and resources for meeting its academic and ethical standards.

Use **IDEA** to introduce and respond to the work of others.

- **I**ntroduce your source to the reader with a brief description and some context.
- **D**ocument your source in the format appropriate for your genre, audience, purpose, and assignment.
- **E**xplain your source, helping your reader to understand what it means.
- **A**ssess the significance of your source, interpreting and showing its relevance to your purpose.

Avoid plagiarism.

- Take careful and accurate notes.
- Document texts directly in your notes.
- Understand your instructor's expectations. When is collaboration acceptable? When is it necessary to work alone?
- When in doubt, ask for clarification.
- When under pressure, ask for help.

TAKEAWAY

ACTIVITIES

1 How do the authors below quote others? What quotation styles do you see? Try to identify each component of IDEA: Introduce, Document, Explain, Assess. Are some components missing? How would you describe the impact of quotation—or lack thereof? Note the genre in each case, and the different conventions these writers follow.

From an argument about all the stuff Zach left at home. Genre: telephone conversation.

Zach: What do you mean you cleaned out my room?

Zach's mom: I mean I cleaned it out.

Zach: And what happened to my stuff?

Zach's mom: Zach, I warned you. On winter break, at breakfast, in front of your father and your brother, I said, and I quote: "If you don't clean up your room, I will."

Zach: Right. You said clean up, not clean out.

Zach's mom: My point was that if you didn't take care of it, then I would clean your room at a time of my choosing.

From a discussion of the life and work of Theodore Seuss Geisel, the author-illustrator who took the name Dr. Seuss. Genre: obituary.

The exact cause of death was unclear, said Jerry Harrison, who oversees children's books for Random House, Mr. Geisel's longtime publishers. Mr. Harrison said the author had been suffering from an infection of his jawbone that had become acute in recent months.

"We've lost the finest talent in the history of children's books," Mr. Harrison said in a telephone interview, "and we'll probably never see one like him again."

Mr. Geisel's work delighted children by combining the ridiculous and the logical, generally with a homely moral. "If I start out with the concept of a two-headed animal," he once said, "I must put two hats on his head and two toothbrushes in the bathroom. It's logical insanity."

Pace, Eric. "Dr. Seuss, Modern Mother Goose Dies at 87." *The New York Time*s, 26 Sept. 1991, p. A1.

From a study of the pursuit of happiness. Genre: journal article.

The pursuit of happiness holds an honored position in American society, beginning with the Declaration of Independence, where it is promised as a cherished right for all citizens. Today, the enduring U.S. obsession with how to be happy can be observed in the row upon row of popular psychology and self-help books in any major bookstore and in the millions of copies of these books that are sold. Indeed, many social contexts in the United States have the production of happiness and positive feelings as their primary purpose, and questions such as "Are you happy?" and "Are you having fun?" fit nearly every occasion (Markus & Kitayama, 1994). Not surprisingly, the majority of U.S. residents rate personal happiness as very important (Diener, Suh, Smith, & Shao, 1995; Triandis, Bontempo, Leung, & Hui, 1990) and report thinking about happiness at least once every day (Freedman, 1978). Furthermore, the pursuit of happiness is no longer just a North American obsession, but instead it is becoming ever more global as people seek to fulfill the promises of capitalism and political freedom (Diener et al., 1995; Freedman, 1978; Triandis et al., 1990). It seems that nearly all people believe, or would like to believe, that they can move in an "upward spiral" (Sheldon & Houser-Marko, 2001) toward ever-greater personal well-being.

Lyobomirsky, Sonja, Kennon Sheldon, and David Schkade. "Pursuing Happiness: The Architecture of Sustainable Change." *Review of General Psychology*, vol. 9, no. 2, 2005, pp. 111–31.

From 1945 to 1946, an international military tribunal tried Nazi leaders for war crimes. In his closing statement, American prosecutor Robert Jackson addresses the Nazis' claim that they were virtually slaves of Hitler, who forced them to commit crimes against humanity. Genre: summation in court.

The defendants may have become the slaves of a dictator, but he was their dictator. To make him such was, as Goring has testified, the object of the Nazi movement from the beginning. Every Nazi took this oath: "I pledge eternal allegiance to Adolf Hitler. I pledge unconditional obedience to him and the Fuhrers appointed by him" (1893-PS). Moreover, they forced everybody else in their power to take it. This oath was illegal under German law, which made it criminal to become a member of an organization in which obedience to "unknown superiors or unconditional obedience to known superiors is pledged." These men destroyed free government in Germany and now plead to be excused from responsibility because they became slaves. They are in the position of the fictional boy who murdered his father and mother and then pleaded for leniency because he was an orphan.

Jackson, Robert. "Summation for the Prosecution." Nuremberg Trials, 26 June 1946. Pace Law Library Research Guide, www.law.pace.edu/library. Accessed 26 Nov. 2018.

From a contemporary assessment of the 1851 novel Moby-Dick. *Genre: book review. Note that at this time in this publication, writers used single instead of double quotation marks.*

We have no intention of quoting any passages just now from *Moby Dick*. The London journals, we understand, 'have bestowed upon the work many flattering notices,' and we should be loth [reluctant] to combat such high authority. But if there are any of our readers who wish to find examples of bad rhetoric, involved syntax, stilted sentiment and incoherent English, we will take the liberty of recommending to them this precious volume of Mr. Melville's.

"Book Notices: *Moby Dick; or the Whale*." *The United States Democratic Review*, vol. 30, 1852, p. 93.

2 Consider the way Anna, Kate, and Jordan use images and multi-media content in these examples. Identify where they Introduce, Document, Explain, and Assess their material.

Kate interviewed a fellow student for a composition assignment to write a profile of a classmate. She weaves in quotations from the recorded interview to illustrate this description of her classmate Maddy.

In a one-hour interview on September 26 at the Student Center, I learned about the life of Maddy Browser, a freshman from Elkhart, Indiana. Maddy drives forty-five minutes each way to get to class. She is living at home in large part to help her parents who are the caregivers of her disabled uncle and elderly grandmother. "I am an only child," Maddy explains. "I am very close to my family and they need me, especially on weekends." Partly because of her experience caring for relatives with medical needs, Maddy hopes to become a doctor. For this reason, she is taking biology and organic chemistry. She records lectures and uses her drive to listen to them "over and over."

Anna's Revolutionary America instructor assigned a short essay in which students write about an image from the Revolution. The assignment read in part: Discuss the choices the artist makes. Who is the audience for this image? What is its purpose? Can you discern a political agenda? If so, what might that be?

Paul Revere's engraving of the Boston Massacre was published in 1770 in many newspapers. The engraving shows British troops firing on American civilians.

Revere, Paul. *The Bloody Massacre*. 1770, hand-colored engraving, Peabody Essex Museum.

The artist makes several decisions to appeal to his rebellious American audience and vilify the British troops. He shows the redcoats standing in formation like a firing squad shooting confused civilians. The British use weapons while the Americans have nothing. Revere draws a cute little dog on the American side to highlight the peaceful innocence of the colonists and the cruelty of the British....

Jordan's Film Studies instructor assigned a brief essay on a newsreel from the early days of cinema. The assignment read in part: What is the purpose of this film? Who do you think the audience might have been? How would you define the "news" in this newsreel? Jordan chooses to write about a newsreel from the Great Depression.

In 1934 a general strike crippled San Francisco. This black and white 1934 newsreel illustrates the dismal effects of the strike (https://archive.org/details/ssfGSTKBEG1?start=0.5.) The brief film shows footage of empty streets and vacant gas stations. Streetcars were not running, and gas stations could not get fuel. Closed shops and restaurants (advertising dinner for 50 cents!) attest to the fact that the city has completely shut down. The people who made this film were clearly trying to show audiences in other states what conditions were like out west. The effect is spooky, as if San Francisco has become a ghost town overnight.

San Francisco General Strike. Directed by Bert Gould, Pathé News, 1934, https://archive.org/details/ssfGSTKBEG1?start=0.5. Accessed 29 Jan. 2019.

3   Practice with IDEA.

While writing his essay on Chinua Achebe, Zach decides to quote the passage where Achebe explains why he decided to become a writer. Here is the text Zach wants to use.

Then I grew older and began to read about adventures in which I didn't know that I was supposed to be on the side of these savages who were encountered by the good white men. I instinctively took sides with the white people. They were fine! They were excellent. They were intelligent. The others were not ... they were stupid and ugly. That was the way I was introduced to the danger of not having your own stories. There is that great proverb—that until the lions have their own historians, the history of the hunt will always glorify the hunter.

Achebe, Chinua. "The Art of Fiction 139." Interview by Jerome Brooks. *The Paris Review*, no. 139, www.theparisreview.org/interviews/1720/chinua-achebe-the-art-of-fiction-no-139-chinua-achebe. Accessed 13 Mar. 2018.

Now look at what Zach has written so far. Where do you think he should place this passage? Consider which part of Zach's text can effectively introduce this passage, and which part might serve as explanation and analysis after the passage. Rewrite Zach's text to include this passage as a block quote.

> Chinua Achebe describes becoming a writer as a gradual process in which he realized some important things about story telling. Probably the most important realization is that story telling is a privilege of those who have power. Achebe compares white story tellers to hunters who have power to kill animals like lions. After spending a lot of time enjoying the hunters' stories, Achebe begins to understand that lions need to have their story tellers too, otherwise only the hunters will go down into history. Only hunters will get the glory.

Write a sentence or two reflecting on why you chose to place the block quote where you did.

Kate is writing an essay on "The Tell-Tale Heart" by Edgar Allan Poe (1809–49). Kate wants to quote from the opening lines of Poe's short story.

> True!—nervous—very, very dreadfully nervous I had been and am; but why will you say that I am mad? The disease had sharpened my senses—not destroyed—not dulled them. Above all was the sense of hearing acute. I heard all things in the heaven and in the earth. I heard many things in hell. How, then, am I mad? Hearken! and observe how healthily—how calmly I can tell you the whole story.
>
> Poe, Edgar Allan. "The Tell-Tale Heart." 1843. www.poemuseum.org/history-of-the-museum. Accessed 28 Jan. 2019.

Now look at what Kate has written so far. How might Kate quote Poe to support her points? Rewrite Kate's text while weaving in Poe's language.

> Edgar Allan Poe grabs the reader right at the beginning of "The Tell-Tale Heart." His narrator seems very jumpy and almost frightened, and he seems concerned that no one will believe him because people might think he is crazy. This makes the reader curious, and perhaps jumpy as well. The effect is intense, partly because the narrator is speaking to the reader directly. At one point the narrator asks the reader a

question. Now the reader starts wondering — is this normal? The whole opening sets the reader off balance.

Write a sentence or two reflecting on the choices you made as you quoted Poe's text. Why did you choose the lines you did? Why did you place them where you did?

Jordan quotes from **Alice's Adventures in Wonderland** *when he writes his analysis of Tenniel's illustration. This is the text from which Jordan wants to quote.*

> The Caterpillar and Alice looked at each other for some time in silence: at last the Caterpillar took the hookah out of its mouth, and addressed her in a languid, sleepy voice.
>
> 'Who are YOU?' said the Caterpillar.
>
> This was not an encouraging opening for a conversation. Alice replied, rather shyly, 'I — I hardly know, sir, just at present — at least I know who I WAS when I got up this morning, but I think I must have been changed several times since then.'
>
> Carroll, Lewis. *Alice's Adventures in Wonderland*, facsimile of first edition, 1865, Engage Books, 2010.

Now look at what Jordan has written so far. How might he weave some of this language into his paragraph to support his points? Rewrite Jordan's text while weaving in quotations from Lewis Carroll.

> The dialogue between Alice and the Caterpillar starts out awkwardly. At first, they just stare at each other, not knowing what to say. Then the Caterpillar speaks to Alice in a confrontational way. When Alice responds, she admits that she does not know exactly who she is. She answers the Caterpillar's demanding questions with a lot of honesty and humility. This is her stance throughout the book. She never pretends she knows what's going on when she does not. She accepts that she is confused and takes each new experience as it comes.

Write a sentence or two reflecting on the choices you made as you quoted Carroll's text. Why did you choose the lines you did? Why did you place them where you did?

9

WRITING AND RESEARCH

Writing a Research Paper.
Crafting a Multi-Modal Portfolio.

JORDAN	I've narrowed my search to sedans under $5,000 with less than 100,000 miles on them from dealers within 20 miles of here.
ZACH	Okay ...
JORDAN	And I found this dealer with 32 five-star reviews.
ZACH	They're probably all by his relatives. I always go by the comments from the three-star reviews. The five stars are too positive, and the one stars are random or crazy. The three-star reviewers write about the pros and cons.
JORDAN	I'm reading *everything*, including the comments on the comments. I need a car!

What Is Research? Where Does It Begin?

Research is investigation beginning with a need—for information, for directions, for advice, for answers. Jordan needs a car. He has limited resources, and he needs to find a used car that is both affordable and reliable. We conduct research like this every day. We research purchases, travel routes, restaurants online. We ask friends to recommend doctors and dentists. We consult reviews to research small decisions like where to go for dinner, and big ones like where to go to school.

Kate needs to find out about Physician's Assistant programs. She researches requirements so that she'll take the relevant courses in college. She looks at the rankings of each program on multiple websites, studies placement records and financial aid packages. Jordan and Kate are highly motivated to gather information. Jordan plans to spend his savings; he can't afford to buy a car that needs expensive repairs. Kate is returning to college in order to change careers, and she thinks carefully about where to invest her time and money as she assesses the risks and rewards of graduate school. Need motivates Jordan and Kate to become meticulous researchers, searching widely—"I'm reading everything!"—and evaluating sources rigorously: *Which comments are useful? Which rankings can I trust?*

If need motivates research in everyday life, what motivates academic researchers? Curiosity is key for scientists and scholars. What causes cancer cells to multiply? How do financial markets work? What is art? How do bees communicate? Questions like these intrigue investigators, who spend years, even whole careers, working on them. A deep desire for knowledge, a *need* to know, drives researchers. Sometimes that need comes from a sense of wonder. *As a child I was a star gazer. I could not stop thinking about the universe.* Sometimes the need to know comes from an ambition to give or to help. Ask a scholar what motivates his or her research and you'll often hear answers like this: *I want to build new tools to save time and energy. I want to understand why students drop out of school. I want to protect endangered species. I want to learn from the past. I want to save lives.* Consider this statement by

Dr. Jim Olson in a film about his work researching new treatments for children with brain tumors:

> First and foremost I'm a parent, and when I know that a child is going to die and the prescriptions I'm writing might make them live a couple of weeks longer but aren't going to save their lives, there's nothing harder than that—and that drives my research.

Olson, Jim. "How Nature and a 9-Year-Old Are Revolutionizing Cancer Treatment." *TEDxSeattle*, 19 July 2013, *YouTube*, www.youtube.com/watch?v=7IWMJhg2Zlc. Accessed 28 Jan. 2019.

Or consider the words of Nobel Laureate Amartya Sen, a philosopher, social theorist, and economist. Asked why he works in so many fields, he articulates the motivation that unifies his diverse projects:

> I am interested in poverty, I am interested in women's deprivation; I am interested in child welfare and child mortality. I'm interested in the bettering of the lives of young women who are constantly bearing and rearing children.

Sen, Amartya. "Humane Development." Interview by Akash Kapur. *The Atlantic*, 15 Dec. 1999. www.theatlantic.com/past/docs/unbound/interviews/ba991215.htm. Accessed 17 Jan. 2019.

Effective research begins with a sense of purpose. For this reason, we urge you to choose a topic or question that interests you. However, not all students enjoy the luxury of choosing research projects. In college you may have to write on topics and questions provided by your instructor. Some research assignments will intrigue you. Some won't. Let's discuss each case.

Starting with the Assignment

Jordan is excited about a research project in his organizational behavior class. He plans to study leadership by observing the shifting power structures in Ultimate scrimmages. He is already playing three times a week, so he's uniquely positioned as a participant-observer.

He will be working and playing at the same time, engaging in the hands-on experiential research known as fieldwork. Anthropologists, sociologists, and journalists often conduct this kind of research, embedding themselves in social groups such as an ethnic group or a neighborhood or a military unit to make careful observations and take notes. In Jordan's case, he will do his fieldwork on the field.

Zach is building on his essay arguing that lotteries tax the poor. He has strong opinions, but he is curious about what the experts say, so he reads several studies of the lottery by economists and psychologists. Researching articles, books, and reports by others who have studied the lottery system, he does a **literature search**, a broad review of sources addressing a question that fascinates him. Why do so many poor people spend their money with so little chance for reward?

Research Materials

As you study your research assignment—ask yourself three initial questions:

- What am I investigating?
- What materials will I study?
- What do others say?

Jordan is investigating the nature of leadership. His materials will be written logs of Ultimate games where he records the movement of players on the field, the number of times each player passes or scores, and even the time outs and changes in strategy that team leaders made. He will also look at books and articles about effective leadership. This means he is using two kinds of material—the material he generates from his own observations, and the material he reads when studying what others have said about leadership.

Zach's materials are quite different from Jordan's. While Jordan studies players leaping and scoring on the field, Zach is studying graphs and charts online. While Jordan attempts to learn about leadership from an Ultimate team with a handful of players, Zach is studying the behavior of huge numbers of lottery players. Careful observation of a few people counts as significant for Jordan's class in organizational behavior, while analysis of spending by millions counts as significant for Zach's sociology class. As we learned in Chapter Five and Eight, what counts as evidence differs, depending on the community for whom you write. What kind of research does this community do? Fieldwork? Experiments? Textual study? Statistical analysis? What material does this community value? One way to answer this question is to look at the work others have done in your area of research. This is why so many instructors ask you to consult scholarly articles when you embark on a research project. It is useful to learn what others have to say on your topic. It is also crucial to look at the materials others use. What kind of data do they gather? What kind of evidence do they find significant?

Identifying a Topic That Motivates You

It's great to get fired up about a research project in college. However, you may not feel the same enthusiasm for every assignment. Indeed, you might need to do a little research in order to spark your curiosity. Kate's instructor hands out this assignment:

> *Explore the cultural significance of a historical event in a research paper. Focus on three to four different contemporary accounts of that event. Choose two or three eye-witness accounts, and consult two scholarly sources — a book and/or journal article.*

Kate

I like this class a lot, but it's not like I wake up every morning thinking I just can't wait to find cultural meaning in a historical event! Also—finding all those sources is a little intimidating.

Her initial response is *hmmmm.*

Whether you are excited about a research assignment or feeling daunted, it helps to look for material that you can make your own.

Often, when an instructor provides the question, the student can choose sources. You might try

- Looking at notes from lectures or class discussion
- Reviewing course material
- Asking your instructor for guidance

Of all the course readings this semester, the one that stands out for Kate is a collection of eye-witness accounts of the Great Fire of Chicago in 1871. (We include some of these in the Activities for Chapter Seven.) It's horrifying to envision an entire city going up in flames, and strange to think that until this class she had never heard of such a huge disaster. She does not know what she will say about the fire, but she wouldn't mind learning more. She decides to take the Great Fire as her topic.

A finished essay in college often begins with an introduction containing a thesis statement—but the research process rarely starts with one. In fact, it usually takes some research to come up with a thesis statement. Kate's instructor encourages this kind of exploration, asking all students to begin work by preparing an **annotated bibliography**, a documented list of sources with a brief summary of each source and an explanation of its relevance. These sources could include not only books and articles, but websites, videos, interviews, pictures, and objects.

Initial Search: Relevant and Reliable Sources

Sometimes assignments provide detailed guidance on sources. A psychology assignment might require two articles in specific journals. Research in a film class might require students to watch three films and read several reviews and critical articles. Instructors often provide students with a list of suggested sources or databases. However, not all assignments spell out expectations or provide possible sources. You may find yourself googling your topic and then trying to figure out which sources you should use and which you should ignore. In your initial search, try testing each source with these questions. Is this source **relevant**? Is it **reliable**?

First, you want to focus on sources directly relevant to your topic or questions. Jordan is looking for cars under $5,000. He won't even glance at those over his budget. Kate is looking for accounts of the Great Fire of Chicago, so she rules out great fires in other cities like London and New York. She also rules out articles on corruption in Chicago, architecture in Chicago, and the origins of Chicago, while she stays focused on the fire. If she gets sidetracked and starts reading everything she can about the city, she'll never begin writing—let alone finish.

Of course, not every relevant source is also reliable. It is important to consider the origin of a source. Who generated this material? If authors are listed, what are their credentials? A scholar affiliated with a research institution could be more reliable than a blogger who calls himself CivilWar Fanboy.

Reliability is not an absolute term. Context and community standards determine reliability. If you are writing a short story about blood and gore at the Battle of Shiloh, CivilWar Fanboy might be a perfect resource. If you are writing a research paper in which you practice the scholarly arts of documentation and discussion of sources, you need to vet your materials, choosing websites, articles, and books accepted by the scholarly community. Such materials include articles published in peer-reviewed journals, publications in which scholars and specialists evaluate submissions, accepting or rejecting articles according to their own professional standards of relevance and reliability.

Wikipedia can be a great starting point for the research process, but most instructors do not accept a Wikipedia article as a source for a research project. First of all, information on Wikipedia is not necessarily compiled or checked by scholars, specialists, and experts. Indeed, a reader has no way of knowing the authorship and affiliation of Wikipedia contributors. Secondly, not all Wikipedia articles are created equal. Some entries are long and detailed, others sketchy, missing information, or incorporating mistakes.

When Kate begins her research, googling the Great Fire of Chicago, she comes up with a long Wikipedia article which she reads quickly for an overview of the dates and major events of the fire. Wikipedia is neither a contemporary account of the fire, nor a scholarly discussion of the event, so it will not count as one of her sources. Kate's instructor suggests viewing Wikipedia as a gateway, no more than a starting point for the research process. Using Wikipedia this way, Kate jots down dates, terms, and names, which she will use to refine her search.

Refining a Question with Key Terms

As Jordan discovered when he was car shopping, a broad search term like *used car* yields massive results. Jordan quickly decides to narrow his search by price, by location, and by mileage. Students can focus a search by studying a general article and identifying certain key terms—words, dates, and names that come up often in discussions of the topic.

Kate notes several words and names repeated in the Wikipedia article. *Origin, Aftermath, Mayor Roswell B. Mason.* Origin and Aftermath stand as headings in the entry for the Chicago fire, as does the phrase The Great Rebuilding. Kate realizes that these are important aspects, or subtopics of the larger event. Searching for these terms, she finds more focused and detailed historical articles.

In addition to searching for subtopics, Kate can refine her search by specifying the kind of source she seeks. *Eye-witness accounts. Newspaper articles Great Fire 1871.* Kate googles *Great Fire of Chicago Eye-Witness* and finds a website called The Great Fire of Chicago and the Web of Memory, where she discovers a digital archive of eye-witness accounts, graphic representations, and newspaper clippings. This seems promising—but before using the materials on this site, she checks to see who put the site together. At the bottom of the homepage she sees that the Web of Memory is a joint project of the Chicago Historical Society and Northwestern University. A historical society and a university seem like reliable resources, representing scholarly and archival interests.

Seeking Expert Advice

Students searching for reliable sources can get help at the college library. Not everyone enjoys asking a reference librarian for guidance, but most librarians will tell you that they enjoy being asked. Librarians are educators dedicated to helping students navigate collections and databases.

Librarians are experts on relevance and reliability. They are also adept at finding sources online and in their own collections. Kate's librarian shows her a number of online collections of scholarly journals. With these databases, Kate can search thousands of journals and abstracts, or summaries, of articles that seem promising. Some of these databases require a paid subscription, but most college libraries subscribe, so as a student you can search for free.

KATE Hi! I'm looking for two scholarly sources on the Great Fire of Chicago.

LIBRARIAN Just two?

KATE Well, I'm required to have two.

LIBRARIAN Do you have a special focus? Historical? Economic? Sociological?

KATE I don't have a focus yet. I'm hoping I'll come up with one!

LIBRARIAN Is there anything in particular you want to find out about the fire?

KATE Um. Its impact? My assignment is to write about the cultural impact of an event.

LIBRARIAN Okay. That's a start! Let's look for journal articles about the cultural impact of the Great Fire.

Kate

The online databases are massive. When I searched for articles on the Great Fire of Chicago, I got over a million citations. A lot of them weren't relevant because they referred to other great fires like London or Boston—but still! I knew I had to narrow down my search, so I tried typing *Great Fire of Chicago 1871*. Now I've got over 100,000 citations. That's a lot, and I don't know what I'm looking for, so I'm going to take notes on some of my eye-witness accounts and then revisit the scholarly articles. Hopefully I'll have a better idea of what I want at that point.

Jordan

Something similar happened to me when I was researching cars. I got flooded with ads as soon as I typed *used car under $5000*. I started narrowing my search by make and model. Then I looked for cars with one owner only so they wouldn't be such wrecks. I got fewer and fewer results until I narrowed them down to 10.

REFLECT on your own experience gathering information either in or out of school. Did you grapple with too much information? If so, how did you narrow your search?

Sorting and Selecting Sources

After gathering sources, it's important to sort them. Sorting allows a researcher to impose order on material without drowning in detail. Sorting also serves as a way to select material for further study. Given the limited time available for research and writing, students need to decide where to focus their energies. To that end, consider the following questions:

1. What kind of source is this?
2. What is the focus of this source?
3. Is this material I want to study further?

WHAT KIND OF SOURCE IS THIS?

Sorting her sources by genre, Kate places scholarly articles in one category and contemporary accounts in another. The scholarly articles include discussions of the fire from a number of different fields, from cultural studies to economics. Kate's contemporary accounts include newspaper articles, cartoons, poems, eye-witness testimonies, and oral histories by survivors of the fire. Kate gathers more material than she can possibly read in just a few days—but she does not have to read it all. Her assignment requires her to use two scholarly accounts and three to four contemporary sources. How to choose?

WHAT IS THE FOCUS OF THIS SOURCE?

Reading titles and abstracts, and skimming paragraphs, Kate identifies the focus of each journal article and contemporary account. There are many ways to sort sources. You could look at date, genre, country of origin. Kate sorts by theme, which is an excellent way to organize information when you are trying to understand a topic. She notices that her sources tend to focus on certain aspects of the fire: Origins. Spread of Fire. Damage. Aftermath. Rebuilding.

IS THIS MATERIAL I WANT TO STUDY FURTHER?

Kate notices that many of her eye-witness accounts focus on the aftermath of the fire. Heart-wrenching and bewildered, the contemporary accounts that intrigue her most are those in which citizens try to come to terms with the tragedy. Kate gathers these together in a folder on her computer and decides these are the sources she wants to study more carefully.

Deciding which material to study further is a great way to narrow a research topic. Kate began with a broad topic. The Great Fire of Chicago. Now she hones in on one aspect of the fire, prioritizing the questions of traumatized survivors. Why this city? Why now? Why did this happen to us?

Taking Notes on Selected Sources

No one has time to study every source that turns up. Careful selection allows you to read and take notes on sources that seem most promising and most relevant to a specific topic.

Kate focuses her reading on sources discussing the aftermath of the Great Fire. In a contemporary magazine article called "Chicago in Distress," Kate reads "Chicago has a weakness for 'big things' and liked to think that it was outbuilding New York." The author goes on to say that the fire spread fast through Chicago's wood buildings, thin walls, and rooftop signs. Kate's instructor suggests that everyone take notes using a T Chart (see Chapter Three), so Kate cuts and pastes this passage, along with documentation, into a new document on her computer, creating a T Chart with the text on the left and her own comments and questions on the right.

Kate pauses here and wonders if this source is reliable. Is this simply a New Yorker who hates Chicago? He writes about urban planning in an authoritative way, but what are his credentials? A quick Google search reveals that the author of the essay is landscape architect Frederick Law Olmsted, the designer of Central Park in New York City, and many other parks, green spaces, and universities throughout the United States.

<u>Chicago has a weakness for "big things," and liked to think that it was outbuilding New York</u>. It did a great deal of commercial advertising in its house-tops. The faults of construction as well as of art in its <u>great showy buildings</u> must have been numerous. Their walls were thin, and were often over weighed with gross and coarse <u>misornamentation</u>. Some ostensibly stone fronts had huge overhanging wooden or sheet-metal cornices fastened directly to their roof timbers, with wooden parapets above them. Flat roofs covered with tarred felt and pebbles were common. In most cases, I am told by observers, the fire entered the great buildings by their roof timbers....

Olmsted, Frederick Law. "Chicago in Distress." *The Papers of Frederick Law Olmsted*. Johns Hopkins UP, 1992, Vol. VI, p. 487.

Is he gloating?? Is he saying I told you so? No, not gloating, but he's saying it's Chicago's fault that it burned because it was built cheap and fast. Wood instead of stone.

Misornamention?? What is that? Ugly architecture?

Kate

Okay, I guess he has the credentials to criticize Chicago's building codes — but he's still pretty harsh!

Kate is fascinated by the notion that Chicago may have brought the fire on itself by overreaching—growing too big, too fast. She starts searching the Great Fire website for other writers who might blame Chicago for its tragedy, and she discovers a poem by W.H. McElroy.

We used to chaff you in other days, Chicago, You had such self-asserting ways, Chicago. By Jove, but you cut it rather fat, With your boastful talk of this and that, As if America's hub was at Chicago. McElroy, W.H. "Chicago." www.greatchicagofire .org/fanning-flames-library/%E2%80%9CCch icago%E2%80%9D-wh-mcelroy/. Accessed 26 Nov. 2018.	Wow, Chicago was "self-asserting" and "boastful" before the fire. Now it's like, how the mighty have fallen. What does chaff mean?

Continuing to read about the aftermath of the fire, Kate finds accounts of chaos in the streets, loss of life and property, but she stays alert for any further references to Chicago's comeuppance. Browsing the official documents section of the Great Fire website, Kate finds a proclamation that stops her cold:

> In view of the recent appalling public calamity, the under-signed, Mayor of Chicago, hereby earnestly recommends that all the inhabitants of this city do observe Sunday, October 29, as a special day of humiliation and prayer; of humiliation for those past offenses against Almighty God, to whom these severe afflictions were doubtless intended to lead our minds....
>
> Given under my hand this 20th day of October, 1871.
> R.B. MASON, Mayor

> *Report of the Chicago Relief and Aid Society.* Riverside Press, 1874, p. 21.

Up until now, Kate has read comments on Chicago's "self-assert-ing ways" by outside observers. However, this is a proclamation from Chicago's own mayor, with a suggestion that the fire might have been punishment for "past offenses against Almighty God." Kate writes in her notes: *Does the Mayor think the fire is a punishment for Chicago's sins? Did other people feel this way?*

Synthesizing Material to Tighten Focus

As we saw in Chapters Three and Four, taking notes is more than a great way to study; note-taking sparks new ideas. While taking notes, students ask questions. *What does this mean? What is going on here? Why does he say that?* As you take notes, you draw connections between this material and class discussion or your own experience. This process of drawing connections is known as synthesis. Making connections and pulling together material in notes, you can delve deeper and narrow a research topic even further.

Kate is shocked by the notion that the Great Fire was a disaster Chicago had coming to it. She herself has spent time volunteering in a homeless shelter and offering her nursing skills to homeless people in a medical van staffed by doctors from her hospital. Now as she studies the aftermath of the Great Fire and sees the finger-pointing going on, she writes in her notes, *It's blaming the victim. Why do people always do that?* She reviews her sources and her notes and she finds that she returns again and again to this theme of blaming the victim. Instead of continuing to read broadly about the aftermath of the fire, she will focus on this question of blame.

For Best Results, Re-Search

The best research happens twice. The initital search is a broad survey. A second search is focused. You return to your material knowing what you want to learn. Many researchers make their best discoveries on later forays. As scientist Louis Pasteur said, "chance favors the prepared mind."

Kate's initial research involved trawling widely for sources on the Great Fire. Sorting through her sources, she decided to focus on the aftermath of the fire. Taking notes, Kate tightened her focus further to investigate the notion that Chicago had it coming. At this point Kate searches online and in the library with a strong sense of direction. She is literally re-searching for material.

Now Kate looks specifically for sources blaming Chicago after the fire. Knowing what she wants, she can search more quickly, ruling out irrelevant information. Equally important, she is becoming increasingly curious about what she can find. For example, the Great Fire website only posts an excerpt from the article "Chicago in Distress." If she can track down the full article, will she find more material about Chicago's shoddy building materials and poor urban planning? She cannot find the complete text online, but she does discover that Olmsted's essays have been published in seven volumes. She goes to the library and reads the full essay in volume six. Here she finds what she was looking for. Olmsted believes that the Great Fire was more than an architectural disaster. It was a financial and moral disaster as well.

It was a maxim in Chicago that a fool could hardly invest in city real estate so badly that, if he could manage to hold it for five years, its advance would fail to give him more than ten percent interest, while there was a chance for a small fortune. Acting on this view, most young professional men and men on small salaries, if they had families, bought a lot and built a small house of themselves, confident that by hook or by crook they should save enough to pay the interest as it fell due on the necessary mortgage, together with the cost of insurance. To accomplish this they lived pinching, and their houses and lots were their only reserves. In thousands of cases, they have lost their houses, their insurance, and their situations all at one blow. Fifty of the insurance companies doing business here have suspended payment, seven of them being Chicago companies, whose directors were men of local influence and often employers.

The Papers of Frederick Law Olmsted. Johns Hopkins University Press, 1992, Vol. VI, p. 487.

He makes Chicago sound like a sleazy get-rich-quick type of place.

Young men bought land and built houses, but never saved money.

The fire destroyed those houses and wiped out their savings.

The insurance companies lost everything too and could not pay out insurance? What??

Is he saying Chicago was a nasty place, worse than other cities? Or just that it had bad luck?

Or is he saying Chicago's get-rich-quick mentality led to its downfall?

Kate re-searches for scholarly articles as well, because she wants to see if others notice what she does. Returning to the online databases, she finds a promising article: "The Great Chicago Fire as a National Event," by John J. Pauly in *American Quarterly*, an academic journal published by Johns Hopkins University Press. She also finds a book in the library called *American Apocalypse: The Great Fire and the Myth of Chicago*.

Developing an Annotated Bibliography

In addition to documentation of sources within the text, longer research-based assignments often require a bibliography, containing full citations for each source consulted. A bibliography typically appears at the end of a research project. However, some instructors require students to turn in at least a partial bibliography early in the research process. Kate's instructor assigns the annotated bibliography first so that he can check students' progress and make suggestions before they start drafting.

There are many bibliographic styles, but Kate's instructor chooses the format of the Modern Language Association, which lists sources alphabetically by author. Kate uses IDEA to introduce, document, explain, and assess each source. (To learn more about IDEA, see Chapter Eight.) Her initial entries look like this:

Mason, R.B. "Proclamation." Chicago, 20 Oct. 1871, *The Great Fire of Chicago and the Web of Memory*, Chicago Historical Society and Northwestern University, 2011, www.greatchicagofire.org/rescue-and-relief-library/official-actions/. Accessed 17 Nov. 2014.

This was a proclamation by the Mayor of Chicago, announcing a day of prayer and humiliation in response to the fire. The mayor refers to "past offenses" by the city and strongly suggests that the fire was a punishment for wrongdoing. I am interested in the way the mayor consistently uses the word humiliation, as though the people might have deserved the destruction of their city.

Pauly, John. "The Great Chicago Fire as a National Event."
American Quarterly, vol. 36, no. 5, 1984, pp. 668–83.

In this article John Pauly describes how news of the
Great Fire was transmitted throughout the country and
the world via telegraph. It was the first disaster of such
great proportions in the age of the telegraph and so word
got out so much faster than in previous disasters. The
fire and the response to the fire was national, not just
regional. I found this article very significant to my own
research because it talks about how disturbed people
were by the fire and how they—like Chicago's own
mayor—wondered if the fire was a punishment. According
to Pauly, sermons all over the country focused on the fire.

Drawing upon Research to Develop a Thesis Statement

After gathering, sorting, and taking notes on several sources,
you may feel in a better position to come up with a thesis statement.

Kate

I hope that's true!

Kate has collected sources with a common theme—a view of the
Great Fire as punishment. The scholarly works she has discovered
provide a historical perspective on this theme. She has a clear focus,
but she needs to interpret the evidence and support her interpretation. She needs a thesis statement.

Kate takes a walk. She rereads her notes. Finally, she rereads her
assignment. *Explore the cultural significance of a historical event....*
Rereading her assignment helps the most, because it provides a
frame for her observations. She can write about blaming Chicago

as a major cultural response to the tragedy. She tries out a thesis statement close to the wording of her assignment.

> The Great Fire of Chicago was culturally significant because after the fire people acted as though the city was at least partly responsible for its own destruction.

At first Kate is relieved that she came up with any kind of thesis. Then as she rereads her own sentence, she thinks, no, this isn't very good. She isn't sure that blaming the city makes the fire culturally significant, and she feels that she is simplifying a complex situation. She needs to set up her idea of blame. Why were people so quick to see the fire as punishment? Kate starts pacing around, talking to herself.

Kate

It's like when things are going amazingly well, you're almost superstitious that everything could fall apart. Chicago was growing so fast. People were making money. Industry and transportation were taking off. Then boom. One fire and literally everything goes up in smoke. That's so traumatic. People think, oh wow. Life is so fragile. This city's success was too good to be true.

With these thoughts in mind, Kate introduces her thesis statement.

> The 1871 Great Fire of Chicago was an important historical event leading to new building codes, insurance laws, and fire awareness, but it was culturally significant as well. Contemporary documents demonstrate that people searched for meaning in the tragedy and began blaming the city for its own destruction, treating the fire as a parable of greed and ambition.

Developing this paragraph, Kate prepares her reader for her thesis:

> People searching for meaning began treating the fire as a parable of greed and ambition.

In her thesis, Kate stakes her claim, announcing her interpretation of primary sources. In her view the fire became a flashpoint, and a warning. People looked at the devastation in Chicago and they said, this is what happens to greedy, ambitious people.

Building a Draft from Notes

The good news about writing up a research project is that you have a lot of material with which to work. Informed by multiple sources, supported by the work of other investigators, and armed with your own notes, you will not write in isolation. The bad news is that you have a lot of material. It can be challenging to organize so much evidence. If you do not know where to start, consider using your introduction and your thesis as your guide. As we saw in Chapter Six, the thesis can provide a blueprint for your paper, setting the parameters of your argument and limiting the scope of your investigation. At times the thesis articulates the order of supporting points within the paper.

Kate's thesis refers to contemporary documents. She decides that she will discuss each in turn to demonstrate the way people blamed Chicago for its own destruction. She builds her draft from her notes on each source.

> Blaming the Victim: The Aftermath of the Great Fire of Chicago
>
> The 1871 Great Fire of Chicago was an important historical event leading to new building codes, insurance laws and fire awareness, but it was culturally significant as well. Using a proclamation, a poem, a newspaper account, and scholarly sources, this paper will show how people searched for meaning in the tragedy and began blaming

the city for its own destruction, treating the fire as a parable of greed and ambition.

One of the first examples of blame came from the Mayor himself, who issued a proclamation just ten days after the fire ended. He called for a day of "humiliation and prayer; of humiliation for those past offenses against Almighty God, to whom these severe afflictions were doubtless intended to lead our minds" (Mason). By referring to past offenses against God, the Mayor takes a very religious perspective on the tragedy which has just happened. He clearly thinks that the fire is a punishment and also meant to serve as a lesson, leading people's minds to think about their wrongdoing.

In another harsh example of blaming the city, the landscape architect Frederick Law Olmsted wrote an article in *The Nation* accusing Chicago of building too much, too fast, and too close together....

Peer Review for a Research Project

It is helpful to show your work to a friend or classmate because you can gauge your reader's response. Is your friend confused? Intrigued? Falling asleep? Peer review supplies an audience and requires you to spell out your findings for someone unfamiliar with your sources. Not all peers provide detailed and insightful comments. However, most can provide a reality check, answering every writer's fundamental question. *Does this make any sense to you?*

After finishing her draft, Kate and her classmate Cole exchange drafts for peer editing. Cole reads and marks Kate's paper, adding several questions. *ID the Mayor? Clarify that this is the Mayor of Chicago—I wasn't sure.*

Kate addresses these suggestions quickly, but she isn't sure what to do about Cole's larger comment at the end of her paper. *Really interesting about the fire. My first reaction was I can't believe I've never heard of it. My main problem is I didn't understand where you were going. There was the Mayor, the architecture, the poem, etc., and I was confused because you jumped around from one source to another so I didn't get the clearest picture. (Sorry! Maybe it's me!) You did a ton of research but maybe it's too much for one paper?*

Kate is frustrated by Cole's comment, because she thinks her examples fit together extremely well. She sees the connections between the parts of her paper and it bothers her that Cole doesn't understand the argument she has been building. Did she actually fail to explain herself? Or is Cole not reading carefully? The more she thinks about it, the more she thinks that maybe the ideas in her mind are not coming across in writing. She brings this up at her conference with her instructor.

KATE I feel like my ideas are not coming across. In peer review, Cole just didn't get what I was trying to say. He thinks my sources are interesting, but they don't fit together.

DR. C. What do you think?

KATE I don't know. I see the connections, but maybe it's because I know my sources so well.

DR. C. You make a good point. You've studied this material, but your reader hasn't. You've got to draw the connections among your sources and spell out how each one contributes.

KATE So I need better transitions between paragraphs?

DR. C. Transitions always help, but in this case I think you need to think about the structure of your paper as a whole.

KATE *thinking—Oh no! He's going to make me rewrite the whole thing!*

DR. C. Right now you jump from one source to the next. You need to explain why you chose these particular examples. You've got terrific supporting points, and you've got an intriguing thesis, but you need to take control of your material. Right now your examples are controlling you.

KATE Okay.

DR. C. And don't forget your scholarly sources. You need to integrate those too.

KATE *Aaaargh*!

Revising a Research Paper

Research involves gathering information. Writing up your findings requires you to show how your material fits together. It's fine to begin with detailed notes, a list of facts, or even a series of paragraphs describing what you've found, but as you write up your work it's important to remember that what seems obvious to you may not seem obvious to your reader. As a writer you need to connect the dots.

After meeting with her instructor, Kate rereads her paper. To her surprise, after time away, she sees that she does jump from one example to the next. It's also true that she neglects to explain how her diverse sources fit together.

Kate

Maybe the reason he doesn't think my sources are as amazing as I do is that I don't show how powerful they are.

CONTROLLING THE EVIDENCE SO THE EVIDENCE DOESN'T CONTROL YOU

Kate believes in her thesis, and she is genuinely interested in her material. She decides that she is going to find a way to control and showcase her examples. As Kate rereads her work, she stops at her introduction. Her instructor suggests that she needs to address the differences among her sources as well as their common theme. Maybe this is the way to go. Kate makes a list of her sources and summarizes each in just a few words.

- Mayor's proclamation: the fire was at least partly our fault; we should repent (moral disaster)
- Olmsted: Chicago brought this on itself with shoddy building practices (technical disaster)
- Poem: Ha ha, they thought they were so great. Serves Chicago right (mockery)

She rewrites her introduction, grouping her sources into three categories. Moral finger pointing, technical finger pointing, and satirical mockery. We underline her additions.

> The 1871 Great Fire of Chicago was an important historical event leading to many reforms of building codes and insurance laws, but it was culturally significant as well. <u>Contemporary documents show how people searched for meaning in the tragedy and began blaming the city for its own destruction. Some took a religious approach, blaming citizens for their sins. Some focused on technical problems, blaming Chicago for building too much too fast with poor construction and shoddy materials. Some satirized Chicago for thinking it was the greatest. Chicago got it from all sides, but in each case, people treated the fire as a parable of greed and ambition.</u>

Kate's new introduction presents a three-part structure. She will discuss three kinds of blame: religious, technical, and satirical. Instead of discussing one source after another, she will organize her paper thematically. The new structure allows her to address differences among her sources even as she demonstrates that they develop the theme of blame. Organizing thematically also allows her to add sources at will. If she wants to discuss sermons or other moralistic interpretations, she can add them to the section on moralistic blame. If she wants to talk about posters and cartoons as well as poems, she can add them to her section on satiric blame.

She begins revising the body of her paper.

> The fire was so dramatic and devastating that many people wondered if it was divine retribution. Roswell Mason, the Mayor of Chicago, issued a proclamation on October 20th, 1871, just ten days after the fire ended. He called for a day of "humiliation and prayer; of humiliation for those past offenses against Almighty God, to whom these severe afflictions were doubtless intended to lead our minds" (Mason). By referring to past offenses against God, the Mayor takes a very religious perspective on

the tragedy which has just happened. He clearly thinks that the fire is a punishment and also meant to serve as a lesson, leading people's minds to think about their wrongdoing. The Mayor seems to think everybody should blame themselves for the fire and take a day to think about their sins.

Not everyone used such religious rhetoric about the fire. The landscape architect Frederick Law Olmsted concentrated on technical issues when he wrote an article in *The Nation* accusing Chicago of building too much, too fast and too close together. However, even this technical analysis begins with language of blame. "Chicago has a weakness for 'big things' and liked to think that it was outbuilding New York" (Olmstead 487). Olmsted focuses primarily on bad urban planning, but even he can't resist speculating about the ambition and greed that motivated overbuilding the city.

Working with a thematic structure, Kate feels less overwhelmed by her sources. Her paper seems less like a list of examples and more like an argument.

Kate

Rereading my first draft I did feel like I was lurching from one source to the next. Now I'm sorting my sources into three bins: religious, technical, and satirical. All the bins have something in common—they are all about blaming Chicago for its own tragedy, but I can talk about the differences among my sources as well.

RESPONDING TO OTHER RESEARCHERS

While it might seem like solitary work on the computer, in the library, or even in the lab, research is actually an extended conversation in which investigators present their work to each other, discussing, debating, and augmenting discoveries. Writing up your research project allows you to enter that conversation. To this end, some research assignments require students to find, read, and respond to scholarly articles on their topic. But where will you find room to discuss these scholarly sources? And how can you enter a conversation with scholars without detracting from your own argument?

Kate goes to the college writing center and speaks to a tutor named Akiko.

KATE I just don't know how to integrate scholarly work. I found a great article, but the author actually says some of the same things I do!

AKIKO What's wrong with that? You can use the article as supporting evidence.

KATE But I found my sources and figured out my thesis state-ment on my own. If I start talking about his paper, it will just look like I copied his ideas.

AKIKO Does he really make the same argument as yours?

KATE Not exactly. He's talking more about the fire as a national symbol, and I'm focused on the way people blamed the city for its own destruction.

AKIKO Why don't you say that in your paper? So and so writes convinc-ingly about the fire as a national symbol. However, I focus on ...

KATE The blame embedded in that national symbol.

AKIKO Exactly!

KATE Hold on. I'm writing that down.

Kate

It was actually kind of empowering to use scholarly sources. I realized it's my paper and mentioning other researchers was not going to change that. Where scholars supported me I pointed that out and it strengthened my argument. Where I had different ideas, I pointed that out too.

Jordan

My instructor told me about this book on organizational behavior which has a theory of leadership that makes perfect sense when you apply it to sports. I cited this theory and used it as a framework for my own observations in my research paper. I gave the author full credit for coming up with the theory, but my instructor said my paper was really creative, because nobody had ever applied this theory to Ultimate before.

REFLECT: Have you consulted the work of other scholars in a writing project? What was your experience? Was it difficult to find useful scholarly work on your topic? How did you use that work? Do you recognize any of your own methods or frustrations in Kate's research process? If not, how has your experience differed?

Kate can use other voices to define and refine her ideas, and she has developed several ways to signal to her reader what she is doing: *I see their point about the proclamation, but I would like to add … I agree with those who write about the fire as a national symbol, but my focus is a little different … This is a compelling discussion, but it glosses over an essential aspect of the crisis …* Phrases like these allow Kate to **pivot**, turning from one idea to another, acknowledging other voices and then asserting her own contribution, qualification, or counter example.

Kate returns to her draft and tries this approach, citing scholar John Pauly to support and extend her observation that many people wondered if the fire was divine retribution.

The fire was so dramatic and devastating that many people wondered if it was divine retribution. In his article "The Great Chicago Fire as a National Event," John J. Pauly writes that the Sunday after the fire, sermons all over the country focused on the tragedy (Pauly 668).

Next, Kate acknowledges Pauly's larger thesis and pivots to explain that her own focus is slightly different. We underline her pivot.

Pauly argues that the fire was not just a local event, but a national one, partly because the telegraph got the news out so fast. He is interested in the scope of the response to the fire, but my focus here is on the content of that response, which was extremely moralistic inside and outside the city. Just ten days after the fire ended, Mayor Roswell Mason issued a proclamation on October 20th, 1871. He called for a day of "humiliation and prayer; of humiliation for those past offenses against Almighty God, to whom these severe afflictions were doubtless intended to lead our minds." By referring to past offenses against God, the Mayor takes a very religious perspective on the tragedy which has just happened....

Multi-Modal Research

Research takes many forms. Research-based writing assignments can take many forms as well. While Kate's instructor assigns a research essay, another instructor may ask students to conduct and transcribe an interview, or to prepare an oral presentation, or to draft a lab report based on experiments conducted in class. You can apply steps of initial search, and re-search, sorting, note-taking, and developing your own perspective to many research assignments. Let's take a look.

Anna's instructor asks students to prepare an online portfolio of materials in multiple formats—not just text or images but audio and video; not just books and articles, but social media and online forums. This kind of research is known as **multi-modal**, because it draws upon—and uses—multiple modes of communication. Anna's assignment reads:

> A question has more than one side, and a debate can take many forms. Create an online portfolio devoted to a current political issue or dispute. Collect and present diverse points of view and draw upon sources in multiple formats.
>
> Your sources should include text, images, audio, and video. You are the curator of this collection, and so it is up to you to organize and introduce us to each exhibit.
>
> Deliverables at the end of this project will include
> - contributions to the class blog in which you post twice a week on your research process and progress;
> - a two-to-three-page introduction to the collection, defining the question or public issue you have chosen, and explaining how you will present your material;
> - a one paragraph discussion of every object in the collection. Use IDEA to identify, document, explain, and assess.

Anna will not be writing a formal research paper, but her process parallels the one Kate follows.

IDENTIFYING A TOPIC

Current political issue? There are so many. Anna begins by jotting down political issues in the news. *Race, immigration, climate change, pollution, homelessness, overcrowded prisons.* All important subjects. She adds a few more topics to the list. *Unemployment, student loans, status of women.* When Anna thinks about the status of women, she considers her own status. She is a woman who will be graduating in a couple of years, and looking for a job. Entry-level salaries are low, and she's heard that women earn even less than men. Is this true? Is it even legal? Anna looks up the phrase *women earn less* and comes up with articles, speeches, and interviews on "the gender pay gap." The more she finds, the more questions she has. This is a topic she finds particularly intriguing.

GATHERING AND SORTING SOURCES

Searching for data on women's salaries, Anna googles *women* and *pay gap*. Immediately she finds several articles asserting that women earn only 78 cents for every dollar a man earns. Graphs and charts illustrate the pay gap as well.

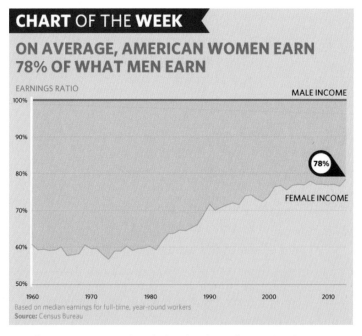

https://www.whitehouse.gov/sites/default/files/image/paygapchart.jpg

Anna's instructor asks students to comment on their research progress on a class blog. Anna posts her first entry on her initial search for information.

> I was looking for the most relevant and reliable sources. When I found this chart on the White House website I decided to use it because the source was official and also the data on the graph comes from the US Census. I also chose this graph because the income gap shocked me!
>
> Then when I went back to document the graph I couldn't find it anymore. It looked like someone took it down from the White House website — but I really wanted to use it. I'm not sure what to do.

Anna's instructor suggests using the graph with the old URL but noting that it is no longer available online. She also provides students with an online portfolio template and directions for using it. Anna uploads news articles about the pay gap, along with video clips of several politicians announcing *It's time to declare an end to the pay gap*.

Many of Anna's sources come from the government. The White House, the Department of Labor, and the US Census seem reliable. However, Anna's assignment requires exploring multiple sides to a question. Are there other perspectives on the pay gap?

Anna refines her search, adding *controversy* as a key term. Now Anna finds radio interviews with writers who talk about the myth of gender inequality. Anna refines her search further with *myth* as a key term and finds an opinion piece in *Time* magazine identifying the pay gap as one of "Five Feminist Myths That Will Not Die." She also finds an opinion piece in *Forbes* magazine with the headline "It's Time to End the Pay Gap Myth."

A cache of articles and interviews emphasize that citizens should look critically at the statistic *78 cents to the dollar*. Anti-pay-gap writers and speakers insist that this ratio falls apart if we consider the fact that more women work part time, and women take lower paying jobs. These writers argue that the so-called pay gap comes from comparing all working women to all working men and not by comparing women and men working the same job. Often, when Anna checks the bio of an author, she discovers that writers on this subject divide along political lines. Those advocating for closing the pay gap tend to identify as feminist, liberal, and progressive. Those arguing that the gap is a myth tend to identify as conservative. However, these categories overlap at times. Some of the writers convinced that the pay gap is a myth identify as feminist as well.

Anna

In my initial research I thought I was just looking for discussions of the pay gap and how to make it disappear. I didn't realize that there are thoughtful people who don't think a pay gap exists! Now I'm starting to think it's important to look at both sides of the issue, and present both points of view in my portfolio because this thing is more complicated than I thought.

Evaluating Each Source for Relevance and Reliability

Politicians, economists, and writers trumpet allegiances and credentials, but Anna realizes that she needs to evaluate each of these sources for relevance and reliability. She asks herself—is this an elected official? An academic expert? An activist? A seemingly rational citizen? What appeals does this person make? And what kind of evidence does this person employ? Anna tries to select sources that support claims with well documented evidence. As a researcher she gravitates toward others who have done research of their own.

After discovering critics of the pay gap concept, Anna finds numerous rebuttals arguing that yes, there IS a pay gap between men and women working the same hours at the same jobs. Political speeches argue that the gap is "math not myth" and insist that even if we take into account all the factors critics mention, women still earn significantly less than men. On a discussion forum at the *Seattle Times*, Anna discovers dozens of citizens debating the issue. At first the forum seems like a great resource because it provides so many voices. However, after the first dozen comments, the debate devolves into an online shouting match.

She wonders whether to include the fan forum. The intense debate is highly relevant but the debaters seem far from reliable. They seem to limit themselves to appeals to pathos and provide no evidence for their claims. She writes in her research blog:

> In this project I have to sort out reliable from unreliable sources. A lot of economists — including people at the Department of Labor — think there is a pay gap. Others, including some politicians, think the pay gap is a myth. Then there are ordinary citizens like the people on the discussion forum. I think I can include them only with a note pointing out that some are coming from an angry and argumentative place!
>
> Another thing I have to think about is what statistics mean. What does 78 cents really measure? Where do these numbers come from? Do they say something important about women? Is the injustice real?

Using IDEA to Prepare an Online Portfolio

Whether writing a research essay, an annotated bibliography or compiling an online portfolio, it is essential to introduce and document material. Just as Kate used IDEA to introduce, document, explain, and assess her sources, Anna uses IDEA to present each source in her online collection. She begins with identification and documentation, including a web link for every online source, then continues with an explanation and assessment of the object. One

Bennett, Clay. "Equal Pay." *Chattanooga Times Free Press*, 31 Jan. 2009., www.timesfreepress.com/news/editorialcartoons/story/2009/jan/31/equal-pay/205834/. Accessed 30 Jan. 2019.

of her exhibits is a political cartoon illustrating the gender pay gap. She introduces the image with the label: Political Cartoon on Gender Pay Gap.

After the cartoon, she describes the image, explains and assesses it.

In this cartoon the artist depicts a man and a woman working side by side. The woman is reading a newspaper with the headline WOMEN PAID 78% OF WHAT MEN MAKE, and with her droopy eyes she looks exhausted and downtrodden. Her male office mate asks, "So, what is seventy-eight percent of doodly squat?" This comment refers to the fact that women earn three-quarters of what men earn, a little over 78 cents on the dollar. The comment also makes a connection between salary and intrinsic worth. Earning three-quarters of what a man earns, then maybe this woman's ideas are worth only three-quarters too? The cartoon shows that man and woman are working at identical desks with identical telephones and computers. Visually they look like they are working at equal jobs. Why then would they be paid unequal salaries? Notice as well that both the workers here are white. Statistics show that the pay gap is even greater between a white man and a woman of color.

She follows the same process with her next exhibit, a graph.

BAR GRAPH ILLUSTRATING GENDER WAGE GAP BY RACE

This simple but powerful graph visualizes how much less women earn than men, but takes it one step further to show that the inequity increases for women of color. A white woman earns 78 cents on the dollar, but an African American woman earns only 64 cents. Latina women earn least of all—only 54 cents compared to a white man's dollar. Asian women earn more than

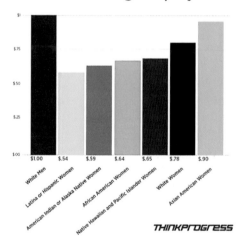

The Gender Wage Gap By Race

Petrohilos, Dylan. "The Gender Wage Gap by Race." *thinkprogress.org*, 18 Sept. 2014, https://thinkprogress. org/the-gender-wage-gap-is-a-chasm-for-women-of-color- in-one-chart-1e8824ee6707/. Accessed 20 Sept. 2018.

other women. Why? Is that because of the jobs they do? Some jobs pay more than others—for example, computer programmers make more than teacher's aides. It is very interesting to see that even within an inequity there can be more inequities. It is also interesting that people who believe the gender gap is a myth do not usually discuss the racial components of the gap. They stick to arguing that women do not really earn less than men.

Organizing the Portfolio

As Kate discovered while writing her research paper, gathering material is just the first step. Organizing that material is essential. A researcher has to make decisions about how to group and prioritize sources.

Anna has compiled a rich archive. Now the question is—how will she introduce and order the collection? She decides to begin by defining the gender gap and then discussing the debate about whether such a gap exists. She will divide her multi-modal collection into two parts: IDENTIFYING THE GENDER GAP and DENYING THE GENDER GAP.

The problem is that Anna has found material that does not fit neatly into either category. She has collected a series of articles by economists and other social scientists who debate how to measure the gender gap. These sources take a step back and deal with research methods. Still other sources make competing claims about what the gender gap means. Several video clips in Anna's collection present political speeches arguing that changes must be made to close the pay gap. However, the speakers disagree about what is to be done. They disagree about what the pay gap represents and, here again, they do not all define the pay gap in the same way. Anna asks her instructor about this after class.

ANNA   I'm just not sure how to organize my portfolio, because it is so diverse.

DR. M.   What have you got?

ANNA   Speeches against the pay gap. Speeches insisting there is no pay gap. Articles debating what method we should use to measure the pay gap. There are so many voices and points of view that I feel like I can't control them.

DR. M.   Anna, what is this portfolio, and what is your role? What is the rhetorical situation here?

ANNA   Well, the portfolio is not a magazine article, or a chapter in a book, or ... It's more like a museum.

DR. M.   Right. It's a virtual museum, and you're the curator. As curator, you get to decide what to present to the viewer. Including multiple points of view is excellent, but it is up to you to take charge in your introduction and frame the debate.

ANNA   So I can present my own point of view?

DR. M.   I think you've got to.

Writing an Introduction to the Portfolio

An introduction to an online portfolio categorizes, describes, and provides an initial assessment of the material the viewer will explore. Anna's introduction explains that she sorts her material into three categories. First she defines the pay gap and provides a tab to access the page of her collection titled WHAT IS THE GENDER PAY GAP? Second, she explains that many experts disagree about how to measure that gap. She provides a tab for viewers to access her collection HOW DO WE MEASURE A PAY GAP? Third, she discusses the debate about whether the gap is real or not. A tab allows viewers to access her collection PAY GAP—MATH OR MYTH? Finally, Anna presents her own point of view as she introduces a fourth category.

People can argue all they want about how to define and measure the gender pay gap. They can also keep arguing about whether the pay gap exists. At the end of the day the pay gap is a way to try to quantify a much larger more complicated problem which extends far beyond how much women earn compared to men. It is not just lower salaries for the same work that is the problem. It is also worse jobs. As critics of the pay gap point out, most women are not even in the same league jobwise as the men, so it is harder to compare their salaries. Worse jobs. Lower level positions. Fewer opportunities. This is the larger injustice, and the pay gap is only part of that. There is a leadership gap between women and men, and there is an opportunity gap. Go here for PART FOUR of the portfolio. THE BIGGER PICTURE.

Anna's introduction orients visitors to her virtual museum. Writing it helps Anna to orient herself as well. The writing process helps her to think more deeply about a political debate. She writes in her research blog.

It was studying other points of view that helped me to define my own. Collecting diverse material pushed me to examine and defend my own opinions. I learned that I could be fair and look at multiple sides, but I could write my own assessment as well.

Research can be an exhilarating process of discovery, but research alone won't inform others. Whether you are writing a traditional research paper or working in a new format, writing up your research allows you to introduce your findings, to explain your thinking, and, above all, to present your own conclusions about your material. Writing clearly and accurately, supporting your assertions with credible sources, you can provide readers with valuable ideas and information. Writing about research, you have a chance to enter into conversation with others who have thought deeply about your topic. You also have a chance to enlighten and inspire those who have not thought about your topic before.

The best research starts with a compelling
desire to know.
Research can take many forms.
Writing about research also takes many forms.

Research Process

- Choose a topic that intrigues you
- Gather information twice: Initial search and re-search
- Select sources for relevance and reliability
- Think about how to organize sources
- Consider which are most useful and informative as you investigate your topic

Presenting Research

- Consider the genre you will use
- Consider how to reach (and teach!) your audience
- If you are writing a research paper, draw upon your research to come up with a thesis statement
- If you are presenting in another format, consider how you want to convey information
- Use IDEA to introduce, document, explain, and assess your sources
- Present your own ideas in response to the ideas of others

ACTIVITIES

1 Each of the following discusses the use of pesticides. Study each source and answer these questions. Who do you think is the intended audience? What is the genre? What is the message? What rhetorical appeals can you identify? Do you think this is a reliable source? Why or why not? If you are unsure, how might you check?

From Food and Water Action.

Petition: Ban Roundup and Dicamba!

Hundreds of millions of pounds of glyphosate, a "probable human carcinogen," are used on farmland across America every year.

We are exposed to this toxic chemical in our food, air and water every day, and the EPA and FDA are not doing enough to protect us.

And dicamba, another Monsanto weedkiller packaged to work with several new GMO crops, is wreaking havoc on farm communities. Dicamba has been drifting to neighboring fields, where it damages MILLIONS of acres of crops and has even been accused of reducing honey production.

We should not be exposed to unsafe or toxic chemicals, pesticides or herbicides in our food, especially not "probable human carcinogens." The EPA and FDA are not doing enough to protect us from these exposures and potential health problems.

Sign the petition to urge the EPA and the FDA to end the use of Roundup and dicamba!

"Petition: Ban Roundup and Dicamba!" *Food and Water Action,* www.secure.foodandwaterwatch.org/act/
    petition-ban-roundup-and-dicamba. Accessed 26 Nov. 2018.

From Pesticides in Perspective.

Crop protection products, also known as pesticides, are chemical or biological substances used to control unwanted pests that can harm our food, health, or environment.

Pesticides are one of the vital tools that help farmers grow healthy crops, protecting our food supply against yield losses and damage caused by weeds, diseases and insects.

Without these products, crop yields and quality would fall, many foodstuffs would be in short supply, and food prices would rise.

Over 97% of UK farms use modern pesticides to deal with a range of pest problems. They can be formulated as liquids, granules or powders. Some are used pre-sowing as seed treatments, but most crop protection products are diluted in water and applied to crops using specialised spraying equipment.

Pesticides are also widely used outside agriculture, for example, to improve the quality of gardens, golf courses, and sports pitches, and to maintain the safety of our roads and railways.

Advances in product development, formulation, and application ensure that modern pesticides are safer, more precisely targeted, and more rapidly degraded in the environment than ever before.

"Introduction to Pesticides." *Pesticides in Perspective,* www.pesticidesinperspective.org.uk/pesticides/ posts/2015/introduction-to-pesticides. Accessed 26 Nov. 2018.

5,000 YEARS OF CROP PROTECTION

3000BC
The Ancient Sumerians use sulfur to control insects.

600BC
Greeks and Romans use oil, ash, sulfur and other materials to control insects.

1600s
Farmers use tobacco infusions (nicotine) and a range of herbs.

1800s
Sulfur and copper compounds are used to protect fruit, vegetables and plants.

MODERN METHODS

1930s
The era of synthetic (man made) crop protection begins, increasing yields far beyond pre-World War II levels and supporting the Green Revolution in India.

1940s
Weed control is revolutionized with the herbicide 2,4-D. Farmers use it to control weeds.

1960s
First generation of pyrethroids is developed to fight insects. Today they are widely used in agriculture and make up the majority of household insecticides.

1970s
The herbicide glyphosate is commercialized and gains popularity for its broad spectrum weed control and low toxicity to animal life.

"5000 Years of Crop Protection." *CropLife International*, https://croplife.org/news/5000-years-of-crop-protection/. Accessed 27 Nov. 2018. We have omitted some of this image for space reasons. See the full image online.

ABSTRACT

During the last 50 years, agricultural intensification has caused many wild plant and animal species to go extinct regionally or nationally and has profoundly changed the functioning of agro-ecosystems. Agricultural intensification has many components, such as loss of landscape elements, enlarged farm and field sizes and larger inputs of fertilizer and pesticides. However, very little is known about the relative contribution of these variables to the large-scale negative effects on biodiversity. In this study, we disentangled the impacts of various components of agricultural intensification on species diversity of wild plants, carabids and ground-nesting farmland birds and on the biological control of aphids.

In a Europe-wide study in eight West and East European countries, we found important negative effects of agricultural intensification on wild plant, carabid and bird species diversity and on the potential for biological pest control, as estimated from the number of aphids taken by predators. Of the 13 components of intensification we measured, use of insecticides and fungicides had consistent negative effects on biodiversity. Insecticides also reduced the biological control potential. Organic farming and other agri-environment schemes aiming to mitigate the negative effects of intensive farming on biodiversity did increase the diversity of wild plant and carabid species, but — contrary to our expectations — not the diversity of breeding birds.

We conclude that despite decades of European policy to ban harmful pesticides, the negative effects of pesticides on wild plant and animal species persist, at the same time reducing the opportunities for biological pest control. If biodiversity is to be restored in Europe and opportunities are to be created for crop production utilizing biodiversity-based ecosystem services such as biological pest control, there must be a Europe-wide shift towards farming with minimal use of pesticides over large areas.

Geiger, Flavia. "Persistent Negative Effects of Pesticides on Biodiversity and Biological Control Potential on European Farmland." *Basic and Applied Ecology*, vol. 11, no. 2, 2002, pp. 97–105.

2 The students in this book grapple with many topics as they complete their writing assignments. Some of these topics suggest areas for further research. Consider the following and write an annotated bibliography and a game plan for a research paper or portfolio for one of the topics.

Visions of Alice. Compare illusrations of the same scene in *Alice's Adventures in Wonderland* or another children's book or fairy tale. (For reference, glance back at Jordan's work on illustrations in Chapter Four.)

The Psychology of Happiness: Truth or Trend? Happiness is a growing field of study in psychology. But is happiness measurable? Are studies of happiness scientific? Create a portfolio and a timeline of this young field. Include results of three experiments and examples of happiness studies in the popular press. Include examples from critics of "happiness studies" as well. (For reference, take a look at Jordan's discussion of an article on unexpected rewards and happiness in Chapter Three.)

Food, Income, and Geography: How America Malnourishes Its Poor. Often the urban poor simply do not have access to nutritious food. They live in what are called "food deserts"—neighborhoods with fast food and convenience stores, but no actual groceries. Create a poster or infographic mapping a food desert. Show the distance between housing and stores, the location of bus and subway stations, and the time it would take to get to different stores. Include prices of snacks in convenience stores versus prices of ingredients from a supermarket. (For reference, consider the discussion of developing a thesis on food deserts in Chapter Six.)

Technology and Cultural Change: How an Invention Changes Lives—for Better and for Worse. How can one appliance, or technological innovation, change so much? Choose an everyday appliance or innovation, and research ways that it has changed lives. Gather images and advertisements, eye-witness accounts by users, a timeline of historical and cultural events, and analyses by scholars. Consider what you think the cultural significance of your chosen innovation might be. Write an annotated bibliography and an introduction with thesis for a research project. (For reference, look at Kate's work developing a thesis on the cultural significance of the refrigerator in Chapter Six, and her work writing a paper on the Great Fire of Chicago in Chapter Nine.)

Literary Lives. How do writers articulate their purpose? Do writers' autobiographical statements shed light on their work? Can those statements also be misleading? Consider some of Chinua Achebe's published work, along with his full interview in the *Paris Review* (Zach summarizes a short passage in Chapter Three). Alternatively, choose another writer to investigate.

10

VOICE AND STYLE

JORDAN   I've got the conclusion for my psych paper. Ready?

ANNA   Sure.

JORDAN   No, are you *ready*? This is good.

ANNA   Ready!

JORDAN   Here's the thing about happiness. For most of us, it's not just about having enough. It's about having MORE. It's not enough if nothing bad happens and nobody screws up. We're only happy if today is the BEST. Anything less than amazing does not qualify. That's how crazy entitled humans are.

ANNA   Hmm.

JORDAN   What? You don't like it?

ANNA   I do, but is it okay to say "screws up" in a paper? I'm not sure about "crazy entitled," either.

JORDAN   So you're saying take out all the personality from my writing.

ANNA   No, maybe just tone it down.

JORDAN   Tone it down? You want me to take out everything that sounds like ME!

What Is Voice?

Think about the people you know. How do you recognize them? By face, by posture, by their hair, their eyeglasses, by the way they walk—those are all visual cues. You also recognize people aurally, by voice. In conversation you can quickly pick out a familiar voice— deep or high pitched, scratchy or smooth, emphatic, or mellow, or strong or breathy. On the phone, you can recognize a friend by voice alone. Every speaker has a voice. Writers have voices too. Voice is the distinctive way a writer has with words.

Voice sets your work apart. Voice is your affinity for certain words and expressions and your avoidance of others. Voice is the rhythm of your prose. Voice reflects your history with language—the way you talk and the way you listen; the way you read and the way you respond to other speakers and writers. Your voice is what you bring to the page. Why, then, does Anna caution Jordan about using certain words and expressions? She worries that Jordan is coming on too strong, and that his language might sound inappropriate in a formal essay. She worries, and Jordan takes offense. It's a tricky question. How much of yourself can you bring to college writing?

HOW CAN I MAINTAIN MY OWN VOICE IN COLLEGE WRITING?
Some students believe that writing in college requires adopting a formal voice that doesn't sound remotely their own. Zach tried this with the opening of his lottery paper.

> Since the dawn of history, gambling has been a part of the human experience, with lotteries playing a large role in society elevating the poor to the very rich with just a stroke of chance. Captivating the imagination, the lottery has become an irrational obsession for millions in the present day who end up contributing to a hugely powerful revenue stream for the state.

Writing in this elaborate way comes across as a bid to impress, and often raises a red flag for instructors. Is Zach padding paragraphs with verbiage, or trying to cover for lack of preparation? What is he actually saying? His writing does not sound authentic or direct.

In contrast, some students write the way they talk, transcribing their casual speaking voice. Writing casually and conversationally can cause problems as well because everyday speech is often less precise and rigorous than the language college instructors expect. Face to face, talking to a friend, you can count on your listener to pick up on all kinds of non-verbal cues—your smile, your self-deprecating gesture. You can also count on a friend to know you're a reasonable person, most of the time. In contrast, on the page, a reader judges you by words alone. In college your instructor does not know you well, and it is up to you to demonstrate that you are a reasonable person, and a prepared student. Broad generalizations (*the book was just BAD*), verbal shortcuts (*know what I mean?*) and colloquial phrases (*yeah, right!*) will not support you the way they do in conversation.

And yet, writing is a form of self-expression. Instructors say that they want to know what you think, and they ask you to use your own words. How can you maintain your own voice in college writing? The trick is to write in your own way while keeping the rhetorical situation in mind. Speakers pitch their voices to the situation, indoors or outdoors, classroom or football field, job interview or party. They adjust, modulate, and sometimes amplify their voices, depending on the audience—three friends sitting at a table, or 3,000 at a pep rally. Writers modulate their voices too, but, ideally, they maintain something of themselves. Consider how Jordan revises his work, modulating but maintaining his voice as a writer.

> **First Draft:** Here's the thing about happiness. For most of us, it's not just about having enough. It's about having MORE. It's not enough if nothing bad happens and nobody screws up. We're only happy if today is the BEST. Anything less than amazing does not qualify. That's how crazy entitled humans are.

> **Revision:** Here's the thing about happiness. For most of us it's not about having enough. It's about having more. We aren't happy with a normal day. We are only happy if today was amazing. Anything less does not qualify. This is how entitled humans are.

Jordan takes Anna's advice, deleting "nobody screws up" and "crazy entitled." He makes other subtle changes as well. Instead of writing MORE, he writes more. He grabs the reader with his first sentence, *here's the thing*, but he does not get up in the reader's face with his colloquial language or yell at the reader with ALL CAPS.

Jordan's challenge is to modulate his writing while maintaining his own voice. Zach needs to strip away the elaborate language he has adopted to reclaim his writing voice.

Anna

When I came to this country in high school, my English was very limited. In fact, I learned to speak English mostly from watching television, rather than from reading books. Now I feel that I speak well and understand everything, but I get nervous at times while writing because this is not my first language. If you say a writer's voice represents her history with language, my history is more with Spanish than English — so I'm still not sure what my so-called writer's voice in English will be!

Kate

As a returning student, I have been away from writing assignments for six years. I always liked writing, but I have not done it for a while, and I sometimes feel pretty rusty. I have been working full time and raising two kids, so I haven't had time to write at all. I enjoy research and organization, but it's not like my words are flowing onto the page. I build my assignments sentence by sentence, and I'm not sure my work expresses a distinctive writing voice.

First Draft: Since the dawn of history, gambling has been a part of the human experience, with lotteries playing a large role in society elevating the poor to the very rich with just a stroke of chance. Captivating the imagination, the lottery has become an irrational obsession for millions in the present day who end up contributing to a hugely powerful revenue stream for the state.

Revision: People have been gambling for a long time because they are obsessed with changing their fortunes in a moment. Currently, state lotteries have become an irrational obsession for millions of ticket buyers. Hoping they'll get lucky, they end up contributing to a huge revenue stream for the state.

Zach's new draft is simple and concise. No more "dawn of history" or "stroke of chance." Zach makes his point with clear precise language. His voice is calm and authoritative, far more effective without the distracting extra flourishes.

REFLECT: What is your history as a reader and writer? How do you think that history contributes to your writing today? Would you describe yourself as having a voice as a writer?

WHAT IF I'M NOT SURE I HAVE A VOICE?

Not all students feel confident that they have a distinctive writing voice. However, as we discuss in Chapter One, every student arrives at college with a distinct history as a reader and writer.

If you are wondering whether you actually have a voice as a writer, it could help to ask a reader to describe your writing.

A reader may notice aspects of your writing that you have overlooked. Consider the following paragraphs. Each student is describing the same event, and yet each description is distinctive.

Jordan

Our education used to be expensive. Now it's just outrageous. As soon as students heard about the latest tuition hikes we mobilized, filling the plaza with cries of protest.

Kate

When I read Jordan's writing I feel like I'm there. His writing voice is very dramatic and personal. He doesn't just say *they* filled the plaza, he says *we*. He doesn't just say the students *protested*; he says *filling the plaza with cries of protest*.

Zach

On Monday after the tuition increases were announced, students gathered to protest the decision. Approximately 20 appeared, demanding an explanation from the administration.

Anna

When I read Zach's work, I notice that he writes in a logical and orderly fashion without appealing to pathos. His voice is calm, almost like a news story.

Kate

Yesterday, the university announced another tuition increase, to the consternation of many students who struggle to pay the current tuition. Students gathered in the plaza to express their very real concerns that they would not be able to stay in school at these new rates.

Jordan

Kate is a serious writer—the opposite of lightweight. She uses heavy words like consternation, but she makes it work! Her voice has a lot of dignity and I respect that.

REFLECT: Show a friend or classmate a paragraph from one of your college essays. Ask your friend to describe your voice as a writer. Do you sound serious? Wordy? Clear and Precise? Witty? What sets your voice apart?

Anna

On Monday students heard that tuition would go up yet again. Dozens of outraged undergraduates gathered to protest the decision outside the president's office. A light rainfall could not dissuade the students from their cause. However, after an hour it became clear that the president was out of town. The rain got worse and the students decided to give up—for now.

Zach

Anna's writing is detailed. She sets the scene. (I never thought of mentioning the rain!) Her description is like a story where she explains the protest's beginning, middle, and end. She has a story-teller's voice, gently drawing people in.

College assignments challenge students to write about new subjects, in new ways. Some assignments ask students to write at greater length than they ever have before. These exercises are not designed to stamp out your individuality as a writer. On the contrary, they are designed to strengthen your writer's voice. Gradually, as you practice writing in different genres, you will develop stamina and versatility. Learning to write in many different situations, you will find new ways to articulate your point of view. Writing effectively, your voice will be heard.

What Is Style?

Voice is what you bring from home. Voice conveys your history with language and your unique way with words. In contrast, style is the manner you adopt. If voice is your sense of self, style is what you wear. When you get dressed, you choose clothes appropriate for the occasion. You wear shorts to the gym, a bathing suit to the pool, everyday clothes to class, formal attire to an elegant party. By the same token, when you write, you choose a style appropriate for the occasion: quick abbreviations in a text to friends, carefully developed sentences in an essay, precise regimented tables in a lab report. The style of your writing refers to the conventions you adopt and the choices you make.

Writers Adopt a Style to Send a Message

Imagine drafting an invitation to a formal wedding. *Mr. and Mrs. Bennet request the honor of your presence at the marriage of their daughter Miss Elizabeth Bennet to Mr. Fitzwilliam Darcy.* Now imagine sending out an invitation for a barefoot wedding at the beach. *Join us as Liz and Darcy tie the knot!* The style of the invitation signals just what kind of an event guests can expect. Full names and titles prepare the reader for a solemn ceremony and an elegant reception. The casual style of the second invitation promises a good time with its exuberant command *Join us*, its nicknames, and exclamation point.

Sometimes adopting a style means writing according to a formula—conforming to fixed conventions and established turns of phrase. You will find formulaic writing in genres such as press releases; traffic citations; death announcements, *Jay Gatsby, beloved son, war hero, and entrepreneur*; political speeches, *My fellow Americans, I come to talk to you tonight about an important question*. Writing according to formula will serve you well when you document sources. As we saw in Chapter Eight, an instructor details exactly what style you should use when citing sources. That style will dictate the order and presentation of author, title, publisher, and date. In similar fashion, science instructors often provide specific instructions about how to draft lab reports, specifying the headings you should use and the kind of content you will need to provide for each section.

Where Does Style Come From?

We say that you adopt or choose a style, but perhaps it is more accurate to say that you make many decisions that add up to style. Organization of information, design and layout on the page, level of detail, even punctuation—each influences the style of your writing. We will discuss two of the most important decisions you will make: diction, the writer's choice of words, and syntax, the writer's arrangement of words in a sentence.

DICTION

Consider the word cat. Mention a cat in conversation, and just about everyone can picture the animal. Speaking in a familiar tone you might call the animal kitty. However, at an official Cat Fancier's Association event, you would signal your animal's lineage with his official show name, Blue Angel's Snowflake. The word cat takes on many shades: technical, formal, ordinary, affectionate. You need to decide which works best in a given situation.

A word's role in a sentence affects its meaning in important ways. Consider the word *scratch*. The word could be used to describe an action: *I have to scratch that mosquito bite*. It could be used to mean basic ingredients: *He baked that cake from scratch*. Or, in a computer class for children, the word could take on quite a different meaning as a proper name, Scratch, a simple programming language.

You see the way context colors words—and words create context. Consider the phrase "take a position." If you're talking about argumentation, "take a position" could mean to make a claim, or take a stand. However, if you're talking about money, "take a position" means you want to buy stock.

Sometimes word choice is a matter of respect. The casual tone you take with a friend won't get you far with the police officer who stops you for speeding.

Sometimes word choice is a matter of emotion. Appealing to pathos, writers use specific words to convey strong feeling. *I'm not just disappointed. I'm outraged. Disgusted!* They repeat individual words for emphasis. *Never, never, never give up.* They use short, hard-hitting words to drive a point home. *What is to be done?*

As we have seen, it is important to choose words with your audience in mind. If you're writing a paper about human anatomy, you need to use correct scientific names for each body part. You enact an appeal to ethos, establishing your credibility as one who speaks the specialized language of a given discipline. However, as with any language, it is not enough to know technical terms in isolation. A writer needs to understand how to use these terms effectively. A computer scientist describes the insect he wants to emulate with a man-made robot. "We found that water striders rotate the curved tips of their legs inward at a relatively low descending velocity with a force just below that required to break the water surface" (Koh 472–73). In this sentence the words *rotate*, *descending*, and *velocity* convey a precise mechanical description of the insect's action. These are movements that the team of scientists will try to mimic as they build their robot. A psychiatrist writes about a study of children with ASD (Autism Spectrum Disorder): "The purpose of the current study was to document cognitive, language, and social function in a group of children diagnosed with ASD at a young age, who no longer carried this diagnosis" (Fein et al. 95–215). The word *document* carries a certain weight, conveying the rigorous observations and record keeping in this study. The words *cognitive*, *language*, and *social function* denote particular categories for evaluation of the children. As a reader you understand more when you note the precise use of words in academic texts. As a writer, you express yourself better when you learn to employ words precisely and accurately.

GUIDELINES FOR DICTION

Consider the Rhetorical Situation

When you hang a picture, you look for a hammer and a nail. You don't run out to buy a pneumatic drill. By the same token, when you are choosing words, you will communicate best when you find those that suit the situation. In a casual note to a friend, you describe the squirrels on the roof as *crazed rodents*. In a formal complaint to your landlord you characterize the squirrels as *aggressive pests compromising the structural integrity of the house*. In a scientific paper on squirrels you specify the variety, Eastern gray squirrel, and use the Latin term *sciurus carolinensis*. In each case, your diction shapes your message. Playful horror to your friends, legal grievance to your landlord, scientific accuracy to the scholarly community. Writing a personal essay about the difficult experience of war veterans you might use the phrase *haunting memories*. Writing on this subject for your psychology class, you choose the technical term *post-traumatic stress*. Consider your diction when you complete your writing assignments. Are your words working hard enough?

Avoid Wordiness and Repetition

Sometimes in conversation people wave their hands to emphasize a point. The equivalent in writing is to pad sentences with excess verbiage and emphatic phrases. Consider this sentence: *The protestors literally could not have been louder if they'd tried; they were deafening in their vehement demands.* The message comes through more effectively when it's short and simple. *The protesters could not have been louder. They were vehement in their demands.*

SYNTAX

Diction is your choice of words. Syntax is the arrangement of words in a sentence.

A **simple sentence** contains a subject, the word indicating who or what the sentence is about, and a verb, or action word. You choose what to do with that subject and verb.

Try a **simple sentence**:

> The cat ran up the tree.

This sentence would work well in conversation or in a factual report. It describes what happened—the cat ran. The sentence also signals where the cat ran with the word *up*, a preposition, a word which indicates a relationship, a location, a direction, or a time.

Perhaps you want to say more. You could write a **compound sentence**, in which you join two simple sentences with a conjunction or a linking word, such as and, or, but.

> The cat ran up the tree, and we couldn't get her down.

This sentence conveys what the cat did and adds the outcome.

You could write a **complex sentence**, elaborating on your simple sentence by adding a dependent clause, a group of words with a subject and verb that does not express a complete idea and begins with a subordinating conjunction like if, although, because, when.

> While we stood on the ground watching, the cat ran up the tree.

You can pile on more dependent phrases and clauses to develop a more elaborate account.

> While we stood on the ground watching in horror, the cat ran up the tree and stayed up there for what seemed like hours, even as we tried to tempt her down.

This sentence takes a complex structure. It conveys a lot of information, and an emotional dimension as well.

All these sentences would work in conversation—but let's consider other possibilities as well. Imagine writing the story of the cat as a police report.

> At 1300 hours, the cat fled the scene and was apprehended in a large oak on the property.

What's different about this sentence? Certainly, the police report uses different diction, "1300 hours ... apprehended ... on the property." The details included contribute to a more formal tone: military time, and the kind of tree, rather than the horror of the cat's owners. Look at the structure of the sentence as well.

Some sentences use the active voice in which the subject takes action.

> The cat fled.

Some sentences take the passive voice, in which the subject is acted upon by the verb.

> The cat was apprehended.

Instead of saying *we caught the cat*, or *I helped the cat down*, the police officer writes that the cat *was apprehended*. Using the passive voice, the officer does not reveal who caught the cat, only that the cat was caught. The very structure of the sentence colors and controls the events of the day in an account that sounds impersonal and guarded.

Try your hand at rephrasing from passive to active voice. We provide the first example.

> **Passive voice:** The medical workers were infected by the virus overseas.
> **Active voice:** The virus infected medical workers overseas.
>
> **Passive voice:** The turtle hatchlings were attacked by predators.
> **Active voice:**
>
> **Passive voice:** By late November, Napoleon's armies had been decimated by the Russian winter.
> **Active voice:**

As we have seen, audience, occasion, and genre influence style. Word choice and sentence structure conform to certain expectations. Imagine writing the story of the cat as a screenplay.

EXT. GARDEN-DAY. Donna stands under huge oak tree.

DONNA
Fluffy? Oh my God! She's gone. Fluffy!
Where are you?

Donna alternates between declarative sentences, which describe, exclamatory sentences, which exhort and invoke—often with exclamation points—and interrogative sentences, which question. Together, Donna's short staccato sentences convey panic, while her font and layout on the page conform to the conventions of a screenplay.

Now imagine a historian recounting the incident in a scholarly book.

We may never fully understand the cat's actions. However, contemporary accounts suggest several possible motives.

This particular historian takes a formal, measured tone. Instead of saying *I have no idea why the cat ran up the tree*, he couches his uncertainty in a broader and more cautious statement: *We may never fully understand ...* After warning the reader that certainty is impossible, the historian uses the word *However*, opening the door to several possible motives for the cat's action. The first sentence lowers expectations, and the second sets the stage for interpretation.

Some writers sound deliberate and reflective. Others sound bold and brash. Consider the cat up a tree as broadcast on television news.

A cat disappears in North Attleboro today. Is your pet safe? More at 11.

A simple declarative sentence announces the event of the day. An interrogative sentence follows in a direct appeal to pathos, inciting the sympathy and fear of the viewer. "Is your pet safe?" Finally, the writer concludes with a brief three-word declaration. Instead of saying *More follows at 11*, the writer clips his sentence down to *More at 11*, saving air time and underlining the urgency of the story—as if to say, we're too busy and the situation is too intense for complete sentences.

Try your hand at rewriting these sentences to suit different genres and occasions. In each case we provide the first example.

Fairytale: Deep in the enchanted wood, the children were growing frightened.
News report: Two children have been missing since Monday. They were last seen walking in the vicinity of Enchanted Wood.

Fairytale: All three ran as fast as their legs could carry them, but the youngest was fleetest of them all, and won the race.
News report:

History book: The events of that day would remain fixed in their memories.
Personal diary: I had the best day! I'm going to remember this forever.

Personal diary: I am crushed. I have never had a grade this terrible, but I'm going to figure out a way to improve. I've got to!
History book:

GUIDELINES FOR SYNTAX

Consider the Rhetorical Situation

A complex, descriptive sentence might work beautifully in a short story. *Long ago, when men worked nine to five, their wives baked casseroles, and the 30-year-mortgage ruled the land.* However, for your economics report, a simple, factual sentence might serve you better. *In 1950, single-income households were the norm.* Short, clipped statements work well in newscasts, but could sound choppy in an essay. Think about your assignment and consider how to trim or tailor your sentences so that they serve you well.

Aim for Clarity

As we have seen, syntax can get complicated. Writers can load down sentences with detail and dependent clauses. *During early childhood the plasticity of the brain is greater than at any other time and so certain kinds of learning are easier than they will be later in life, when, for example, it becomes so much more difficult to master a new language.* This sentence makes the reader work, following its contours to figure out what is going on. If the writer unloads this material into shorter sentences, the message will come across more clearly. *Early childhood is the best time to do certain kinds of learning. Later in life the brain is not so plastic and it is more difficult to master a new language.*

Extensive use of the passive voice can cloud a writer's meaning as well. There is nothing inherently wrong with the passive voice. Many excellent points have been made with it. However, the passive voice can obscure a writer's meaning and force the reader to back up and reread paragraphs to understand who or what is meant. *Several military options were discussed.* Well, who is discussing these options? What is the writer talking about? The active voice makes this clear. *President Roosevelt discussed several military options with his cabinet.*

Adopt a Style, Maintain a Voice

Text messages, status updates, news clips, reports—these are just a few of the diverse writing styles we hear, read, and view every day. It is important to understand that you will read and practice diverse styles in college as well. There is no single style of academic writing. In fact, the best academic writers are often the most versatile, adapting themselves to different situations and different audiences. By the same token, the most effective student writers are those who adapt their language to the specific requirements of an assignment. However, even while adapting to specific expectations, the voice of the writer comes through.

Look at Anna's first-person account of her work volunteering as a translator.

> The hot dusty day I arrived at the Legal Aid society I found a very tiny old couple. Their son, who usually helped them, had moved to a different state. I began speaking to them in Spanish and explaining the different lines and the Legal Aid hours. Suddenly the husband spoke to me in English. He demanded, "Good student?" I was surprised by this change of subject, but he began speaking to me as a grandfather. "Study hard in school!"

Anna writes to tell a story. Notice the adjectives she uses—*hot, dusty, tiny, old*. Anna's style here is first-person and conversational. She uses long flowing complex and compound sentences, and she includes dialogue as well. She could have paraphrased her conversation with the old man. Instead she chooses to quote him directly, dramatizing his interjections and sharing her own surprise with the reader.

Now look at another of Anna's writing assignments. This passage comes from her research project on unequal pay for women.

> Historians and economists have documented inequality in the workforce. It is no secret. It is a well-known fact. A gap exists between the salaries of women and men. Even today, women in America earn 78% of what men earn for doing the same job. The question then is what can be done to change this situation?

Anna's style here is factual and emphatic. She drives home her points with short sentences and repeated structures: *It is no secret. It is a well-known fact.* This is not a first-person essay. Anna never uses the pronoun I. However, her emphatic language conveys an intense concern with the injustice of unequal pay for equal work. Anna's phrase *Even today* signals her frustration with this injustice. The rhetorical question engages the reader in her argument. *The question then is what can be done?* In both passages, Anna adapts to the requirements of the assignment. At the same time, she maintains her voice, conveying her strong interest in inequality, and her sense of narrative. Notice that Anna speaks of inequality as a historical fact, a current problem, and a question for the future. She brings to the discussion her own sense of structure—beginning, middle, and end.

In college you can expect to practice new styles for diverse assignments. Bring a sense of adventure to this enterprise, and a willingness to experiment. Bring an inquiring mind, and ask for models when you aren't sure what style your instructor expects. Bring a sense of humor and flexibility as you hone your craft, revising and refining your work. Above all, bring yourself, your own voice and your own history, your ideas, opinions, and affinities. When you bring yourself to an assignment, the work takes on a new life, and your writing becomes purposeful and necessary.

You can maintain your voice while adapting your style to different situations.

Voice is a writer's particular way with words. Voice reflects a writer's

- Experience
- Ideas
- Affinities
- History with language

Style is the manner a writer adopts. Many small choices contribute to a writer's style. Among the most important are

- Diction — word choice
- Syntax — sentence structure
- Use of passive or active voice
- You can maintain your voice while adapting your style to different situations

ACTIVITIES

1 Consider the following paired sentences. What is the purpose of each?
How might you characterize the intended audience? How would you
describe the style of Sentence A? How about Sentence B? How do
word choice and sentence structure contribute to that style?

A. It is not my intention here to depress your spirits unduly.
B. I don't want to get you down.

A. Step right up! Step right up to play the greatest game on
earth! Everybody plays; everybody wins!
B. Would you please try this game? If you play, you'll win a prize.

A. Measure twice, cut once.
B. If you want to make sure you don't waste time and material,
double check all your measurements before cutting.

A. Reasons swimming is good for you: 1) aerobic exercise 2) easy
on joints 3) known to relieve stress ...
B. There are three main reasons to include swimming in your
exercise program. First, swimming is excellent aerobic exercise,
good for your entire cardio-vascular system. Second, swimming
will not stress your joints. Third, swimming is known to relieve
stress.

A. We found that as the temperature rose, so did the numbers of
horned caterpillars.
B. A strong correlation was demonstrated between unseasonably
warm weather and the unusually large population of horned
caterpillars.

2 Read the following openings. Each responds to the same event. How would you describe the style in each case? How do choices in diction, syntax, and layout contribute to that style?

> Hello, NBC. Hello, NBC. This is KTU in Honolulu, Hawaii. I am speaking from the roof of the Advertiser Publishing Company Building. We have witnessed this morning the distant view [sic] a brief full battle of Pearl Harbor and the severe bombing of Pearl Harbor by enemy planes, undoubtedly Japanese. The city of Honolulu has also been attacked and considerable damage done. This battle has been going on for nearly three hours. One of the bombs dropped within fifty feet of KTU tower. It is no joke. It is a real war. The public of Honolulu has been advised to keep in their homes and away from the Army and Navy. There has been serious fighting going on in the air and in the sea. The heavy shooting seems to be ... a little interruption. We cannot estimate just how much damage has been done, but it has been a very severe attack. The Navy and Army appear now to have the air and the sea under control.

> History Matters: The U.S. Survey Course on the Web. historymatters.gmu.edu/d/5167/. Accessed 28 Jan. 2019.

WASHINGTON, Dec. 7…

Oahu was attacked at 7:55 this morning by Japanese planes. The Rising Sun, emblem of Japan, was seen on plane wing tips. Wave after wave of bombers streamed through the clouded morning sky from the southeast and flung their missiles on a city resting in peaceful Sabbath calm.

"WAR! OAHU BOMBED BY JAPANESE PLANES." *Honolulu Star Bulletin Extra*, 7 Dec. 1941, p. 1.

*President Franklin Delano Roosevelt addresses Congress
and the nation via radio in response to the bombing of Pearl
Harbor.*

Mr. Vice President, Mr. Speaker, Members of the Senate, and of
the House of Representatives:

Yesterday, December 7th, 1941—a date which will live in
infamy—the United States of America was suddenly and
deliberately attacked by naval and air forces of the Empire of
Japan.

The United States was at peace with that nation and, at
the solicitation of Japan, was still in conversation with its
government and its emperor looking toward the maintenance of
peace in the Pacific.

Indeed, one hour after Japanese air squadrons had commenced
bombing in the American island of Oahu, the Japanese
ambassador to the United States and his colleagues delivered
to our Secretary of State a formal reply to a recent American
message. While this reply stated that it seemed useless to
continue the existing diplomatic negotiations, it contained no
threat or hint of war or of armed attack.

It will be recorded that the distance of Hawaii from Japan
makes it obvious that the attack was deliberately planned
many days or even weeks ago. During the intervening time, the
Japanese government has deliberately sought to deceive the
United States by false statements and expressions of hope for
continued peace.

The attack yesterday on the Hawaiian islands has caused severe
damage to American naval and military forces. I regret to tell
you that very many American lives have been lost. In addition,
American ships have been reported torpedoed on the high seas
between San Francisco and Honolulu.

Yesterday, the Japanese government also launched an attack
against Malaya.

Last night, Japanese forces attacked Hong Kong.

Last night, Japanese forces attacked Guam.

Last night, Japanese forces attacked the Philippine Islands.

Last night, the Japanese attacked Wake Island.

This morning, the Japanese attacked Midway Island.

Japan has, therefore, undertaken a surprise offensive extending throughout the Pacific area. The facts of yesterday and today speak for themselves. The people of the United States have already formed their opinions and well understand the implications to the very life and safety of our nation. As commander in chief of the Army and Navy, I have directed that all measures be taken for our defense. But always will our whole nation remember the character of the onslaught against us.

No matter how long it may take us to overcome this premeditated invasion, the American people in their righteous might will win through to absolute victory.

I believe that I interpret the will of the Congress and of the people when I assert that we will not only defend ourselves to the uttermost, but will make it very certain that this form of treachery shall never again endanger us.

Hostilities exist. There is no blinking at the fact that our people, our territory, and our interests are in grave danger.

With confidence in our armed forces, with the unbounding determination of our people, we will gain the inevitable triumph—so help us God.

I ask that the Congress declare that since the unprovoked and dastardly attack by Japan on Sunday, December 7th, 1941, a state of war has existed between the United States and the Japanese empire.

Roosevelt, Franklin D. "Address to the Congress Asking That a State of War Be Declared between the United States and Japan." 8 Dec. 1941.

3   Read the following abstracts and introductions to three academic articles. How would you characterize the word choice and sentence structure? How do these contribute to style? How would you describe that style?

Jumping on water is a unique locomotion mode found in semi-aquatic arthropods, such as water striders. To reproduce this feat in a surface tension-dominant jumping robot, we elucidated the hydrodynamics involved and applied them to develop a bio-inspired impulsive mechanism that maximizes momentum transfer to water. We found that water striders rotate the curved tips of their legs inward at a relatively low descending velocity with a force just below that required to break the water surface (144 millinewtons/meter). We built a 68-milligram at-scale jumping robotic insect and verified that it jumps on water with maximum momentum transfer. The results suggest an understanding of the hydrodynamic phenomena used by semi-aquatic arthropods during water jumping and prescribe a method for reproducing these capabilities in artificial systems.

Koh, Je-Sung, et al. "Jumping on Water: Surface Tension-Dominated Jumping of Water Striders and Robotic Insects." *Science*, July 2015, p. 472.

The grounding of the oil tanker Exxon Valdez on Bligh Reef in Alaska's pristine Prince William Sound on March 24, 1989, was one of the greatest environmental disasters in the United States prior to the explosion and subsequent wellhead leak of BP's Deepwater Horizon oil rig and the Macondo prospect in the Gulf of Mexico. In Alaska, between 11 and 32 million gallons of crude oil poured into the Sound. Four days later, a storm with winds of seventy miles per hour drove the oil onto the sand and rock beaches and then southwest from the Sound along Alaska's outer coast on the Gulf of Alaska, eventually spreading nearly five hundred miles from the spill site and fouling one thousand miles of irregular shoreline. As a result of the spill, scientists estimate mass mortality among sea otters and harbor seals, and an unprecedented number of seabird deaths. Macroalgae and benthic invertebrates were also killed by a combination of chemical toxicity, smothering, and physical displacement from their habitat by the pressure washing used to clean the oiled shores. For people living in communities on the Sound, including two native villages whose residents depended on the subsistence harvest of the water's resources, the impact of the spill constituted an emotional, psychological, and economic tragedy. Its effects linger: oil still lying around rocks and in sand, and a profound sense of loss among people.

Haycox, Stephen. "'Fetched Up': Unlearned Lessons from the Exxon Valdez." *Journal of American History*, June 2012, p. 219.

Autism spectrum disorders (ASDs) are generally regarded as lifelong conditions, affecting communication, relationships, adaptive skills, academic and vocational attainment (Piven, Harper, Palmer, & Arndt, 1996). While children with ASD exhibit outcomes that vary widely (Eaves & Ho, 2008), moving off the autism spectrum into social and communicative function that is within normal limits is not generally considered a realistic goal, and, indeed, is not a common outcome (Billstedt, Gillberg, & Gillberg, 2005; Venter, Lord, & Schopler, 1992). The purpose of the current study was to document cognitive, language, and social functioning in a group of children diagnosed with an ASD at a young age, who no longer carried this diagnosis. This report is part of a larger study designed to better understand the phenomenon of 'optimal outcome' (OO) in ASD, to explore possible persistent cognitive and emotional difficulties in this population, to document the range of treatments they received, and to explore biological characteristics in these individuals through structural and functional imaging.

Fein, Deborah, et al. "Optimal Outcome in Individuals with a History of Autism." *The Journal of Child Psychology and Psychiatry*, Feb. 2013, p. 195.

4 Each of the following passages introduces the opinion of a Supreme Court justice on whether or not the US government should allow same-sex marriage. Justice Anthony Kennedy presents the majority decision to allow same-sex marriage. Chief Justice John Roberts and Justice Antonin Scalia present dissenting arguments. The justices write on the same topic and delivered their opinions to the same audience — the nation — on the same day, 26 June 2015. Each justice adopts a public formal style, befitting his position on the Supreme Court. However, each justice treats the topic in a different way. How would you characterize the claims each justice makes? What appeals does each justice use? When you read these passages, do you hear a voice come through? How would you describe that voice? Consider the word choice and sentence structure that each justice chooses.

Introduction to decision to allow same-sex marriage by Justice Anthony Kennedy.

From their beginning to their most recent page, the annals of human history reveal the transcendent importance of marriage. The lifelong union of a man and a woman always has promised nobility and dignity to all persons, without regard to their station in life. Marriage is sacred to those who live by their religions and offers unique fulfillment to those who find meaning in the secular realm. Its dynamic allows two people to find a life that could not be found alone, for a marriage becomes greater than just the two persons. Rising from the most basic human needs, marriage is essential to our most profound hopes and aspirations....

The petitioners acknowledge this history but contend that these cases cannot end there. Were their intent to demean the revered idea and reality of marriage, the petitioners' claims would be of a different order. But that is neither their purpose nor their submission. To the contrary, it is the enduring importance of marriage that underlies the petitioners' contentions. This, they say, is their whole point. Far from seeking to devalue marriage, the petitioners seek it for themselves because of their respect — and need — for its privileges and responsibilities. And their immutable nature dictates that same-sex marriage is their only real path to this profound commitment.

Introduction to dissenting opinion by Chief Justice John Roberts.

Petitioners make strong arguments rooted in social policy and considerations of fairness. They contend that same-sex couples should be allowed to affirm their love and commitment through marriage, just like opposite-sex couples. That position has undeniable appeal; over the past six years, voters and legislators in eleven States and the District of Columbia have revised their laws to allow marriage between two people of the same sex.

But this Court is not a legislature. Whether same-sex marriage is a good idea should be of no concern to us. Under the Constitution, judges have power to say what the law is, not what it should be. The people who ratified the Constitution authorized courts to exercise "neither force nor will but merely judgment." The Federalist No. 78, p. 465 (C. Rossiter ed. 1961) (A. Hamilton) (capitalization altered).

Introduction to dissenting opinion by Justice Antonin Scalia.

I join The Chief Justice's opinion in full. I write separately to call attention to this Court's threat to American democracy.

The substance of today's decree is not of immense personal importance to me. The law can recognize as marriage whatever sexual attachments and living arrangements it wishes, and can accord them favorable civil consequences, from tax treatment to rights of inheritance. Those civil consequences — and the public approval that conferring the name of marriage evidences — can perhaps have adverse social effects, but no more adverse than the effects of many other controversial laws. So it is not of special importance to me what the law says about marriage. It is of overwhelming importance, however, who it is that rules me. Today's decree says that my Ruler, and the Ruler of 320 million Americans coast-to-coast, is a majority of the nine lawyers on the Supreme Court. The opinion in these cases is the furthest extension in fact — and the furthest extension one can even imagine — of the Court's claimed power to create "liberties" that the Constitution and its Amendments neglect to mention. This practice of constitutional revision by an unelected committee of nine, always accompanied (as it is today) by extravagant praise of liberty, robs the People of the most important liberty they asserted in the Declaration of Independence and won in the Revolution of 1776: the freedom to govern themselves.

For the full text of these and other Supreme Court opinions, see http://lp.findlaw.com/.

Obergefell v. Hodges. 576 U.S. (2015): 3–4, www.supremecourt.gov/ opinions/14pdf/14-556_3204.pdf. Accessed 20 Sept. 2018.

---

5 Read each of these reflections on writing in college. What do these passages have in common? How would you describe their style? How does word choice and sentence structure contribute to that style? Does an individual voice come through? How would you describe each student's voice? Write and share your own paragraph on your writing this semester.

Anna

I arrived seriously interested in writing, and I still like it, despite frustrating moments. What I like most is using writing to think through how something works. I feel like writing is actually a way to look at something more closely. What was painful at times was dealing with longer essays such as the research project, where I collected so many points of view. At first, putting together my portfolio felt like a puzzle with a million tiny pieces. It was challenging to introduce my own ideas while keeping so many other ideas in mind. In the end, it was a relief to express my own point of view!

Kate

I came back to school feeling fairly confident about what my writing skills *used to be*. I was probably a little rusty when I started out, because I had not done writing assignments in several years. What I did have going for me was some maturity—not that I'm so old! Let's just say I'm old enough to know some things. For one thing, I am probably more open to asking for help than some other students. When writing my research essay on the Great Fire, I went straight to the reference librarian to ask for advice on finding sources. I also went to the Writing Center and to office hours. I'm not afraid to use my resources. That said, my best resource was myself, because I really worked hard. I did get bogged down and discouraged, but I took a deep breath and revised my essay. That was my biggest accomplishment. It was hard, but the essay really did come out better.

Jordan

So, I still prefer poetry, public speaking, and improv. I am still more of the think on your feet give me a prompt and let me run with it type of writer. What surprised me was how much I like analysis IF it's a subject I enjoy. Analyzing Sir John Tenniel's illustration of Alice meeting the caterpillar was definitely weirder than I ever thought it would be. The more I looked at that picture the crazier it became. If I learned anything, it's write about what fascinates you. You might hate something. You might love something. It's all good if you have the passion. That's where my inspiration comes from.

Zach

Three lessons I have learned about writing. 1. Do not try to write five pages in one night. 2. Imagine an audience besides your instructor. 3. Talking about it helps. Number three is the most important. I have learned that I do my best work when I try out ideas on a friend.

Works Cited

"5000 Years of Crop Protection." *CropLife International*. https://croplife.org/news/5000-years-of-crop-protection/. Accessed 27 Nov. 2018.

"A Product No One Wants." *PETA*, 18 Mar. 2014, www.peta2.com/news/canadian-seal-slaughter/. Accessed 26 Nov. 2018.

"Account of the Great Fire." *Chicago Evening Post*, 17 Oct. 1871, www.greatchicagofire.org/eyewitnesses/anthology-of-fire-narratives. Accessed 26 Nov. 2018.

Achebe, Chinua. "The Art of Fiction 139." Interview by Jerome Brooks. *The Paris Review*, no. 139, www.theparisreview.org/interviews/1720/chinua-achebe-the-art-of-fiction-no-139-chinua-achebe. Accessed 13 Mar. 2018.

Adams, Abigail. "To John Adams." 31 Mar. 1776. *Familiar Letters of John Adams and His Wife Abigail Adams, during the Revolution.* New York, Hurd and Houghton, 1876, p. 150.

Anthony, Susan B. "Is It a Crime for a Citizen of the United States to Vote?" National Woman Suffrage Association Meeting, Washington, DC, 16 Jan. 1873.

"Attack Made on Island's Defense Areas." *Honolulu Star Bulletin Extra*, 7 Dec. 1941, p. 1.

"Attack of the Killer Tomatoes (1978) Trailer." *YouTube*, uploaded by moon howler, 23 Feb. 2014, https://www.youtube.com/watch?v=aXoWch1UNuw.

Bark cloth (maro), early 20th century. Museum of Fine Arts, Boston.

Bennett, Clay. "Equal Pay." *Chattanooga Free Press*, 31 Jan. 2009, www.timesfreepress.com/news/editorialcartoons/story/2009/jan/31/equal-pay/205834/. Accessed 30 Jan. 2019.

"Black Holes." *NASA Science*, www.science.nasa.gov/astrophysics/focus-areas/black-holes. Accessed 20 Sept. 2018.

"Bold, Modern, Life Insurance Newspaper Ad Design for a Company in Australia." *DesignCrowd*, 12 Feb. 2013, uploaded by shpaolin, www.designcrowd.ca/design/1456620. Accessed 20 Sept. 2018.

Book Notices: *"Moby Dick; or the Whale." The United States Democratic Review*, vol. 30, 1852, p. 93.

Boylan, Jennifer Finney. "Save Us from the SAT." *The New York Times*, 6 Mar. 2014, p. A25.

Bradwell, Bessie. "1926 Account of the Great Fire of Chicago." *Great Chicago Fire*, www.greatchicagofire.org/eyewitnesses/anthology-of-fire-narratives.

Carroll, Lewis. *Alice's Adventures in Wonderland*, facsimile of first edition, 1865, Engage Books, 2010.

Charles, Robert. "If the Second Amendment Falls, Our Entire Bill of Rights Falls." *Fox News*, 29 Mar. 2018.

Coleman, Mary. "GITS Q&A, Part 4: Mary Coleman (Pixar)." Interview by Scott Myers. *Go into the Story* blog, 28 Feb. 2012, www.gointothestory.blcklst.com/gits-q-a-part-4-mary-coleman-pixar-cfea02a390e5. Accessed 20 Sept. 2018.

Cook, Captain James. "21 April 1770." *Captain Cook's Journal*, www.southseas.nla.gov.au/journals/cook/17700421.html. Accessed 26 Nov. 2018.

Dalí, Salvador. *Advice from a Caterpillar*. 1969, lithograph, Dallas Museum of Art.

Daniele, Guido. "WWF Elephant." *guidodaniele.com*, Oct. 2006, www.guidodaniele.com/hand-painting/handpaint-advertising/category/47.html. Accessed 20 Sept. 2018.

Douglass, Frederick. *Narrative of the Life of Frederick Douglass, an American Slave*, 1845. Broadview Press, 2018.

Eakins, Thomas. *The Agnew Clinic*, 1889. Philadelphia Museum of Art.

Ebert, Roger. "Gone with the Wind." Rev. of *Gone with the Wind*, dir. David O. Selznick, 21 June 1998, www.rogerebert.com. Accessed 9 Sept. 2015.

Episcopal Church. *The Book of Common Prayer and Administration of the Sacraments and Other Rites and Ceremonies of the Church: Together with the Psalter or Psalms of David According to the Use of the Episcopal Church*. Seabury Press, 1979.

Farmer, Paul, et al. "Reduced Premature Mortality in Rwanda: Lessons from Success." *BMJ*, Jan. 2013, pp. 346–65.

Fein, Deborah, et al. "Optimal Outcome in Individuals with a History of Autism." *The Journal of Child Psychology and Psychiatry*, Feb. 2013, pp. 195–215.

Fields, Debbie. "Blue-Ribbon Chocolate Chip Cookies." *Mrs. Fields Cookie Book: 100 Recipes from the Kitchen of Mrs. Fields*. Time-Life Books, 1992.

Freud, Sigmund. "Childhood and Concealing Memories." *The Psychopathology of Everyday Life*, edited and translated by A.A. Brill. T. Fisher Unwin, 1914.

Friedan, Betty. "Betty Friedan Interview." Interview by Ben Wattenberg. www.pbs.org/fmc/interviews/friedan.htm. Accessed 17 Jan. 2019.

Friedman, Milton. *Capitalism and Freedom*. University of Chicago Press, 1962.

Gaiman, Neil. "Why Our Future Depends on Libraries, Reading, and Daydreaming." *The Guardian*, 15 Oct. 2013, www.theguardian.com/books/2013/oct/15/neil-gaiman-future-libraries-reading-daydreaming. Accessed 26 Nov. 2018.

Geiger, Flavia. "Persistent Negative Effects of Pesticides on Biodiversity and Biological Control Potential on European Farmland." *Basic and Applied Ecology*, vol. 11, no. 2, 2002, pp. 97–105.

Gould, John. "Four Types of Finch." *Journal of Researches into the Geology and Natural History of the Various Countries Visited by H.M.S. Beagle,* by Charles Darwin. J. Murray, 1845.

Grandin, Temple. *Thinking in Pictures: And Other Reports from My Life with Autism*. Vintage Books, 2006.

Grant, Adam. Slide from Ted Talk on Original Thinkers. *YouTube*, www.youtube.com/watch?v=fxbCHn6gE3U. Accessed 17 Jan. 2019.

Haycox, Stephen. "'Fetched Up': Unlearned Lessons from the Exxon Valdez." *Journal of American History*, June 2012, pp. 219–28.

Hegel, G.W.F. *Phenomenology of Mind*. Translated by J.B. Baillie, Dover, 2003.

Herrick, Robert. "To the Virgins, to Make Much of Time." *Hesperides*. London, John Williams, 1648.

Hiroshige, Utagawa. "Driving Rain, Shono." *Fifty-Three Stations of the Tokaido*, 1833–34.

Hopkins, Gerard Manley. "Binsey Poplars." 1879. *Gerard Manley Hopkins: Poems and Prose*. Penguin Classics, 1985.

"In S.F., It's B.Y.O.B: 'Bring Your Own (Water) Bottle.'" *Los Angeles Times*, 6 Mar. 2014, www.latimes.com/opinion/editorials/la-ed-bottled-water-ban-san-francisco-20140306-story.html. Accessed 9 Sept. 2015.

The International Table Tennis Federation. "The Laws of Table Tennis." *Handbook 2018*, ITTF, 2018, www.ittf.com/handbook/. Accessed 20 Sept. 2018.

"Introduction to Pesticides." *Pesticides in Perspective*, www.pesticidesinperspective.org.uk/pesticides/posts/2015/introduction-to-pesticides. Accessed 26 Nov. 2018.

Jackson, Robert. "Summation for the Prosecution." Nuremberg Trials, 26 June 1946. Pace Law Library Research Guide, www.law.pace.edu/library. Accessed 26 Nov. 2018.

Johnson, Lyndon B. "Address before a Joint Session of the Congress, November 27, 1963." *The American Presidency Project*, compiled by Gerhard Peters and John T. Woolley, www.presidency.ucsb.edu/ws/?pid=25988. Accessed 20 Sept. 2018.

Josh. "How to Deal with an Alcoholic Husband." *Clean and Sober Live*, www.cleanandsoberlive.com/how-to-deal-with-an-alcoholic-husband/. Accessed 20 Sept. 2018.

Keller, Helen. *The Story of My Life*. Doubleday, 1903.

Kennedy, John F. "Inaugural Address," 20 Jan. 1961. *American Rhetoric*, www.americanrhetoric.com/speeches/jfkinaugural.htm. Accessed 29 Jan. 2016.

Kogan, Marcela. "Where Happiness Lies: Social Scientists Reveal Their Research Findings in the Realm of Positive Psychology." www.apa.org/monitor/jan01/positivepsych.aspx. Accessed 11 Nov. 2018.

Koh, Je-Sung, et al. "Jumping on Water: Surface Tension-Dominated Jumping of Water Striders and Robotic Insects." *Science*, vol. 349, no. 6247, pp. 517–21.

Lange, Dorothea. *White Angel Breadline, San Francisco*. 1933, gelatin silver print, Museum of Modern Art, San Francisco.

"Largest Bike-Sharing Programs Worldwide, Early 2013." *Permaculture News*, 26 April 2013, www.permaculturenews.org/images/update112_largest.PNG. Accessed 26 Nov. 2018.

Lewis, Ray. "Ray Lewis Addresses the University of Miami Football Team." 2 Sept. 2011, *YouTube*, www.youtube.com/watch?v=uu4aVQ-qR8U. Accessed 26 Nov. 2018.

Lin, Grace. "In-depth Written Interview." *Teachingbooks.net*, 23 May 2011, www.teachingbooks.net/interview.cgi?id=95&a=1. Accessed 20 Sept. 2018.

Lumenick, Lou. "'Gone with the Wind' Should Go the Way of the Confederate Flag." *New York Post*, 24 June 2015, nypost.com/2015/06/24/gone-with-the-wind-should-go-the-way-of-the-confederate-flag/. Accessed 9 Sept. 2015.

Lyobomirsky, Sonja, Kennon Sheldon, and David Schkade. "Pursuing Happiness: The Architecture of Sustainable Change." *Review of General Psychology*, vol. 9, no. 2, 2005, pp. 111–31.

Machiavelli, Niccolo. *The Prince*. Trans. George Bull. Penguin, 2003.

Marsalis, Wynton. "What Jazz Is—and Isn't." *The New York Times*, 31 July 1988, pp. 20–21.

Marwick, Alice E., and danah boyd. "The Drama! Teen Conflict, Gossip, and Bullying in Networked Publics." *A Decade in Internet Time: Symposium on the Dynamics of the Internet and Society*, *University of Oxford, Sept. 2011*. SSRN, Sept. 2011, http://ssrn.com/abstract=1926349.

Mason, R.B. "Proclamation." Chicago, 20 Oct. 1871, *The Great Fire of Chicago and the Web of Memory*, Chicago Historical Society and Northwestern University, 2011, www.greatchicagofire.org/rescue-and-relief-library/official-actions/. Accessed 17 Nov. 2014.

Mason, R.B. *Report of the Chicago Relief and Aid Society*. Riverside Press, 1874.

McCullough, David. "The Art of Biography No. 2." *The Paris Review*, no. 152, Fall 1999, www.theparisreview.org/interviews/894/the-art-of-biography-no-2-david-mccullough. Accessed 17 Jan. 2019.

McElroy, W.H. "Chicago." www.greatchicagofire.org/fanning-flames-library/%E2%80%9Cchicago%E2%80%9D-wh-mcelroy/. Accessed 26 Nov. 2018.

"MNA: 'State of Patient Care in Massachusetts' Survey Released for National Nurses Week Finds Nurses Sounding the Alarm over Deteriorating Conditions for Hospitalized Patients and Need for Safe Patient Limits." CISTON PR Newswire, Massachusetts Nurses Association, 8 May 2018, 07:00ET. Accessed 23 Jan. 2019.

Muir, John. "The American Forests." *The Atlantic*, 1 Aug. 1897, pp. 145–57.

National Oceanic and Atmospheric Administration (NOAA). "Nautical Chart." www.oceanservice.noaa.gov/facts/chart_map.html. Accessed 20 Sept. 2018.

Nightingale, Florence. *Notes on Nursing: What It Is and What It Is Not*. D. Appleton and Company, 1860.

Nugent, Frank S. "David Selznick's 'Gone with the Wind' Has Its Long-Awaited Premiere at Astor and Capitol, Recalling Civil War and Plantation Days of South—Seen as Treating Book with Great Fidelity." *The New York Times*, 20 Dec. 1939, p. 31.

O'Neil, Dennis. *The DC Comics Guide to Writing Comics*. Watson Guptill, 2001.

Obergefell v. Hodges. 576 U.S. (2015): 3–4, www.supremecourt.gov/opinions/14pdf/14-556_3204.pdf. Accessed 20 Sept. 2018.

Olmsted, Frederick Law. "Chicago in Distress." *The Papers of Frederick Law Olmsted*. Johns Hopkins UP, 1992, vol. VI, p. 487.

Olson, Jim. "How Nature and a 9-Year-Old Are Revolutionizing Cancer Treatment." *TEDxSeattle*, 19 July 2013, *YouTube*, www.youtube.com/watch?v=7IWMJhg2Zlc. Accessed 17 Jan. 2019.

"One in Four MA RNs Report Patient Deaths That Are Directly Attributable to Unsafe Patient Assignment," Massachusetts Nurses Association/National Nurses United, Press Release, 6 May 2015. Accessed 23 Jan. 2019.

Orwell, George. "Politics and the English Language." *Horizon*, vol. 13, no. 76, pp. 252–65.

Pace, Eric. "Dr. Seuss, Modern Mother Goose Dies at 87." *The New York Times*, 26 Sept. 1991, p. A1.

Paine, Thomas. *Common Sense*, 1775–76. Broadview Press, 2004.

Papdimitrious, Michael. Audio Guide, Museum of Fine Arts, Boston, MA, 20 Sept. 2015.

"Paul Farmer's Graph of the Year: Rwanda's Plummeting Child Mortality Rate." *Wonkblog*, 29 Dec. 2013, www.washingtonpost.com/news/wonk/wp/2013/12/29/paul-farmers-graph-of-the-year-rwandas-plummeting-child-mortality-rate/. Accessed 26 Nov. 2018.

"Petition: Ban Roundup and Dicamba!" *Food and Water Action*, www.foodandwaterwatch.org/act/petition-ban-roundup-and-dicamba. Accessed 26 Nov. 2018.

Petrohilos, Dylan. "The Gender Wage Gap by Race." *thinkprogress.org*, 18 Sept. 2014, www.thinkprogress.org/the-gender-wage-gap-is-a-chasm-for-women-of-color-in-one-chart-1e8824ee6707/. Accessed 20 Sept. 2018.

Poe, Edgar Allan. "The Tell-Tale Heart." 1843. www.poemuseum.org/history-of-the-museum. Accessed 28 Jan. 2019.

"Protect Trees." *Thomson Multiwood*, www.multiwood.in/blog/protect-trees. Accessed 26 Nov. 2018.

Rackham, Arthur. *Advice from a Caterpillar*. *Alice's Adventures in Wonderland* by Lewis Carroll. Easton Press, 1907, p. 50.

Rembrandt. *The Anatomy Lesson of Dr. Nicolaes Tulp*. 1632. Mauritshuis Museum.

Revere, Paul. *The Bloody Massacre.* 1770, hand-colored engraving, Peabody Essex Museum.

Roosevelt, Franklin D. "Address to the Congress Asking That a State of War Be Declared between the United States and Japan." 8 Dec. 1941.

Rosen, Kenneth H. *Discrete Mathematics and Its Applications.* 4th ed., McGraw-Hill, 2011.

Ross, Alex. "Beethoven's Bad Influence." *The New Yorker,* 20 Oct. 2014, pp. 44–49.

Ross, Alex. "Listen to This." *The New Yorker,* 16 Feb. 2004, pp. 146–55.

Rothko, Mark. *Light Red Over Black.* 1957, oil on canvas, Tate, London.

San Francisco General Strike. Directed by Bert Gould, Pathé News, 1934, https://archive.org/details/ssfGSTKBEG1?start=0.5. Accessed 17 Jan. 2019.

Sandberg, Sheryl. *Lean In: Women, Work, and the Will to Lead.* Knopf, 2013.

Sen, Amartya. "Humane Development." Interview by Akash Kapur. *The Atlantic,* 15 Dec. 1999. www.theatlantic.com/past/docs/unbound/interviews/ba991215.htm. Accessed 17 Jan. 2019.

Shaw, George Bernard. *Pygmalion: A Romance in Five Acts.* London, Constable, 1920.

Siege of Temesvár, 1552. Turkish miniature. Topkapi Palace, Istanbul.

"Signal Flow Transistor AM Radio." *YouTube,* uploaded by AllAmericanFiveRadio, 24 Feb. 2011, www.youtube.com/watch?v=qlx7KRSiPM4. Accessed 17 Jan. 2019.

Sotomayor, Sonia. *My Beloved World.* Vintage Books, 2014.

Stevens, John Paul. "Repeal the Second Amendment." *The New York Times,* 27 Mar. 2018, p. A23.

Stillwell, John. *Prince George of Cambridge First Birthday.* 2014, Getty Images.

Sustermans, Justus. Portrait of Cosimo de' Medici III. 17th century.

Tenniel, John. Illustration for *Alice's Adventures in Wonderland* by Lewis Carroll, 1865. Dover, 1993, p. 44.

Thomas, Dylan. *Under Milk Wood.* New Directions, 1954.

Tverberg, Gail. "World Energy Consumption by Source, Based on Vaclav Smil Estimates from Energy Transitions: History, Requirements and Prospects Together with BP Statistical Data for 1965 and Subsequent." www.ourfiniteworld.com/2012/03/12/world-energy-consumption-since-1820-in-charts/. Accessed 26 Nov. 2018.

"Unemployment Rates and Earnings by Educational Attainment, 2017."
Bureau of Labor Statistics, 27 March 2018, www.bls.gov/emp/chart-
unemployment-earnings-education.htm. Accessed 26 Nov. 2018.

US Anti-Doping Agency (USADA). Statement Regarding the U.S. Postal
Service Pro Cycling Team Doping Conspiracy, 10 Oct. 2012, www.
cyclinginvestigation.usada.org. Accessed 20 Sept. 2018.

Vonnegut, Kurt. "Letter to Charles McCarthy, November 16, 1973."
Letters of Note: Correspondence Deserving of a Wider Audience,
compiled by Shaun Usher. Canongate, 2014, pp. 193–194.

Welty, Eudora. *Dolls*, Jackson. 1936, Mississippi Department of
Archives and History.

The Whole Duty of a Woman, Or, An Infallible Guide to the Fair Sex. T.
Read, 1737.

"Why Give Blood." *Community Blood Center*, www.givingblood.org/
donate-blood/why-give-blood.aspx. Accessed 20 Sept. 2018.

Willis, Jay, "What Justice Stevens' Op/Ed Gets Wrong about the Second
Amendment," *GQ*, 27 Mar. 2018, https://www.gq.com/story/repeal-
second-amendment-counterproductive-justice-stevens, Accessed 29
Jan. 2019.

Wolters Kluwer Tax and Accounting US. "Plan for Life: Finance and
Estate Planning." *SlideShare*, 24 Sept. 2015, www.slideshare.net/
WoltersKluwerTAAUS/plan-for-life-finance-and-estate-planning-
infographic. Accessed 20 Sept. 2018.

Yong, Ed. "Not Exactly Rocket Science: The Writing Process." *Discover
Magazine*, 30 March 2011, http://blogs.discovermagazine.com/
notrocketscience/2011/03/30/the-writing-process/#.XEDMtGllDIU.
Accessed 17 Jan. 2019.

Yousafzai, Malala. "Nobel Lecture." 10 Dec. 2014, Oslo, Norway, www.
nobelprize.org/prizes/peace/2014/yousafzai/26074-malala-yousafzai-
nobel-lecture-2014/. Accessed 20 Sept. 2018.

About the Authors

Allegra Goodman is a novelist. Her books include *Kaaterskill Falls, The Family Markowitz, Intuition, The Cookbook Collector*, and *The Chalk Artist*. Her short fiction has appeared in *The New Yorker* and *Best American Short Stories*. Her essays on writing have appeared in *The New York Times, The Boston Globe, The Wall Street Journal*, and many composition readers. She has taught first year composition at Stanford, and creative writing at Boston University.

Michael Prince is the founding director of the Arts and Sciences Writing Program at Boston University, where he is associate professor of English, specializing in Writing Studies and early modern literature and philosophy. His essays on rhetoric and composition appear in *College English, The Chronicle of Higher Education*, and *The Journal of Education*, and on literary theory and criticism in *Modern Language Quarterly, New Literary History*, and *Essays in Criticism*. His books include *Philosophical Dialogue in the British Enlightenment* (Cambridge University Press, 1997) and *The Shortest Way with Defoe:* Robinson Crusoe, *Deism and the Novel* (University of Virginia Press, 2019). He serves on the Modern Language Association Committee for K-16 Alliances.

About the Illustrator

Emmeline Pidgen is an illustrator creating books, comics, and commercial illustration in North West England. Emmeline has worked with a wide range of clients internationally, and was named "UK Freelancer of the Year" in 2016.

Permissions Acknowledgments

Boylan, Jennifer Finney. "Save Us from the SAT." *The New York Times*, 6 March 2014. Copyright © 2014, The New York Times. Used under license.

Community Blood Center. "Why Give Blood," www.givingblood.org/donate-blood/why-give-blood.aspx. Reprinted with permission.

Ebert, Roger. Excerpt from *Gone with the Wind* review, 21 June 1998, https://www.rogerebert.com/reviews/great-movie-gone-with-the-wind-1939. Reprinted with the permission of the Ebert Company, Ltd.

Fein, Deborah, et al. Excerpt from "Optimal Outcome in Individuals with a History of Autism," in *The Journal of Child Psychology and Psychiatry* (Feb. 2013): 195–215. Copyright © 2013 The Authors. Journal of Child Psychology and Psychiatry copyright © 2013 Association for Child and Adolescent Mental Health.

Food and Water Action. "Petition: Ban Roundup and Dicamba!," https://secure.foodandwaterwatch.org/act/petition-ban-roundup-and-dicamba. Reprinted with the permission of Food and Water Action Fund, Washington, DC.

Gaffney, Elizabeth, and Benjamin Ryder Howe. Excerpt from "David McCullough, The Art of Biography No. 2," *The Paris Review* 152, Fall 1999. Reprinted with the permission of The Paris Review, Elizabeth Gaffney, and Benjamin Ryder Howe.

Gaiman, Neil. Excerpt from "Why Our Future Depends on Libraries, Reading, and Daydreaming," copyright © 2013 by Neil Gaiman. Reprinted with the permission of Writers House LLC acting as agent for the author.

Geiger, Flavia, et al. Abstract: "Persistent Negative Effects of Pesticides on Biodiversity and Biological Control Potential on European Farmland," from *Basic and Applied Ecology* 11.2 (2002): 97–105. Reprinted with permission from Elsevier.

Josh. "How to Deal with An Alcoholic Husband," from *Clean and Sober Live*, www.cleanandsoberlive.com/how-to-deal-with-an-alcoholic-husband/, 2013. Copyright © cleanandsoberlive.com.

Los Angeles Times Editorial Staff. "In S.F., It's B.Y.O.B: 'Bring Your Own (Water) Bottle,'" published 6 March 2014. Copyright © 2014, Los Angeles Times. Used with permission.

Lumenick, Lou. Excerpt from "'Gone with the Wind' Should Go the Way of the Confederate Flag," *The New York Post*, 24 June 2015. Copyright © 2015 The New York Post. All rights reserved. Used under license.

Marsalis, Wynton. Excerpt from "What Jazz Is—and Isn't" *The New York Times*, 31 July 1988. Copyright © 1988 by Wynton Marsalis. Reprinted with the permission of Wynton Marsalis.

Myers, Scott. Excerpt from *Go into the Story Q&A, Part 4: Mary Coleman*, posted 28 Feb. 2012. Reprinted with the permission of Scott Myers.

Nugent, Frank S. Review of *Gone with the Wind*, directed by David O. Selznick. *The New York Times*, 20 December 1939. Copyright © 1939, The New York Times. All rights reserved. Used under license.

Stevens, John Paul. "Repeal the Second Amendment," from *The New York Times*, 27 March 2018. Copyright © 2018 The New York Times. All rights reserved. Used by permission and protected by the Copyright Laws of the United States. The printing, copying, redistribution, or retransmission of this Content without express written permission is prohibited.

TeachingBooks. Excerpt from interview with Grace Lin, 23 May 2011. www.teachingbooks.net/interview.cgi?id=95&a=1. Reprinted with the permission of Nick Glass.

Excerpt from "This Is No Joke: This Is War": A Live Radio Broadcast of the Attack on Pearl Harbor, *History Matters: The U.S. Survey Course on the Web*, http://historymatters.gmu.edu/d/5167/. Courtesy of the Michigan State University, G. Robert Vincent Voice Library. Reprinted with permission.

Vonnegut, Kurt. "Letter to Charles McCarthy, Chairman of the Drake School Board, November 16, 1973," from *Palm Sunday: An Autobiographical Collage*. Copyright © 1981 by Kurt Vonnegut. Used by permission of Dell Publishing, an imprint of Random House, a division of Penguin Random House LLC. All rights reserved.

Wattenberg, Ben. Excerpt from "Betty Friedan Interview," *The First Measured Century*, PBS (air date unknown), http://www.pbs.org/fmc/interviews/friedan.htm. Reprinted with the permission of Andrew Walworth.

Yousafzai, Malala. Excerpt from the Nobel Prize Lecture, 10 December 2014, Oslo, Norway. Copyright © The Nobel Foundation, 2014.

Images

Page 30 Yong, Ed. "Not Exactly Rocket Science: The Writing Process," *Discover Magazine* blog, 30 March 2011. Reprinted with permission.

Page 100 Rothko, Mark. 1903–1970. *Light Red Over Black*. 1957, oil on canvas. Copyright © Kate Rothko Prizel and Christopher Rothko/SOCAN/DACS 2018. Photograph copyright © Tate, London 2019.

Page 102 Bark cloth (maro), Teluk Yos Sudarso (Humboldt Bay), Papua Province, Indonesia. Early 20th century. Gift of William E. and Bertha L. Teel. Photograph copyright © Museum of Fine Arts, Boston.

Page 106 "A Product No One Wants." *PETA*, 18 March 2014, www.peta2.com/news/canadian-sealslaughter/. Courtesy of People for the Ethical Treatment of Animals.

Page 111 Lange, Dorothea. *White Angel Breadline, San Francisco*. 1933. Copyright © The Dorothea Lange Collection, The Oakland Museum of California, City of Oakland. Gift of Paul S. Taylor.

Page 122 "Bold, Modern, Life Insurance Newspaper Ad Design for a Company in Australia." *DesignCrowd*, uploaded by shpaolin, 12 Feb. 2013. www.designcrowd.ca/design/1456620.

Page 123 Wolters Kluwer Tax and Accounting US. "Plan for Life: Finance and Estate Planning." Reprinted with the permission of Wolters Kluwer.

Page 124 Welty, Eudora. *Dolls, Jackson*. 1936. Copyright © 1936, Eudora Welty, LLC. Reproduced courtesy of the Eudora Welty Collection, Mississippi Department of Archives and History, and Russell & Volkening as agents for the author's estate.

Page 125 Daniele, Guido. "WWF Elephant," reproduced with the permission of Guido Daniele.

Page 126 Earth Policy Institute, Rutgers University. "Largest Bike-Sharing Programs Worldwide, Early 2013," http://www.earth-policy.org/plan_b_updates/2013/update112. Copyright © 2013 Earth Policy Institute.

The publisher has made every attempt to locate all copyright holders of the material published in this book, and would be grateful for information that would allow correction of any errors or omissions in subsequent editions of the work.

Index

From the Publisher

A name never says it all, but the word "Broadview" expresses a good deal
of the philosophy behind our company. We are open to a broad range of
academic approaches and political viewpoints. We pay attention to the
broad impact book publishing and book printing has in the wider world;
for some years now we have used 100% recycled paper for most titles.
Our publishing program is internationally oriented and broad-ranging.
Our individual titles often appeal to a broad readership too; many are
of interest as much to general readers as to academics and students.

Founded in 1985, Broadview remains a fully independent
company owned by its shareholders—not an imprint
or subsidiary of a larger multinational.

For the most accurate information on our books (including
information on pricing, editions, and formats) please
visit our website at www.broadviewpress.com. Our print
books and ebooks are available for sale on our site.

broadview press
www.broadviewpress.com

FSC
www.fsc.org

MIX
Paper from
responsible sources
FSC® C103567